A Practical Approach
to
Professional Writing:

Technical and Business

Revised Edition

Douglas W. Brooks

For Eleanor

Special Thanks to Dr. Philip Snyder

Printed in the United States of America

ISBN 1-58692-411-7

Erudition Books
Courier Custom Publishing, Inc.
15 Wellman Avenue
North Chelmsford, MA 01863
877-408-5027

Please visit our website at www.eruditionbooks.com

CONTENTS

INTRODUCTION

This book will approach professional writing from a practical point of view. It will deal with how to apply the concepts of effective communication in an industrial setting. In order to become a better communicator, it is extremely important that practice and exercise are an integral part of the learning process. Therefore, much of what is offered in this book will culminate in putting that knowledge to the test.

To a certain extent, the term "Technical Writing" could almost be considered a misnomer. When used, the term is often associated with the career field of professional writing. Professional writing is a career field, but it is also a relatable discipline everyone working in industry or the private sector should be familiar with. Maybe the term "Professional Writing" would more clearly define what one might expect to practice on the job.

A Practical Approach to Professional Writing will primarily deal with necessary communication skills for the technologies, and will be geared towards industrial and business application. Emphasis is on the preparation, organization, audience and the effective use of formats and supplements. (More on all of this good stuff later.)

Much of what is required to understand the importance of communicating in industry today can be found in the majority of textbooks on professional writing. One thing lacking in most books is an element that will be included here. That element is the Human Factor. This will be discussed along with all chapters in this book. The Human Factor is simply understanding that although we are often dealing with complicated professional data we are always communicating with people who have good days, bad days, likes and dislikes; not unlike ourselves, the communicators. Understanding and appreciating the human factor can help us better reach and inform our intended audience. (More on the Human Factor will follow.)

As a technical writer for a number of years, I came to understand and appreciate just how important effective communication in industry really is. I came to understand how communicators double their value to the company and their employer. I came to appreciate that we get paid for doing our jobs, whatever the discipline, but we succeed if we can also communicate.

YOU CAN BE THE BEST IN YOUR DISCIPLINE, BUT IF YOU CAN'T COMMUNICATE, NO ONE WILL KNOW IT BUT YOU

As a rookie professional writer, I was assigned to work with a mechanical engineer I'll call Rich. The projects we were collaborating on weren't terribly difficult or complicated; they mostly consisted of rewriting some standards and specifications. Rich provided the data and I included it in audience directed documents. Rich knew his stuff. His primary area of expertise was in the field of fasteners. We dealt with screws and bolts and grommets and rivets and all kinds of fasteners related to industrial applications.

During the course of our collaboration, Rich became comfortable enough to ask me for a favor. He was putting together a proposal offering a way to decrease costs in his department. He asked me if I would mind looking it over, giving it a quick proof; maybe editing it for him. I agreed. Rich left the document with me and went back to his office to do what engineers do. As I removed the document from the intercompany envelope, I expected to see a rough but coherent draft of his proposal. I expected to be able to understand the elements of the proposal and the prescribed plan of action. What I found was a jumbled, confusing and sloppy document that made little if any sense at all. I was, to say the least, surprised.

There are a number of things a proposal is required to accomplish. It should provide a certain amount of background information, a detailed plan of action, including time involved, availability of data and expected results, among other things. Rich's proposal (term used loosely) failed to provide any of these essential details. Rich obviously failed to research the requirements of a proposal—one of the first steps in writing for industry—find out the general requirements for the document you're putting together. What does the document look like? What information will meet the needs of your audience? Questions Rich failed to answer; failed even to ask.

The information he did provide was sketchy at best. It did little to offer anything of substance that I could work with. Eventually I had to sit down with Rich and spend far more time than I could afford to try and make sense out of what he was trying to get across. Rich came to me many times after that. He brought letters, memos, reports and many other documents familiar to the industrial communicator for me to proof and edit. Rich lacked the necessary skills required of all industrial communicators—the ability to communicate one's thoughts and ideas effectively. How he made it through college is anybody's guess. How he will succeed in his career is just as questionable, considering I'm no longer with the company. Unless he found someone else to help him with his documentation, his prospects are quite limited.

Remember: **IF YOU CAN'T COMMUNICATE YOUR THOUGHTS AND IDEAS, NO ONE WILL KNOW THEM BUT YOU.**

C h a p t e r   O n e

The Writing Process

PROCESS > PRODUCT

In order to achieve a desired product, the communicator in industry must follow the accepted steps in a particular process. All professional craftsmen know how important the process is. To get the best product possible, a particular process must be adhered to. Cabinet makers don't make it up as they go along; they know what works best, what's required to get the product their customers have come to expect. They have, through trial and error, the best, most efficient way to construct their product. The professional will only realize the most effective product when the process works to that end.

For example, let's look at the process of making a simple table. There can be many steps in a process, whether making a table or writing a manual. The Professionals will consider the possible steps and choose those that work best for them; help them to realize a desired product.

The various steps involved in the process of making a table could include:

* drawing up the plans
* choosing the material
* gathering the material
* making preliminary cuts, shaping the material
* shaping the top
* attaching the legs
* adding supports
* making certain each part relates to the whole
* applying the finishing coats
* testing the finished product

Certainly this list of steps is not conclusive but does serve to illustrate how a process might work. Each one of these steps could also be compared to the process of professional writing, from gathering material (conducting research) to applying the finishing coats (a good thorough proof and edit of the document). Remember, if the process is followed each time, the product will reach the intended audience.

THINKING AND PLANNING, WHATEVER THE PRODUCT, ARE THE FIRST STEPS IN THE PROCESS

The first step is THINKING. Thinking about a project gives us time to become comfortable with it, to try and understand, to ask ourselves some questions, because questioning is still another important element in the communicating process. Think about it, ask yourself some questions: What do I know? What do I need to find out?

THINK COMPILE CONSTRUCT VISUALIZE REALIZE

How to Begin

When confronted with a writing assignment in industry, no matter how unfamiliar we are with the subject, we have taken the first step; we are thinking about it. One of the first assignments I received as a professional writer had to do with writing and rewriting some standards and specifications. Briefly, standards and specifications govern material and procedure in manufacturing. I have to admit, although I didn't at the time, I had absolutely no idea what a standard or specification was. I had two choices when my boss gave me the assignment: I could have expressed my confusion and refused the assignment or I could have accepted it and proceeded as best I could. Refusing it probably wouldn't have done a lot by way of enhancing my career but would have relieved some pressure. But I didn't refuse it; I accepted it. In accepting the assignment, I learned some very important lessons about communicating in industry.

With this first assignment, I began to develop a philosophy about writing as a professional. I learned that if you have the ability to communicate, confidence and the enthusiasm to reach your audience, there are very few topics you can't write about. That's where the process comes in. Ask yourself what you know about the assignment. I didn't know the first thing about standards and specifications. Ask yourself what you need to find out. I needed to find out all I could.

The first thing I did was to dig out old standards and specifications. I studied them, became familiar with what they were all about: what they were meant to accomplish, how the audience might employ the data and how I might approach collecting and presenting the data. That was an important lesson. I discovered that there are very few writing assignments one might face in industry that haven't been done before. So, if you're unfamiliar with the document you have to produce, go to a file, hard copy or computer, take a look at a previously produced document. As you study the old document and come to understand it, note what seems to work, note what seems like it wouldn't work as well with this new assignment. Now you're into the process; keep going.

Gathering Data — Where to Look — Who to Speak With

Now that you've been given the assignment, thought about it and answered those two important questions—what do I know, what do I need to find out—you can move on to the next step in the process.

Gathering Information — Research

Any industry professional will attest to the importance of finding the right information in order to best serve the needs of your audience. (This audience thing keeps coming up—don't worry about it now, we'll get to that later.) Again, the best place to begin is to take a look at a similar document already produced and disseminated; become familiar with the basic requirements of the document. Take notes, always take notes; keep track of the process. The next step in the information gathering process could depend on the intent of the document, but there are basically two paths we could take: consult the available professional periodicals and books relating to the topic or interview the appropriate industry professionals. Note: the effective communicator will more often than not follow both of these paths.

PRINTED RESOURCE MATERIALS

In any given organization, there are generally a wide variety of printed materials available to consult for appropriate resource material. These organizations, as well as individuals employed by the organization, probably subscribe to a number of professional periodicals relating to many different disciplines. They may even be collected in a particular area, a library or a shared resource room. Find out where they are stored and make use of them.

Many organizations also maintain a professional library. These libraries usually include a wide variety of discipline related books as well as periodicals that are current and up to date. It is important to remember that these resources should be used for a number of different reasons. We, as communicators in industry, don't only use these materials to discover information necessary for a particular document, we also should use these resources to familiarize ourselves with disciplines that might not be in our area of expertise.

As mentioned before, if we are confident in our ability to communicate, there are very few subjects that we can't write about. One way to ensure that we effectively reach our audience is to understand, even if only on a limited basis, the topic we are writing on. When faced with putting together a document that deals with an area that might be somewhat unfamiliar to us, we can rely on a technical library to gain some background in this area. Begin with the basics; give yourself a mini-course, if you will, in the area of concern. Study some current periodicals; learn about the current changes in an area, recent innovations prior to constructing the document.

Interviewing Industry Professionals for Information

Remember, the process of research in industry generally begins with consulting books for background information relating to a particular discipline.

The next step in the research process would be to consult periodicals. Periodicals come out on a somewhat regular basis and probably have the most current information contained therein. We bring ourselves up to date. So, with books we begin with background, some basic familiarization, next we consult periodicals to discover the most current innovations and information on a particular area of concern. The next step in the industry-related research process would be the interview of professionals.

BOOKS — PERIODICALS — PROFESSIONALS = COLLECTED DATA

The communicator's primary source of professional data generally comes from the industry professional. The professional should have most of the information we need available to him or her. In school, they studied the theoretical background in their discipline—classroom instruction that utilized books and practical application. Since becoming professionals, they undoubtedly subscribe to and study a variety of particular kinds of specific publications. Therefore, it can be assumed that these professionals are current and up to date in their areas of interest. When you think about it, how much confidence would we have in a doctor who didn't stay up with the current issues in medicine, be familiar with new medications and treatments? Not long, I bet. That's why it is important to search out those industry professionals who do stay current with the innovations in their particular disciplines.

Interviewing The Professional

One of the benefits of collecting information from individuals is that not only are they familiar with the area of interest, they are probably also familiar with the specifics of the organization and the mission of the company.

In preparing for the interview, we take a few steps back here. Let's say you're charged with putting together a document that requires some in-depth electronic information. Unfortunately, at this point, electronics is not one of your strongest areas of knowledge. It would be unwise to interview professionals when you are basically uninformed about their discipline. Their time is valuable; they won't appreciate having to give you a quick and dirty mini-course in the subject area.

All that is really required at this point is some basic research. Study some books on basic electronics; consult some general interest electronic periodicals. Take a course in electronics if time permits. As a new professional writer, that's just what I did: took some basic courses in electronics, instrumentation, blueprint reading and so on.

Why Familiarize Ourselves With the Basics of a Discipline?

Understanding the basics of a discipline will not only help us better design questions for the professional, it will also assist in our understanding of the information provided. Remember, the industry professional's time is valuable; he or she won't have the time to explain concepts in great detail, give definitions of terms or explain all of the details of the application of the data provided. Possessing basic background information in an area of interest also goes a long way in establishing your credibility as an industry professional whether as a professional writer or a discipline-related communicator.

Designing Questions

Once we are familiar with some of the basics of an area of interest, such as definitions of terms, basic applications, and recent innovations, we can construct questions leading to the information required for the document in question.

Plan for the interview ahead of time. Don't just show up at the professional's office or work area; make an appointment far enough in advance that will serve your purpose, and is convenient to the professional. As you set up the interview, give the professional some general information relating to what you need to know. This allows them the opportunity to prepare, if necessary, for answering your questions. It also allows them time to discover specific data that's not immediately available. Again, plan for the interview, know exactly what you need and how to ask for it.

Don't design questions that merely require a yes or no answer, because that's all you will get, and yes or no provides very little information. It's much easier to reject information at a later stage in the process than to discover that you're lacking data and have to go back for more. For example, if you were to ask an electrical engineer a question like, "Is there more than one kind of resistor on this circuit?" Their response would be "yes," or "no." That would require additional questions. A more appropriate question might be, "Please explain the variety of resistors associated with this circuit." That requires an in-depth response and provides the detail you probably need for your document. Retrieving information from an industry professional is not always an easy process for a number of different reasons.

The Reluctant Professional

The professional's main concern, of course, is his or her area of expertise and position. Providing you with information may be necessary but it's not always considered a major portion of their responsibilities. This is where the human factor comes in. Why might a professional be reluctant, less than enthusiastic to offer information?

There could exist any number of reasons why a professional may be a bit less than enthusiastic to provide information necessary for you to produce your document:

Reason: time constraints—contact any experts as far in advance as possible; discuss the most opportune time for both of you to meet. Remember, they are providing you with the essential data you need for your document, work within their schedule, set up meetings to satisfy yours, but most importantly, their needs.

Reason: discipline allegiance—experts may occasionally be reluctant to provide information because they feel their positions could best be ensured if they remain the expert in their particular areas. In other words, the more people who know what they know diminishes their worth to the organization. Of course this is rarely if ever true, but considering the human factor, this could be a problem the industrial communicator may encounter. Remember, the simple point here is they are being paid for their knowledge and expertise and should always be afforded the courtesy their position calls for.

Solution: mission first—your priority as well as the expert's should always be what is best for the organization and the project at hand. Explain your intent to the expert and clarify specifically what you are trying to accomplish. It might help to detail the elements of the document and why their information is vital to its success.

Put Your Source at Ease

When interviewing for data, it often helps not only to detail and explain the project you are working on, but to show a certain amount of understanding. Let the expert know that you understand their position and the value of their time. It never hurts to show appreciation prior to the interview; thank the expert for setting up the meeting as well as for providing the information necessary for your project.

There may be other reasons that experts may not readily provide you with the essential information required for your project, but if you are aware of the human factor, the difficulties relating to gathering information will be limited. Respect their position and knowledge and understand the constraints they may be working under. Give your sources the benefit of the doubt; allow them the time they need to provide you with the data. To them their job is just as important as yours is to you; remember that.

BOOKS — PERIODICALS — EXPERTS = INFORMATION

AUDIENCE

Who you are producing a document for is one of the primary questions that needs to be addressed and answered within the professional writing process.

While involved in the various stages of the process, the order in which to pursue particular steps relates to a number of factors. For example, should the research be accomplished prior to deciphering our audience's needs or should we figure out the audience first?

The General Audience

The general audience mainly consists of individuals from a variety of professional disciplines. The professional communicator can make very few assumptions about the members of this audience. About the only thing one can be sure of is that they all probably work for your organization and have its best interests at heart.

Types of general interest documents:

Personnel announcements
Safety regulations
Adopted suggestions
Training materials
Company policies

Of course these are not conclusive, but do demonstrate the intent of general audience documentation.

The Discipline Specific Audience

This audience is usually concerned with a particular area of professional interest. They may be electronic engineers or food service workers. More accurate assumptions can be made with the discipline specific audience and the professional communicator can go as far as is necessary to research them and their particular needs.

First, the communicator should discover the general elements of this type of audience, then become familiar with the specific needs a particular document must fulfill.

General elements:

Educational background
Professional discipline
Group mission

Those are only a few audience related questions the writer may ask when researching a proposed audience. (More in-depth questions later.)

Researching the Audience

It is not difficult to determine the make-up of a particular audience. Just as communicators may be encouraged to do some basic research in a discipline, they may also find it important to research a prospective audience.

Contact a variety of possible readers of the document you're charged with producing; do a general, over-the-phone interview. It helps to briefly explain the document you're putting together as well as what you hope it will accomplish. Ask for their suggestions and inquire as to their needs in the specific document related area.

If this particular audience is in a centralized area, go and visit where they work, talk with the people you encounter, become familiar with the way they operate and what their needs and concerns may be.

Contact personnel and request a general profile of the group and what their primary mission in the company may be. The more you find out about a specific audience, the better you can meet their needs and produce an effective document.

Questions to Consider
When Evaluating an Audience

1. What are the basic characteristics of the audience: Education? Professional Discipline? Experience? Primary Mission? Position within the Company? Individual Responsibilities?
2. What does the audience know about this specific, discipline related subject: Shared Knowledge? What do they need to be informed of?
3. Who, other than the members of our audience, might be interested and read our document?
4. How might our documentation be regarded and used in the future? Does it have immediate and lasting value?
5. To what extent is the audience involved in reading documentation? What would encourage them to read all of ours?
6. What basic assumptions can we make about our audience without stereotyping?

Again, these questions are not conclusive, but do offer some suggestions to help us begin evaluating an audience.

THE HUMAN FACTOR

Practicing professional writers consider topics from various points of view for a number of different reasons: from the general to the discipline specific. There is rarely a singular line of thought that goes through one's mind when considering a professional document and its value. Through experience, I learned to address each task and its audience's needs individually, considering the facts and needs as they might relate to a desired product. Remember: PROCESS > PRODUCT. A document should contain pertinent facts, and like all forms of writing, those facts should be organized in a particular way and serve the needs of a particular audience. Once we address our audience's needs, and research the best way to reach their needs, we must ask whether or not we have sufficiently considered our readers.

We have sufficiently considered our readers, their needs and how to meet their needs only after we have reviewed them considering the "Human Factor." Remember, our readers, no matter how disciplined and professional they may be, are still people. This may sound somewhat simplistic, but this factor is too often disregarded and sacrificed because as writers we believe the facts, the information will suffice, float to the surface so to speak, in spite of the human factor. To a certain extent this may be true, but why take the chance of not reaching and convincing our audience? If they don't positively react to our documentation and act upon it, we've wasted their time as well as ours.

Time

Time, to say the least, is an important factor in industry. There are only so many hours in a day to accomplish what often seems insurmountable. The communicator not only has to reach his or her audience, but must also encourage interest in the documentation. Considering the human factor can help us reach our goals. Like ourselves, our readers have good days and bad days, likes and dislikes; in short, they are people too. When analyzing your audience, go beyond the obvious, find out who they are, what interests they may have, where, yes where they live and play and so on. Much of this can be assumed, but the assumption should be made.

- Don't Offend.
- Avoid Stereotypes.
- Consider Economic Status.
- Consider Social Status.
- Is Gender a Factor?
- Are Outside Activities a Factor?
- Are Affiliations a Factor (Professional and Otherwise)?

The Human Factor and Document Rejection

One truth that most industry professionals can agree on is that time is a commodity. We are bombarded, whether on or off the job, with information at every turn; it often seems everyone is interested in our time, knowledge or money. Information is essential to our professional lives as well as our private lives. Fortunately, we can pick and choose, edit most of what the media throws at us in our private lives. But our professional lives are a different story altogether.

- What Should We Read?
- What Do We Need to Retain?
- What Should We Watch?
- Who Should We Listen To?
- What Information Should We Act Upon?

??????????????????????

These are questions the professional must deal with on a regular basis. Granted, some of the time it is quite obvious what information is important to our jobs and careers, but when it isn't, the questions arise.

As communicators, one of our primary responsibilities is to ensure that our audience reads our documentation. It's important; that's why we wrote and disseminated it. Considering the human factor is one way to be sure our documentation isn't rejected, at least initially. The key is to get our audience to read and process our information and then consider its value. Remember, busy people pick and choose what they will invest their time in.

Aesthetics—the document should be well formatted, attractive to look at, encourage reader interest.

On Time—the audience should receive the information in time limits that allow them the opportunity to absorb and act upon it.

Product—know your audience and what they require; give them information that is pertinent to their needs.

KNOW AND REACH YOUR AUDIENCE

Note: We will look at how we might evaluate the possible audiences for the documents detailed in this book.

Targeting The Audience

Remember, knowing your audience and their needs is one of the primary roads to effective communication in the technologies today.

Communicators are becoming more concerned than ever before about identifying readers and their specific needs. Who are the readers, the audience of a professional document? With the continued growth of technology, the audiences for professional information are becoming less defined. With this growth comes an increased need for information by readers who had not previously required information. These readers can be as diverse as the documents. How best to serve the specific reader should be a primary concern of the professional communicator.

In many cases, the readers targeted for information are as important as the documentation being presented. As stated before, the audience should be researched, regarded and studied as intently as the data in question. The needs of the reader have to be determined, and how to meet those needs should always be an integral part of the research process.

Audience Background

Part of the communicator's responsibility is to consider reader background:

• What level of knowledge regarding the information does the reader possess?
• Is the reader a technician with rudimentary knowledge?
• Is the reader someone with little or no working knowledge?
• Is the reader an experienced technician?
• Is the reader an experienced engineer?

These are, once again, questions that need to be considered when evaluating an audience—target your reader.

Researching the background of a particular audience can be accomplished in a number of effective ways. Most organizations have employee lists and job descriptions that can be obtained and studied.

An industrial communicator can study documented information previously supplied to a particular audience, consider and pinpoint its effectiveness. The communicator should consider the steps by which to present information based, in part, on its complexity and the audience's level of knowledge. In other words, would the information be best served by offering it on a one-shot basis or by disseminating it over a period of time? The pace in which information is presented is important when considering audience needs.

Readers don't always act upon or study information when it is presented or received; there is often a time lapse for a number of different reasons.

• Schedules don't always allow for immediate action.
• Information may need to be considered and discussed prior to action.
• Other information may take precedence.
• The reader may be reluctant to act.
• The document may be filed away until a later date.

WHAT TYPES OF DOCUMENTATION MIGHT THE COMMUNICATOR EXPECT TO FACE?

As a technical writer, I produced a wide variety of documents. I learned early not to refuse an assignment, to accept the project and take it from there. Again, research and understanding are the keys to effectively communicating on almost any subject. Is there an inclusive list of probable documents? Probably not, but there are certainly standard industrial types of documents.

• Standards
• Specifications
• Letters

- Memos
- Instructions
- Procedures
- Proposals
- Reports
- Manuals

These are some, but certainly not all, of the possibilities. As a professional writer I began working primarily with basic documents such as standards and specifications. But as time and experience progressed I was working with a wide variety of documentation. I continued to work with the basic type of documents but I also worked with documents that had a marketing angle. I researched and produced and disseminated information meant to inform and convince a reader to consider everything from products to services. This was industry-related marketing. I produced everything from brochures to scripts for industrial commercials. Be open and be ready.

What's New?

There exist few totally new forms of documentation in industry today. If you do happen to come across a previously untried form of documentation, don't panic; set the precedent. The process has to begin someplace, and looking at what was produced in the past is often a good place to begin. More often than not, something already exists to serve as a point of focus, a point of departure when approaching a task.

Look it up—study it—adopt what works—reject what doesn't.

If it's been done before, then it can be done again; if it hasn't, set the precedent.

One of the first manuals assigned to me as a professional writer concerned an employee incentive system. There existed a fair amount of material available for consideration, but not to the point of satisfaction or completion. This particular system had been operating without a company-wide accepted manual for guidance and uniformity. The material available dealt with the system and was employed by the majority of participants in the incentive system. The problem was that very little of what existed, the scattered elements of the system, addressed all of the pertinent facts in a single, useful publication.

Lots of Voices, Little Coordination

Everyone involved, the systems coordinators, possessed parts of the rules, guidelines and regulations, but no one group had all of it. What resulted was increased confusion and decreased equity for those involved. The system could only hope to succeed as it was meant to when each and every employee was treated equally based on complete, conclusive and acceptable practices.

AN INCENTIVE SYSTEM CAN ONLY WORK WHEN EMPLOYEES ARE RECOGNIZED AND REWARDED FOR THEIR SUGGESTIONS FAIRLY.

The need was finally recognized and the task was clear: ONE SYSTEM.

Bringing all of the elements of the system together was not as difficult a task as it was initially perceived. My job was to consider my options, rely on established resources, and decipher the audience's needs.

COORDINATING A TASK CAN OFTEN BE THE COMMUNICATOR'S PRIMARY RESPONSIBILITY.

It was partly my responsibility to decide what information was pertinent and then assemble it according to audience need. As I began the process, I realized what little I knew about this particular incentive system. Remember, writing is a questioning process.

WHAT DO I KNOW? WHAT DO I NEED TO FIND OUT?

What I basically knew was from the same perspective as most employees. With this limited knowledge I found I was better able to relate to and appreciate the needs of the targeted audience. To consider the information from the user's point of view benefited the process.

The process itself involved incorporating all extraneous material into a cohesive and workable whole. I began by considering the various voices, contributors to the manual. My primary task involved rewriting, revising that which already existed into one voice— bringing the fragmented parts together to create a complete, workable document.

- What remained pertinent?
- What was no longer factual?
- What was the collective intent?
- What was the average employee's perception?
- What was management's perception?

HOW COULD IT SERVE ALL EMPLOYEES?

All elements needed to come together to create the desired product. This incentive system had to serve the electronics group, and the health care facility as well as the manufacturing elements within the organization.

THE COMMUNICATOR AS COORDINATOR

As previously stated, it is often the responsibility of the communicator in industry to act as document coordinator. Disseminating information is rarely a singular effort. There can be more than a few professional disciplines involved.

- The writer, or writers
- The editor
- The proofreader
- The technical illustrator
- The CAD operator
- The technical expert, or experts
- The print shop
- The document's designer
- The responsible implementer
- The distributor

It is the coordinator's responsibility to bring all of these professionals together to successfully complete the task.

In a typical writing situation, information would generally pass through a number of stages before actually being reviewed by the customer or expert source. The policy instituted by the responsible team could deal with the information and related elements before leaving the coordinating communicator.

Each document could be passed on to a colleague not directly connected to the project. He or she could review the material based on his or her knowledge, or discipline, looking for inconsistencies overlooked by the coordinator.

ALWAYS SHOW YOUR DOCUMENTATION TO SOMEONE
WHOSE OPINION YOU RESPECT AND TRUST.

The reviewer could offer suggestions, question the coordinator about sources, relevancy and scope of the documentation including audience need and background. The uninvolved reader can often provide invaluable assistance when striving to produce an effective document.

Always give the technical expert the opportunity to review the document for factual accuracy and completeness. It doesn't hurt to double check their information in either resource materials or with an additional technical expert.

Discuss the inclusion of graphics and illustrations with the technical illustrator—determine location and complexity based on audience need and data complexity. If your organization doesn't employ such an individual, locate someone with artistic ability and solicit their talents in the production of your document.

Work with reviewers, editors and proofreaders to ensure consistency of voice, style and overall consistency and cohesiveness. Work with members of the audience to ensure that the product meets their needs. In short, consult and work with those professionals who share, on one level or another, in the production of your document.

DOCUMENT DESIGN

Information sharing is a primary responsibility in industry today. People rely on information in order to effectively do their jobs, and often require this data quickly and efficiently. With this plethora of computer generated and hard copy documents, it can be difficult to determine what to read. It can be difficult to decide not only what to read, but what to read completely. What a document looks like can play a large part in encouraging reader participation.

The aesthetics of documentation should lend themselves to reader involvement and use. As communicators, it is important to understand that what a document looks like can go a long way toward ensuring the success of our efforts. Along with the aesthetics of a document, the communicator also needs to appreciate how effective organization encourages reader interest and involvement.

To fully understand reader awareness, the communicator should also consider the importance of aesthetics and organization, and how they serve the reader's needs.

One of the most beneficial ways to accomplish logical organization in any writing task is to produce an outline. The outline helps the communicator consider relative and sequential steps in documenting information. It can point out discrepancies even before detailed information is compiled; it serves as an indicator for researching information in a logical order. Consider the readers and the most effective way to sequence information to meet their needs. An outline assists in avoiding redundancy and over-simplification. With an outline, the technician can see what information should go where and how much of that information to provide for optimum clarity. The outline encourages the process of revision (to be discussed in Chapter 2) before the actual information has been compiled and the document has been completed. It helps to establish what the readers need to know and in what order they need to know it.

IF IT LOOKS GOOD, IT WILL ATTRACT ATTENTION

The communicator needs to consider throughout the process how a document looks; does it encourage reader interest? The information contained in professional documents often offers less than exciting reading, and sometimes is considered dry or clinical by nature. Therefore, how it looks, the aesthetics, is an important consideration when presenting technical information.

Because of its nature, the purpose of the information is most certainly not entertainment. A document should be produced as attractively as time constraints and production capabilities allow.

ASSEMBLE A PERSONAL LIBRARY OF PREVIOUSLY PRODUCED DOCUMENTS

Headings, White Space and Graphics

Headings should be included to maximize the reader's ability to locate information: make each section stand out. Data should not be heaped onto pages, but spread out adequately and properly identified. Lists should be provided as often as appropriate. The rule in technical communication is to list when possible. Information can be separated for readability and easy access.

Bullets: ◆   ●   ◆   ■
Dashes: -   –   —
Numbering Systems: 1a, 3c
Divisions and Subdivisions
Varying Type Sizes: Type Type
Varying Type Styles: Technical *Technical*

Design the document as attractively as possible. It should be easy to read and access information. Too much text on a page can be offensive to the eye; allow for white space, break up the text. In short, if the technique helps readers, give it to them. In the past, how a document looked was often greeted with, "It's the content, the information that matters." To a certain extent, that is still true. But if readers aren't initially attracted to the document by what it looks like, the chances of their becoming involved with the information are limited. What good is the information if the readers can't find what they're searching for, or are reluctant to use it because it is presented in an overly complicated manner?

The communicator needs to be as concerned with reader awareness as with precise professional documentation. If the information fails to serve its intended audience for any reason, then the process has failed. Audience awareness is the rule rather than the exception. Remember the Human Factor.

Graphics and illustrations more often than not play an important role in professional documentation. Graphics can be used to enhance or take the place of overly complicated, reader-directed information. Graphics can be specific, text related, or graphics and illustrations can be merely for aesthetic reasons, encouraging reader participation.

TECHNOLOGY AND THE COMPUTER'S ROLE IN PROFESSIONAL COMMUNICATION

The introduction of the computer into the private sector is no longer current news. They are all over the place. You can't walk into an office today and turn around quickly without bumping into a terminal of some kind.

Computers are here to stay; they've been integrated into most areas of industry. They are used in applications ranging from running assembly lines to running programmed machining operations. Few industry communicators rely on the standard typewriter. Organizations of all sizes are incorporating the use of word processors and more complex computer systems into publishing efforts. In the past, efforts might have included draft typing and forwarding to other areas or out of plant for production, generating illustrations and graphics for inclusion and other complicated production techniques. Today, with the proliferation of publishing systems, the majority of document production can be relegated to a single area.

With the advent of affordable publishing systems, organizations are realizing the benefits over more tedious methods. Even the use of computers as word processors in professional communication is changing. Often, documentation can go from the terminal screen to being typeset, formatted and organized, graphics included, without generating a single preliminary hard copy.

The use of computers as sophisticated publishing systems is following an ever increasing course. In certain respects, computers are making the job of the communicator easier. It's understood, communicators deal with timely information and deadlines on a daily basis, and computers are effectively meeting these concerns. The computer encourages the communicator to increase his or her knowledge and job effectiveness.

In the past, communicators would receive an assignment and follow the initial process of research and interviewing before generating the physical document. They would then compose the documentation on a standard typewriter. The next step included a copier, where the communicator would reduce and enlarge specific material for inclusion in the document according to prescribed dictates. Then the material would be cut and pasted on boards for additional copies before it could be distributed to the appropriate experts for review. If illustrations or graphics were required, an entire step would be added to the process. Following review, the communicator would receive the information and make necessary changes, conduct additional research, and proceed through the same typing, copying, and reducing process as before. The communicator would then take the relatively clean, error-free document and submit it to a proofreader, who in turn would submit it to the editor, who in turn would submit it for illustration analysis before even going to the generator; where it would then, hopefully, be okayed for preliminary production to be distributed to the intended audience. If there was a single change or question within any of these steps, the entire process would probably have to begin again.

This overall effort was always time consuming and quite often frustrating. But publishing systems introduced many changes to the methods by which professional communicators produce documentation. No longer do they have to deal with mountains of paperwork.

The introduction of the computer virtually eliminated many of the problems once faced by the professional communicator. Rarely does information have to physically change hands today; it can proceed from one area to the next electronically. Changes can be made to screen without the need for generations of hard copy. In addition, messages and ideas can be shared in conjunction with the document, graphics can be included through "CAD" (Computer Aided Design) and other systems. The documented information can proceed through the entire process, from writing to typesetting and organization, without having to spend hours cutting and pasting.

The computer offers the opportunity to be more creative to concentrate more fully on the information and how that information is presented to the audience. The communicator in industry is required to be familiar with computers and their uses for disseminating important information. The computer is a tool; the communicator needs to learn it and use it; it can only enhance the product.

EXERCISES

1. Choose one of the following topics and conduct research to discover what you don't know. Consult books, then periodicals, and finally, interview an expert in the area.

   ✔ High Definition Television ✔ Laser Imaging   ✔ Ozone Depletion

   ✔ Cellular Phones   ✔ Compact Disc   ✔ Automotive
                                Development   Innovations

   ✔ Career Opportunities   ✔ Medical   ✔ Individual
                                Advancements   Interests

   Where to begin? Start with the Readers' Guide to periodical literature, check the library's card catalogue, speak with a professor on campus, ask the librarian and begin taking notes right away.

2. Research a general interest and a discipline specific audience. Begin by making some initial assumptions, then take it from there.

   ✔ Electronics Students   ✔ Various Clubs   ✔ Fellow Employees
                                on Campus

   ✔ Lottery Players   ✔ Sports Fans   ✔ Dog Owners

   ✔ Liberal Arts Students   ✔ Computer   ✔ Dental Hygienists
                                Programmers

3. Research the variety of documentation in a given organization on or off campus. What kinds of documents are common to their tasks and goals?

4. Research computer systems in use on and off campus. In particular, discover how many types of publishing systems are in use right on your own campus.

5. Detail the process that results in a particular product. How can this process be compared to the process of documenting and disseminating information?

6. Outline the process of communicating particular information to a specific audience. Where and how does it begin, and where and how does it conclude?

Editing and Revising

REVISING

Once all the pertinent information has been collected, organized and formatted, there remains an extremely important step in the process of communicating: revising for accuracy, coherency and intent. Does the document do what it is supposed to do and reach the intended audience?

Revise to Perfect

The objective of communication is to convey information to a reader in a style and format which is easy to understand and use. The style and format should make it as easy as possible for the reader to understand and retain the information. The communicator ensures success and meets his or her objectives through revision.

Preparation

Establishing the process ahead of time allows for more efficient revision. This allows adequate time for review and revision. You must first analyze the writing task, collect source material—research, organize ideas and research the audience and its needs. This preparation can best be accomplished beginning with a detailed outline. A detailed outline encourages revision.

Revise for Audience Need

- Use words and ideas the reader will appreciate and understand.
- Unfamiliar terms should be defined when initially used.
- Determine audience's level of knowledge and experience.
- Review similar publications; consider format, organization and overall style.
- Be consistent and reach your audience.
- Use concise language, particularly for description: This can consist of short, incomplete sentences which begin with active verbs, drop articles, omit verbs when understood and imply subject.
- Simplify long or complex sentences when appropriate by using lists.

Revising Text

Text is usually the most difficult, time consuming element of documentation to revise. Where text is required, it should be carefully researched and detailed to be as easy as possible for the audience to understand and retain.

Revise complicated text by using alternatives to conventional sentence/paragraph text when possible:

- tables
- lists
- illustrations
- charts
- graphics

When it is necessary to use conventional text:

- Limit paragraphs to a single idea
- Limit sentences to a single thought
- Never use two words when one will do
- Never use a big word when a smaller one will serve

Revise text to encourage reader interest:

- Locate illustrations on the same or facing page with text
- Organize text in a logical order
- Ensure text is consistent in style, terminology and format

Inadequate attention to revision can result in overlooking problems and not completely meeting the needs of the audience.

What to look for:

- writing style is difficult to understand
- paragraphs and sentences are overly lengthy
- specific information is difficult to locate quickly
- frequent cross-referencing (avoid requiring reader to jump around document)
- illustrations and graphics are not directly associated with text

Revising for Style

Style is often referred to as voice. The "voice" of the document should more than anything else relate to cohesiveness and consistency. Style should not supplement official, professional language that applies to any given text.

Use idiomatic language in preference to formal language; use the jargon of the reader when it makes the information easier to understand, and more interesting. Pay attention to the words used in the document and revise to meet intent:

- use a word that is concrete rather than vague
- use words that are specific rather than general
- use words that are familiar to the reader rather than formal
- avoid words or phrases that could be subject to interpretation
- define key words that may be open to interpretation
- avoid using verbs that may be misinterpreted
  - ✔ ascertain bolt is tight   ✔ be sure bolt is tight
- avoid trite phrases
  - ✔ for the purpose of   ✔ for
  - ✔ in the event that   ✔ when
  - ✔ attached please find   ✔ attached

Revise for Clarity and Voice

The proper use of verbs in communication is essential for clarity of thought and expression.

- Be sure each verb agrees with the subject in number.
  - ✔ Two machine assemblies were removed
  - ✔ The operator is required to check safety features.
- Always strive to employ the active verb form (imperative) rather than the passive.
  - ✔ (not good) A singular switch is used with a singular machine.
  - ✔ (good) Use a singular switch with a singular machine.
- Use the passive verb form only in selected circumstances.
  - ✔ The receiver of the action of the verb must be emphasized over the doer.
  - ✔ The doer related to the action is unknown.
  - ✔ Emphasis must be placed on the receiver of the action.

Standard Rules

Generally, in communication, the standard rules of proper English usage apply. But when dealing with information there are certain points that need to be addressed. It is important to consider the complexity of professional data and audience need, and how the standard rules may apply.

The Basics as They Could Apply to Professional Communication.

Sentences

- The key to constructing reader directed, effective sentences is clarity.
- Arrange the parts of the sentence so that the meaning is clear with the first reading. Time is a factor here; industry professionals don't always have the time to reread documents.

Short/Concise/Simple

- Revise sentences that are confusing, awkward, not logical, or obscure.
- Revise by breaking up long, complex sentences into shorter ones.
- Revise by eliminating words, phrases or clauses that have no direct relationship to the main point of the sentence.
- Revise by eliminating unrelated thoughts in a compound or complex sentence.

Revise For Proper Sentence Construction

- Check to be sure there is only one main thought or idea per sentence.
- Check to be sure that closely related points in a sentence are only linked when they explain a point or advance the focus.
- Be sure the antecedent of the pronoun is clear.
    - ✔ (not good) After connecting the wire to the assembly, remove it.
    - ✔ (good) Remove the assembly.

Note: As a very basic discussion of proper usage related to communication, there is much that is not touched upon here. For those communicators with particular difficulty, there are many very good English handbooks available for study. The best, most effective way to become more comfortable with the language is by reading and writing.

Revising the Paragraph

- Overly long paragraphs don't encourage reader interest. Keep them short, probably no more than 5 sentences.
- Revise to be sure that each paragraph deals with only one clear idea.
- Be sure each paragraph contains specific, concrete details to interest and hold reader's attention.
- Check to be sure paragraphs contain only as much information as the reader can grasp in one reading.
- Revise all paragraphs that don't flow from the topic sentence.
- Just like the document itself, paragraphs should flow in a logical, reader-directed order. Revise if they don't.

Style and Professional Communication

There are some special circumstances in communication that contradict some elements of proper usage. Much of the information in professional documentation is directive by nature. Intent is clear and exceptions to proper usage are acceptable.

- Incomplete sentences when called for—articles are dropped, for example.
- For clarity, sentences can begin with the active verb form.
- Subject is implied, not always stated.
- Certain unique ways to spell particular words; usually employed with space constraints.
- Numbers are rarely if ever spelled out.
- Elliptical Constructions—acceptable sentence fragments—used primarily when further emphasis is called for.

In short, if it serves the requirements of the document and the needs of the reader, it will probably be acceptable. But it must be understood without question. Check, revise and be certain.

Revision Stimulates Thought

Revision, more often than not, in professional documentation lends itself to effective communication, a desired product and reaching the needs of the audience. REVISE, REVISE, REVISE.

EDITING THE DOCUMENT

Where revision gives the communicator the opportunity to change the document, check professional data, ensure clarity of thought, conciseness and reader understanding, editing perfects the document: provides the final, finishing touches required for effective communication.

Definition—When editing, the writer checks the manuscript for professional accuracy, conformity to standards, information presentation and clerical accuracy.

- The writer does whatever is necessary to ensure the document is a reliable, reader directed product.
- The editor's responsibilities include discovering inaccuracies, problems with style, professional specifications and reliability and overall mechanics.
- When editing, the writer should edit for one thing at a time to ensure a thorough job is done. Although editing for just one thing at time may seem time consuming, the majority of violations will be found and corrected.
  - ✔ Read for professional accuracy
  - ✔ Read for grammatical problems
  - ✔ Read for logical organization
  - ✔ Read for consistency of style
  - ✔ Read for mechanics
  - ✔ Read for spelling (Checking for spelling can often prove difficult because the reader is involved with the material, not necessarily aware of each individual word. Therefore, reading the document backwards allows for optimum attention to each word.)

- Remember, a less than thorough edit will cost time and money; find the problems and fix them.

Discovering clerical and factual discrepancies in a document is the first step in the editing process; the second step of course is to correct these problems.

- Correct all elements of questionable data.
- Rewrite information to improve accuracy and readability.
- Mark-up manuscript, clearly pointing out all changes to ensure an accurate final document.

All Communication Requires Editing to Some Degree.

What communicators are striving to do when they edit is to make the document or presentation as suitable for dissemination as possible.

Everyone's An Editor

✔ Professional Letters
✔ Personal Letters
✔ Homework, Ours & Kids
✔ Verbal Communication (Will what we say be understood?)

The Communicator's Responsibility

Whether you have the luxury of having a professional editor to check your work or you have to rely on a colleague, it is important that you make it as easy for them to do their job as possible. Keep their role in mind as the document is being produced.

- Don't overcrowd the page. Leave plenty of room for future changes.
- Be sure the document's intent is clear—be consistent.
- Keep lines of communication open during the editing process.
- Be open minded—consider suggested changes and act accordingly.
- Work together and let the process produce the most effective product required.

It's important to keep in mind that the editing process can often take more than one or two back and forth reviews. When editing a document, plan for additional reviews.

- Don't discard original data—it could prove accurate.
- Make changes in a variety of colors, pen or pencil, to distinguish from original input.

- Avoid excessive editing marks on original—document on separate page and indicate.
- The most important thing to remember is to avoid confusion.

Remember,
Thorough PROCESS = Effective PRODUCT

Editing and the Human Factor

When editing a document, keep in mind that the readers you are editing for have particular needs and responsibilities. Understanding that a collective group of readers, the audience, is also made up of individuals who can have particular likes, needs and responsibilities. A document's worth is based on how seriously it is regarded.

- Keep the reader in mind when editing—know your audience.
- Question data—always check information for accuracy.
- Be objective—support and explain suggested changes.
- Be the expert—know what you're doing when editing a document.
  - ✔ Standard usage and mechanics
  - ✔ Accepted style guide rules
  - ✔ Consistent editing style
  - ✔ Safety regulations
  - ✔ Specifications and standards
  - ✔ Technical knowledge when required
  - ✔ Audience needs
  - ✔ Organization's rules, regulations and publication requirements

The editor should be aware and informed in order to effectively edit a document and present incorporated changes efficiently and professionally.

Having confidence in one's ability and reason for suggested changes can limit the time a document spends in the review part of the process. Remember, in industry, time is money.

Getting the Document Ready for Dissemination

No matter how long the review process takes, eventually the document reaches a point where it is nearing completion. You have discussed the document with the experts, certain members of the audience and maybe even reviewed it with a colleague. It looks good, seems to offer the right information to the right audience and the deadline is quickly approaching. The document is now ready for that final edit, one last proof to perfect and finalize.

Understandably, each document is unique and should be regarded as such. But a final, general type of edit is necessary to complete the job.

That final check should include:

- ✔ Spelling
- ✔ Punctuation
- ✔ Format
- ✔ Organization
- ✔ Grammar
- ✔ Illustrations and graphics
- ✔ Readability
- ✔ Style
- ✔ Technical data unique to document

The editing process continues until all errors have been eliminated from the document. It's good practice to compare each version of the document with previous versions in order to ensure accepted accuracy is retained.

Editing Hints

- Use two people when editing a document. Have one check the document as the other reads.
- Always check previously produced documents for consistency and accepted format.
- Use reference books—thesaurus, dictionary, English handbooks and any professional reference guides necessary.
- Question changes—a matter of right or wrong, or among a number of possibilities?

Perfecting a document is obviously one of the most important steps in the process. Many members of a given audience will not have the benefit of knowing the communicator personally. With this in mind, their knowledge of you is based solely on the document. Any problems discovered by the audience, spelling, punctuation, inaccurate data, will most certainly reflect poorly on the communicator or coordinator of the project. Protect your credibility—Edit to Perfection.

Revision and editing in communication are, again, important steps in the process, and are, more often than not, the key concluding elements. Technology changes quite rapidly, and what was new yesterday can become old and obsolete today. Documents that fail to keep up with changes become not only worthless but costly. Revise and edit—create reliable products.

EXERCISES

1. Locate a set of instructions, possibly those which came with a product you've purchased. Revise and edit the instructions to make them more readable and useful to the reader. Considering instructions, it shouldn't be terribly difficult to locate a poorly written set.

2. Write a personal letter to a friend or someone you haven't seen in a while. After the first draft has been completed, go back and proof, employing the check for one thing at a time rule. Keep track of the number of problems you discover.

3. Locate a fellow student who has a term paper of some kind due in one of their classes. Ask to edit their paper, and employ the suggestions detailed in this chapter.

4. Revise the following sentences to make them more readable.

   - Dented or crushed cans may cause them to jam in the crusher or extracting problems.

   - The fly wheel should be turned all the way around slowly inside the housing in order to engage the rotor.

   - The image won't become sharp and clear until the focus ring is rotated.

   - There is three safety checks on the machine that should be engaged near the start housing.

5. Locate a discipline-specific professional document or a brief section in an advanced textbook and revise to meet the needs of a general audience.

6. Revise and edit the following document. The document's intent is to announce a service offered by a electronics group.

Electronic Special Services Group is currently ready to begin and start offering its services outside of our company to the local industrial community. We are a group of 9 technicians and one supervisor who believe Quality is our main objective.
We offer quality at a reasonable cost and can diagnose and solve a variety of electronic problems like circuit boards devices and systems. We will replace faulty components at a reasonable cost, instead of entire boards. We offer competitive turn around, repair history review, programmed test equipment and shared training. The group's technologies include, class 1 ESD protected facility, component level repair, cost effective repairs, design and build fixtures. We also make every effort and strive to offer documentation maintenance, field repair and documentation of repairs for the customer to keep track.
Our goals are involvement, planning and customer support to better serve your electronic repair needs. Contact Electronic Special Services Group for more information. 555-8849.

The Résumé and Related Issues

THE RÉSUMÉ

Why do the majority of technical and professional communication books deal, to one degree or another, with the résumé and related documents?

The résumé is probably one of the most important documents individuals will be required to construct. It's a document that continues to be important even after it serves its purpose and you land that ideal job. It assists professionals in keeping track of their careers. It encompasses many aspects of what a professional document is all about.

✔ Format
✔ Organization
✔ Document aesthetics
✔ Audience
✔ Content choices

The résumé is basically a summary of an individual's professional and educational experience.

- The résumé telegraphs who you are and what you want right up front.
- The résumé contains evidence of your past performance that forms part of your sales pitch for a desired position.
- The résumé emphasizes what you think is important about you as a candidate for a position.
- The résumé uses a format of your making, not theirs.

The résumé, like all professional documentation, must meet the needs of a prescribed audience. But, even before that audience's needs are met, purpose must be considered and addressed.

The Résumé's Purpose

The résumé is a catalog of what you have to offer a particular employer for a specific job. Or, if you do not have one particular employer pinpointed, it serves to present your qualifications to several prospects. The way you construct your résumé should be goal oriented, like all professional documentation. And the goal or purpose of the résumé is to get an interview, not to land a job. You land the job. The résumé is just the first step in that process.

In considering the purpose of the résumé, getting the interview, only that which is pertinent to that purpose should be included in the résumé. All factors related to the production of the résumé should be considered according to the established goal: purpose.

ONLY THAT INFORMATION WHICH IS PERTINENT TO PURPOSE SHOULD BE INCLUDED IN THE RÉSUMÉ.

While understanding and accepting that the résumé is designed solely to get you that interview, some preliminary considerations should be kept in mind while involved in the process. Think about it, take notes, ask questions and allow the document to serve its purpose.

Initial Pointers

- ✔ Keep it simple (easy to read).
- ✔ Inventory your contributions.
- ✔ Action verbs start each sentence.
- ✔ Draft it first and second and third, whatever it takes to perfect.
- ✔ Eliminate information not pertinent to purpose.
- ✔ Have it critiqued.
- ✔ Make it look good.
- ✔ Meet the needs of the audience.

Audience

Like all documentation, it is important to analyze the potential readers. Determine who they are and what they are basically looking for in our documentation. Understanding our potential readers will lend itself to determining what information is pertinent to purpose: getting the interview.

Some general assumptions can be made about the potential readers of the résumé. When considering intent, it is obvious that at least one aspect of the audience will probably be made up of those individuals involved in personnel, or human resources.

Note: Understandably, when involved in the job search the individual should research target companies to discover how best to meet their needs through the résumé. Here we will take more of a general look at the potential audience and its probable requirements relating to the résumé.

Generally when a position becomes available the solicited résumés are usually funneled through the staff at the personnel or human resources office. They are more often than not the first to see and evaluate the résumés received. While it is quite important to find out what specifics might relate to this member of our audience, some general assumptions can be made that will assist in facilitating the purpose at hand: getting the interview.

REMEMBER, ONLY THAT INFORMATION THAT IS PERTINENT TO PURPOSE AND MEETS THE NEEDS OF THE AUDIENCE SHOULD BE INCLUDED IN THE RÉSUMÉ.

It is probably accurate to assume that Human Resource personnel have particular knowledge and talents in common. Their primary motivation probably relates to finding the best possible candidates to be interviewed for an available position. That is their job, selecting the right candidates for the right reasons.

Generally speaking, when a professional position becomes available more than a few applications in the form of résumés are received. It is the primary responsibility of the human resource reader to decide, at least initially, what candidates meet the basic requirements for the position. They determine whose résumé goes in the "maybe" pile and whose goes in the "forget about it" pile. With this in mind, our résumé should, in part, strive to meet their needs. If your background meets their requirements, then no problem exists here. But what if the candidate doesn't quite have what the position calls for? Should the writer not take the chance and apply, reject the potential opportunity? No.

If your background doesn't quite encompass exactly what they are looking for, substitute what you do have for what you don't have. Allow the reader to make the final decision, determine whether or not you might make a viable candidate for the position.

For example, let's say an advertised position requires 2 years experience in electronic repair, but you have no professional experience. What you do have is 1 year in a co-op program where the thrust of the experience involved the repair of certain electronic components. Maybe you have a special interest in repairing VCRs or stereos in addition to your co-op experience. Well, emphasize what you do have on the résumé, not what you don't have. Again, allow the reader to make the final determination. Don't close yourself out of potential opportunities.

Always emphasize and subordinate according to the reader's needs. Emphasize that which is most pertinent to purpose and subordinate that which is least pertinent to purpose: meeting the individual needs of your audience. (More on how organization can help to accomplish this later.)

Okay, Human Resource personnel have the best interest of the company in mind and one of the things they will be looking for is whether or not you meet the basic requirements. You're aware of this and have even gone so far as to substitute what you do have to encourage their offer, they have to first look at your résumé, be drawn to it and take the time to discover your talents. Getting their attention is the first step in meeting their needs.

Encourage Reader Interest—Make It Look Good

Creating an attractive résumé is one of the first steps in ensuring success with this document. Keep in mind, a job opening with professional possibilities will probably attract more than a few interested applicants. One of the primary duties of Human Resource personnel is to compile these résumés and determine, at least initially, who might prove to be a viable candidate to interview. One of the first things they notice is how professional the résumé looks and if it attracts their attention for the right reasons.

Attracting their attention for the right reasons does not encompass anything cute or out of the ordinary. Do not print your résumé on paper that is not acceptable, like a bright red or blue. It will attract attention, but not for the right reasons. The only thing with these résumés that stands out is the color of the paper, not the content of the document. Don't include graphics or fancy type styles. Again, it may attract attention, but not for its content.

One of the assumptions that can be made on behalf of these members of our audience, Human Resource personnel, is that they probably see quite a few résumés on a fairly regular basis; that's part of their job. They know what a good résumé looks like; they know what works. Give them what they expect; they don't expect surprises.

Maybe this is your first professional résumé and you're not quite sure what your potential audience might appreciate. Again, as discussed earlier, take a look at previously produced résumés. Locate professionals already practicing in your chosen profession. Take note of what seems to be standard or acceptable in meeting the needs of the audience. Consider the general elements of the résumé, then determine what might work specifically for you. Determining what is acceptable and expected by Human Resource personnel is the first step to success.

- Standard paper color—white, off-white, light grays & tans.
- Standard, easily read type style.
- Include plenty of white space—encourages interest.
- Use headings to distinguish important sections.
- Use a balanced format.

In short, don't give the reader any reason to reject your résumé, at least initially. The human factor should also be taken into account here. Anytime a document is being produced, the communicator should ask a number of important questions when considering audience reaction. How will choices be received positively and how might they be received negatively. If there are any negative ways a choice might be received, that choice should probably be reconsidered. (More on this as we go through the résumé step-by-step.)

More on the Résumé's Audience

Another potential member of the audience for your résumé besides Human Resource personnel will probably be the professional, the expert in your field. Where Human Resource personnel are looking for those specifics relating to the discipline and how they might be applied to the available position, the expert will be looking for those specifics that might be applied to the opening.

What can we assume about these potential readers? They are probably in a supervisory capacity or have a direct interest in the group, department, or section within the company that is looking to fill a particular position. These members of the audience will most likely get a chance to review potential candidates after Human Resource personnel have completed the initial screening process. The experts are familiar with your field, they know what might fill their specific needs relating to the opening. They can determine the value of specifics relating to experience as well as education.

- Emphasize and subordinate according to field and job requirements.
- Include professional affiliations familiar to experts.
- Detail experience, duties and responsibilities when pertinent.
- Concentrate on discipline specifics, but also portray diversity.

Remember, these potential readers are probably experts in your discipline and they know what they're looking for to fill the position. They're looking for the best candidates to interview. Construct your résumé to meet their needs as well as those of the Human Resource member of the audience. All possible readers are basically looking for the same information, just for different reasons.

There are certainly other potential readers of your résumé, but the two detailed here are probably the primary decision makers in the process. Remember, the intent of this document is to get the interview. Every consideration and choice should work toward that end.

Take a look at practicing professionals' résumés—what works for them?

Include only that which is pertinent to purpose.

Consider the positive and negative ramifications relating to choices.

Meet human resource personnel's general requirements.

Meet expert's specific requirements.

Getting Started

Like any other professional/technical document, writing the résumé should follow a process that leads to the intended product. We begin by determining what the purpose of this document is and who might be potential readers.

- Purpose—to get an interview.
- Audience—Human Resource personnel and professional experts.

The next step in the process is to determine what information will be pertinent to your purpose and what information will serve the needs of our audience.

Here, we'll take the communicator through producing a résumé as though they haven't had the opportunity to compile and disseminate a résumé. As with all professional documents, we begin the process by thinking, contemplating what the résumé might be all about. Accepting that writing is, in part, a questioning process, we begin by asking two essential questions.

- What do we know about the résumé?
- What do we need to find out?

Collecting information is an important initial step in the documentation process. Since the résumé is basically a summary of our background, we start collecting information dealing with what we might have to offer a potential employer.

Note: It's much easier to reject information at a later stage than to discover we lack information and find ourselves needing to go back.

Begin by considering what might prove beneficial to the members of our predetermined audience. Ask and answer questions.

WHO AM I? LIST AS MANY RESPONSES AS POSSIBLE

- Personality traits—"self-starter" as example: relates to personal initiative.
- Interests/Activities—relates to personal commitment & transferable responsibility.
- Performance abilities—relates to situation adaptability.
- Experience/Education/Training—previous learning experience & potential.
- Contributions—enhances description of duties & responsibilities.

Responding to "Contributions," for example, could deal with a number of issues. Responses often depend on individual background and experience.

✔ any activity performed which resulted in a tangible benefit to an organization and demonstrated a productive use of your skills.

- Skills/Strengths/Talents—languages, specific areas of proficiency.
- Community activities—ability to supervise, run a program, self motivated achievements.
- Emotions/inner issues—positive approach to personal history.

Responding to these considerations is an effective first step, but the responses will most probably be somewhat general by nature. In addition to the responses, we'll also have to include specific examples that support and clarify.

Once all of these issues are covered, supported by specific examples from the individual background, concentrate on those that best reflect background and how it might relate to job performance abilities.

What we're doing here is collecting data that might prove useful when constructing the résumé. This pre-writing stage encourages the communicator to think in terms of the specific document and its purpose, and how it might come together to satisfy the needs of the audience.

GENERAL OVERVIEW—THE BASICS

- Developing and preparing the résumé

  ✔ analyze yourself and your background
  ✔ identify those, in general and specifically, to whom you will submit your résumé
  ✔ Organize and prepare the résumé (Note: we will take a more detailed look at the individual sections later in this chapter.)

- Gathering information—a thorough analysis

  ✔ experience
  ✔ education
  ✔ training
  ✔ professional skills

More on the Basics

- It helps to list the major points for each category before actually beginning to organize and write.
- Analyze and evaluate appropriate information (select and reject).
  ✔ What exact job are you seeking?
  ✔ What information is most pertinent to that job or career area?
  ✔ Add appropriate, related details.
  ✔ How are you going to present your qualifications most effectively to get an interview?
- With all communication tasks, it's a good idea to place yourself in the shoes of the reader—see yourself through the eyes of your audience. Try and determine what information it might find useful and pertinent to the purpose of the document.

Note: No matter what subject requires you to communicate, it's essential that you get to know your topic as thoroughly as possible. The better you know your subject, the more effectively you can relate information to your readers. Here, the subject is you and you might be surprised how much you may learn about your subject when taking the time to ask questions and compile the pertinent, necessary information.

Once you've collected all the important information that relates to your subject—you—you can begin determining how this data might find its way into your résumé. (Note: you can always add data later—the process allows for change.)

The résumé, like all documentation, is made up of many elements. One of these elements deals with the sections that might be included on the résumé to fulfill the needs of the audience. Individually, we will probably choose particular sections that best highlight specific backgrounds. Considering the diversity of individual backgrounds, we'll take a look and consider the sections a résumé might include.

The Sections of the Résumé

✔ Work History	✔ Special Skills
✔ Awards	✔ Hobbies (Interests)
✔ Experience	✔ Goal
✔ Salary History	✔ Objective
✔ Education	✔ Personal Information
✔ Military Experience	✔ Professional Affiliations
✔ Name, address, phone number	✔ Volunteer
✔ References	✔ Training

Again, these are general possibilities. Specifically, individual background will dictate what sections are chosen to be included on the résumé.

Headings

In order to distinguish one section from another on your résumé, headings are used to indicate the separate sections. Headings are also used to make the résumé attractive, and encourage reader interest. Headings also allow the reader to quickly find particular information without the hassle of scanning the entire document.

The résumé, as opposed to the application form, is of your construction; it involves your choices as they pertain to a particular job that may be available. It allows you to include only that information that you choose to include. You're not limited to filling in the spaces that might appear on the application. Therefore, let headings work to this advantage. Choose the heading that best introduces the information you wish to present in your résumé.

Everyone will have either a work history or experience section on their résumé, maybe both for some. The heading should indicate what the section contains. Work History suggests those experiences where we were compensated; jobs held where you received a pay check. If there are sufficient items to include under this heading, then work history will do the job. But what if your individual work related experiences are limited, and one or two entries under this heading seem lost; they limit your background.

Rather than risk a negative review of your résumé for this reason, use a heading that will better serve the purpose. Maybe you do have limited work related experiences, but you do have a number of other kinds of experiences. Maybe you've participated in a co-op program, volunteered for a local community activity or service where you gained some valuable experience, except you weren't compensated in the traditional way, like with money. Head this section "Experience" rather than "Work History." This way, the heading works to your benefit, points out your background without limiting the value, or relying solely on traditional job type entries.

Use Headings to Your Benefit Selecting the Right Sections For the Résumé

When determining what sections will work best for you on your résumé, there are a couple of things to keep in mind. Consider the Human Factor throughout the process; remember the readers of your résumé are people just like you and have good days, bad days, likes and dislikes. Put yourself in the place of the reader and ask what would work best if the roles were reversed. Another thing to keep in mind is the questioning part of the process.

Every choice you make when documenting information for dissemination to an audience should be questioned initially by you. Chances are that the reader may have a question or two regarding the information offered. Every choice made when documenting information should have a reason; you should be able to explain that choice if called upon to do so.

- Why did you organize the information the way you did?
- Why did you choose a particular format?
- What dictated your content choices?

Have the right reasons; know why and you can be confident that you probably made the best choices under the circumstances.

The Positive/Negative Question

In addition to having well thought out reasons for documenting information in particular, you should also address the positive and negative ramifications regarding your choices. As you put yourself in the position of your reader, consider to what extent your information will be regarded in a positive way.

- Will the data be accepted as presented?
- Is the data open to interpretation?
- Is there any way your data could be regarded in a way not intended?
- Could the data possibly cause your document to be rejected in part or in whole?
- If any of these questions can be answered in the affirmative, maybe you'll want to reconsider including that particular data.
- If, as best you can considering the circumstances, you determine the data being presented can probably only be regarded as positive and serve the purpose of the document, you have probably made the right choice.

Name, Address, Phone Number

It's obvious that all résumés will include the writer's name, address and phone number. This is the most important information on your résumé and should be emphasized and highlighted to catch the reader's attention. You are who this document is all about and where you can be contacted.

Include your full name and middle initial. Don't use nicknames or condensed versions. A good rule to follow is to use the name you would use to sign an important document such as a marriage license or a release to make a movie out of your life story.

Include your full address, including complete zip code and apartment number when applicable. The address included should be that address where you can be reached at any given time.

Not all documents are acted upon when received and the résumé is no exception. It may find its way into a file for action at a later date. So, if you're away at school or have more than one address for any reason, it is best to indicate only the one where you are sure to be contacted at any given time.

Including two addresses on a résumé requires the reader to figure out where you may be if they decide to contact you by mail. If you include a school address, the reader has to figure out whether or not you may be on a break, taking summer classes. It requires the reader to do more than they're possibly willing to do. Remember the negative. Could including more than one address cause your résumé to be rejected?

The same considerations apply to the phone number also. More than one phone number requires the reader to figure out where you may be at any given time. It requires that they make more than one call. If there are more than a few applicants for the position you are applying, maybe including two phone numbers could encourage the reader to move on to the next résumé. Oh yes, don't forget the area code.

SUGGESTED

Michael C. Carpenter
386 Ridgelawn Ave.
Rochester, New York 14615
Phone: (716) 555-8849

As the most important information on your résumé, make it stand out: center the entry, boldface your name, surround it with white space. Do whatever it takes, but keep it neat and professional.

NOT SUGGESTED

Mike Carpenter
386 Ridgelawn Ave.
Rochester, N.Y.
555-8849

OR

Mike Carpenter

124 Campus Drive   386 Ridgelawn Ave.
Rochester, N.Y. 14615   Rochester, N.Y. 14615
College Town, N.Y. 12315   (716) 555-8849
(213) 555-7733

Make it as easy as possible for the reader to get in touch with you when they need to. Don't require them to do more than is necessary and you shouldn't have to worry about your résumé being rejected for this reason.

Objective

The next section that might be included on a résumé is the objective. The objective is exactly what it states. It would generally address a particular kind of job or area of interest relating to the professional desires of the writer.

An objective certainly isn't always necessary to include on your résumé. Not everyone has an objective or particular area of interest. In fact, a too specific objective could limit the applicant's opportunities.

Include an objective if you happen to have a specific job you are interested in. Don't include an objective if your needs are more general in nature. Leave it up to the reader to interpret your education and experience to determine where your talents can best be put to use within the company. If you have a degree in electronics and two years professional experience, chances are they won't offer you a job in their cafeteria. If, by chance, they do, turn it down.

Be specific about your objective, but leave your options open.

SUGGESTED

Objective: Entry level position in Accounting where my skills and education can best be utilized.
Objective: Position as Electronic Technician where my skills and education can best be utilized.

NOT SUGGESTED

Objective: Position where my skills and talents can be enhanced.
Objective: A position that gives me the opportunity to discover the focus of my talents.

Goal

A goal statement can take into account those elements that define, in part, the objective statement, but project beyond the immediate. A goal is, again, exactly what it suggests. The goal adds an eventual plan, future opportunities to the immediacy of the objective. It deals with where you would like to be in your career in the future, where you would like this position to lead.

Just like the objective, only include a goal if you have one. Don't include a goal if you don't. It's not always necessary to document where you would like a job to lead. To a certain extent, this can be determined in the interview.

SUGGESTED

Goal: Position as an account representative leading to management.
Goal: Entry level position in electronics where increased experience supports design opportunities.

NOT SUGGESTED

Goal: Position quickly leading to management.
Goal: Position as computer programmer where my talents will be rewarded.

Don't forget the questioning in the process. If you do choose to include an objective or a goal, ask how it will be regarded by your audience, positively or negatively; think like your reader. Imagine what their needs are and how an objective or a goal might begin to meet their needs.

An objective or goal gets your message across quickly. If you choose to include either one, make it brief and interesting. It basically answers the reader's immediate questions, like what are you seeking.

There are a variety of other sections that could follow your name section, such as the summary statement. Most individuals who choose to include this section have an extensive professional background and decide it is necessary to summarize their experiences. It accomplishes taking the specific successes from various positions and condenses and highlights those that best support immediate intent.

Education

The education section of the résumé is probably one of the two most important sections on the résumé. (The other is work history or experience.) No matter what the extent of educational background, everyone will include an education section; it's expected by the audience.

Detailing education indicates a number of different things to your audience.

- Education indicates an understanding of discipline theory.
- Education indicates a basic understanding of a particular field or discipline.
- Education demonstrates ability to apply oneself to the specifics of a discipline.
- Education supports a desire to dedicate one's professional career objectives to a particular discipline.
- Just like in any other document, the communicator emphasizes what is most pertinent to the purpose at hand: what might most interest the reader. Education is emphasized when there is little or no experience relating to a chosen

discipline. It displays commitment to a particular profession. What specifics will be included under the education heading depends on individual background and career plans.

Content Choices

Again, choices are dictated by an individual's background, but could include everything from high school to scholarships awarded for post-secondary education.

High school should only be included when there are no educational experiences beyond that level. Everyone has a high school education, particularly those interested in a professional career. Is it really necessary to point it out?

Whatever might have been accomplished in high school is probably less than pertinent once you begin thinking in terms of career goals and construct your résumé and detail professional qualifications. Sure, maybe you were the president of your class, but who cares? Maybe you participated in 42 clubs in high school, but who really cares, except maybe mom and dad. Okay, maybe one of those clubs is pertinent to career goals, but it was in high school. Consider the extent and depth of instruction and how it might interest potential readers.

If the high school was in-depth and hands-on, then consider including it under a separate section: additional training, for example. If you do have an individual or personal reason for including high school, then go ahead and include it; just don't emphasize it, particularly when you have a college degree or college credit. Even if you have yet to complete the degree you're currently working on, it should be included and detailed with the reader in mind.

Detailing College With the Positive and Negative in Mind

Just as the communicator should decide how to organize an entire document, so should you determine how to organize and emphasize each section of that document. The résumé is no exception. Emphasize the most important facts based on background and reader's needs.

Emphasizing College Data

The most important information regarding college is the degree itself. Whether it's completed or not, point out the degree in question: A.S., B.A., M.A. or certificate programs that indicate commitment and completion.

The field or major would follow the degree itself. That indicates the discipline and a commitment to completing the requirements for a particular program. Again, detail information in order of importance. The degree comes first, followed by the major.

After the degree and major have been listed, detail the institution where you are pursuing the degree. It's important for the reader to know that you are pursuing an education at an accredited institution of higher learning. Believe it or not, there are organizations out there, they don't deserve to be referred to as colleges, that are less than reputable and are not recognized as respected, accredited places of higher learning.

Many of these pseudo-colleges are advertised in a variety of magazines. They'll even send you a slick looking catalogue that can be quite impressive. Some of these institutions are very good at what they do. They will even require you to do some work to make you feel as though you legitimately earned the degree. The only problem is, most of these degree granting organizations are not accredited, recognized by an agency offering accreditation. Therefore, the degrees they offer are all but worthless. Like with anything else, when it comes to education, "let the buyer beware."

DEGREE—MAJOR—INSTITUTION

Again, as best as you can in any given situation, place yourself in the reader's position and determine how you would react. What information regarding this entry is most important and how should that information be organized?

SUGGESTED

A.S. Electronic Technology, Monroe Community College
B.S. Mechanical Technology, Rochester Institute of Technology
(Note: One of the few instances where it's acceptable to abbreviate on the résumé is with the degree.)

NOT SUGGESTED

Associate in Science, M.C.C., Rochester, Electronic Tech.
(Too confusing; requires reader to spend more time than is necessary to figure out what your education is all about.)

Bachelor of Science, Mech. Tech. R.I.T.
(Again, doesn't reach the uninformed reader.)

Dates

Including dates along with the degree is rather simple, particularly if the education has been completed and the degree is in hand. It simply follows the name of the institution. It's generally not necessary to include the month or day, the year is sufficient information.

A.S. Electronic Technology, Monroe Community College, 1993

This indicates to the reader the year you received your degree, what the degree is, the major, as well as the institution. This entry is clear and to the point. The most important data has been properly emphasized and the reader is not left to figure out what the degree is all about or whether or not you received it.

SIMPLE—CONCISE—TO THE POINT

What about if you have yet to receive your degree? Maybe you're getting ready to graduate and want to begin your job search, but don't want to present false information. Maybe you're already in the work force and going to school to increase your marketability, or going to school part-time. How can you indicate this without holding back information or creating a false impression? Again, consider the reader, their needs and the logic behind emphasizing and subordinating information.

It's always important to be honest and up-front with your readers, especially in a document like the résumé. Don't give the reader any reason to reject; consider the positive and the negative ways the data may be regarded. Include the date, but be specific about the status of your degree. Subordinate the date by placing it beneath the degree entry within parentheses. Point out that you anticipate or expect to receive the degree at a particular point in time.

As best as can be determined, project when you think you might complete the requirements for the degree. Be as accurate as possible, but don't be terribly concerned if for some unforeseen reason you don't meet that date. Remember, the purpose of this document, the résumé, is to get the interview. You can always deal with a missed personal goal when the time comes, if necessary.

A.S. Electronic Technology, Monroe Community College
(Anticipated Spring, 199ʹ)

B.S. Mechanical Technology, Rochester Institute of Technology
(Expected Fall, 199 ̆)

As with all entries, be honest, accurate and to the point, but don't emphasize what you don't have. Subordinate what you don't have, and lead with what you do have. Emphasize according to intent, the purpose of the document.

Academic Honors

There are many ways to stand out, demonstrate special achievement in education. The variety of opportunities to be recognized for academic excellence are many.

- Grade point average
- Clubs and organizations
- Dean's list
- Leadership
- Scholarships
- Awards
- Athletics

These are certainly not conclusive, but do represent some of the ways you can enhance your educational experience and be recognized for your hard work, commitment and dedication.

What else to include under the education heading should be determined based on the purpose of the document and on the reader's needs. Remember, for everything you consider including in your résumé, consider the positive and negative ways that information may be regarded.

When to include grade point average (GPA)? If your GPA is above 3.00 should you include it on your résumé? It is certainly a respectable average, indicates academic achievement and a certain amount of success. But what if it's below 3.00, should it be included?

When trying to determine whether or not to include GPA on your résumé, consider the Human Factor, the positive, negative reactions to this entry. Put yourself in the place of the reader and question their possible reactions.

You come across a résumé, the nineteenth you've looked at, and the individual's GPA is 4.00. Maybe you're impressed, envious of the applicant. You recall your fellow students when you were in college who maintained such an excellent average. What were they like? Who were they? They were certainly excellent and dedicated students; they were good at what they did: go to school. They were probably respected for their academic achievements, but was their educational experience balanced?

You can't do much better than a 4.00 average; it suggests something positive about the applicant. It suggests they can apply themselves and achieve academically. It could also suggest a certain rigidity, a lack of balance. How well someone does in school doesn't necessarily mean they can succeed on the job. Consider the reader. How would you react?

In order to avoid trying to second guess your reader regarding the GPA, it's probably a good idea not to include this data on your résumé. If you determine it's pertinent, bring it up at the interview. Don't give the reader any reason to reject your document; keep the purpose in mind. Besides, generally, how well you did in school becomes unimportant five years after you're out of school. By that time you've got some practical experience behind you and you have proven your ability to succeed at your profession. If you do decide to include your GPA, remember to emphasize what is most pertinent to the reader's needs and subordinate that which is least important.

When it comes to determining when and when not to include other academic achievements, consider the Human Factor, the positive, negative reactions. If it's pertinent to your field of study, it's probably a good idea to include it.

- If you're a member of the Society of Mechanical Engineers and you're majoring in engineering, include it.
- If you're the student body president and you want to point out your leadership skills, include it.
- If you received an award for the most innovative computer program and you're a computer major, include it.
- If you're a physical education major and you participate in sports, include it.
- If you've received a scholarship, determine how well the type of scholarship you received (academic, financial, athletic) will be perceived by your readers.

If you want to demonstrate a well-rounded, diverse background, determine the positive and negative ways the information may be regarded by your readers, then emphasize or subordinate according to purpose. If the particular academic achievement is pertinent, include it.

Course Work

Among the other items that could also be included under the Education heading is course work. Here, again let the heading work to benefit, serve the purpose at hand. The heading, course work is general in nature and almost any course completed could be included here. The heading, related course work is a bit more specific and suggests courses directly and indirectly related to a major field of study.

When and when not to include additional courses under the education heading depends on a number of factors. A variety of courses can be listed if only to show a well-rounded, diverse educational background. Choosing the right course to add can enhance meeting the goal of this document.

List courses that aren't traditionally associated with your particular program. If your major is accounting, you're certainly not going to list courses like Accounting I, or Fundamentals of Accounting, or Economics. It's understood by your reader that these courses are a necessary part of your program; there's no point in listing the obvious.

List those courses that go beyond a traditional course of study, show a broad educational experience. Consider your readers and what might impress or interest them. What might they be looking for in an employee?

- Computer courses—most jobs today require you to use a computer.
- Writing courses—one of the main things employers would like in more of their employees is the ability to write.
- Communications courses—again, employers appreciate employees who have the ability to communicate.

THE ABILITY TO COMMUNICATE EFFECTIVELY DOUBLES YOUR VALUE

- Psychology courses—they indicate an understanding of people.
- Any unique course—courses that indicate a diverse education.
  ✔ Literature courses if you're a math or engineering major.
  ✔ Many advanced humanities courses for the same reason
  ✔ Science courses or math courses if you're a humanities major.

Additional Education

Include any other education experiences, particularly if they prove to be pertinent to purpose. Generally any and all education indicates something positive about an applicant. Completed programs, of course, would be emphasized, but that doesn't negate including other education.

Before settling on a program that is or will eventually be completed, maybe you attended some other institutions but for one reason or another didn't complete the program and receive a degree. Include these also, unless you determine they may be regarded as negative by your reader, but be sure to subordinate these entries. Be specific about the facts and details associated with these particular entries.

Accounting, University of Rochester, 1992

This entry indicates the program, the institution and the year of study. It's straightforward, concise and to the point. It suggests you studied accounting at a particular school for a specified period of time. Of course if you have more than a couple of these experiences to list it could indicate an inability to complete what you've started. Again, consider the positive and the negative reactions by your readers and base your decision on the perceived reaction.

Industrial Education

After being in the work force for a period of time, many of us have taken advantage of the courses, and educational opportunities offered by the companies we work for. Various companies offer a variety of training opportunities to employees to improve not only productivity, but also theoretical understanding related to practical performance.

As a writer, I took advantage of a variety of in-plant courses that were offered to employees. The main reason I took these courses was to enhance my ability do my job better.

I took some courses in basic electronics in order to facilitate producing documents that encompassed electronic elements. I wanted to understand what I was writing about. I wanted to be able to communicate with the experts I was expected to interview for information. I didn't want to require them to give me a mini-course in their field every time I asked a question. I wanted to understand terms and concepts and how to apply those terms and concepts in documentation. I took courses in instrumentation, blue print reading and optics for the same reasons. These courses certainly belong on the résumé, particularly if they are pertinent to purpose.

If you have more than one of these in-plant courses, you might want to consider giving them their own section on your résumé. Make them stand out and serve the purpose at hand.

Industrial Education

Basic Electronics, Eastman Kodak Company, 199

Basic CAD Operation, Flugel Industries, 199

Again, emphasize and subordinate as is appropriate to purpose. If these experiences are limited, include them under the traditional education heading.

Go ahead and initially collect all the data you can think of for the education section. It's much easier to reject information at a later date than it is to discover you lack sufficient information to serve the purpose.

Remember, education indicates to your reader an ability to apply yourself and commit to goals. Success is realized when the process has been completed. Education indicates to the reader a theoretical understanding of the subject matter, the discipline, but doesn't necessarily support practical application. Fully detail your educational background according to the purpose; meet the reader's needs. But it is also important to present a balanced background, and the rest of the résumé accomplishes that.

SUGGESTED

A.S., Electronic Technology, Monroe Community College

(Anticipated Spring, '   ) GPA 3.63

Note: use your discretion when entering honors—remember the possible positive and negative reactions. THINK LIKE YOUR AUDIENCE.

Related Courses:	Professional Writing	Computer Programming
	CAD Basics	Public Speaking

Sociology, Columbia University, 199

B.A., English, New York University, 199

New York City, New York

Note: It's not necessary to include any more than the city and state when indicating the address of the college.

B.S., Electrical Engineering, Rochester Institute of Technology

(Expected, Fall, '   )

Certificate, Industrial Management, Eastman Kodak Company

Creative Writing, University of Iowa, 199

Note: all entries on your résumé, education section included, should be detailed in a concise and accurate manner that doesn't require your reader to interpret your information.

NOT SUGGESTED

Associate in Science, M.C.C., 1000 E. Henrietta Road, Rochester New York. Currently attending

–hope to graduate about 199

BS, Elect. Eng. R.I.T. Rochester, New York, 199

Deans's List 4 separate semesters, GPA 2.80

Roosevelt High School, Diploma, 1989

    Class Secretary

    Drama Club

    Yearbook Staff

Note: Who really cares about high school when you have post secondary education?

B.S., Accounting, University of Rochester

(Expected, Spring, ')

Course Work: Accounting 1 & 11, Micro & Macro Economics

Statistics 107, 211, 302

Note: course numbers are obscure to the uninformed.

The best way to determine what to include under the education heading is to anticipate your reader's reactions. What's pertinent to purpose? What's going to help get you that interview? When trying to decide what to include, remember the positive and negative. If all possible reactions on behalf of your readers are positive, then the entry is probably pertinent. If you can anticipate a possible negative reaction to an entry, it's probably best to reconsider whether or not that particular entry is pertinent to the purpose at hand.

MEET YOUR READER'S NEEDS—DON'T PROVIDE A REASON TO HAVE YOUR DOCUMENT REJECTED

Work History

Work history is another section that is essential to everyone's résumé. Detailing work related experiences indicates a number of different things to your readers. Even if your employment background is not pertinent to your chosen career field, it is important to include this section.

First of all, allow the heading to work to your benefit. Work history indicates particular jobs you've held in which you were compensated. Another possible heading for this section could be, Employment; although this might sound somewhat more specific; it may indicate professionally related jobs. Experience is another possible heading for this section, but could indicate more than traditional kinds of jobs. (More on this possible heading later.)

Again, it is essential to include work history on your résumé for a number of different reasons. It's not always possible to practice our chosen profession, or have hands-on experience in our field while attending college. Often, all we have to indicate to a reader that we are a viable candidate for a position is our education. In this case, we certainly will emphasize the education on our résumé. But that doesn't negate including a work history section. In fact, this dictates that we include a work history section on our résumé.

Include unrelated work history to indicate an ability to be employable. What does unrelated work history indicate to your reader?

- It indicates commitment.
- It indicates a sense of responsibility.
- It indicates a desire to apply yourself.
- It indicates an understanding of compensation for effort.
- It indicates an ability to get up in the morning.
- It indicates an ability to obtain and hold a job.

These points may seem simple in scope, but they do offer your reader some essential information. Even unrelated work history provides the reader with information that will assist in the decision making process. This information helps the reader decide whether or not to take a chance on you and your ability to learn and to perform effectively on the job.

Put yourself in place of the reader when trying to decide what information to include in the work history section of your résumé. You come to Education and it meets the requirements for the position, next you move on to the work history section, but the applicant has little if any practical experience, but they have held a number of unrelated jobs.

6/89–5/94   Cashier, Leigh Supermarkets, Inc. Mossberg, Ontario Canada.

Duties: Supervised front end cashiers, including closing and cashing out responsibilities.

This job listing may initially seem less than encouraging for the reader along with your degree in electronics, but it does provide some essential information. How would you regard this entry if you were the reader? What does it suggest about the applicant? It indicates all those things necessary for a new employee. It indicates that they can obtain a job, learn, take on responsibility and succeed when presented with an opportunity.

Related Work History

As indicated, any and all work history entries provide essential information to your reader. Remember to put your best foot forward here and emphasize your employability. Beyond general, non-discipline related jobs are, of course, those positions held that connect either directly or indirectly to your career goals.

It is not out of the question for those of us with more than a number of years in the work force to have some career-related experience behind us. But then there are those who have little discipline-oriented experience. The key here is of course to emphasize what you do have. If you have or are working on a degree in Accounting and you're only related job was as a counter person, make it fit.

Inventory counter coordinator, Camshaft Auto Parts, Detroit, MI.

Duties: Dispensed the complete range of auto parts to customers and dealerships. Estimated and determined daily receipt totals, including cashing out and closing responsibilities.

This is a bit exaggerated, particularly the job title, but should indicate how language can work to your advantage. Be accurate and truthful always on this and all other documents, but remember to use words to serve the purpose at hand. What sounds more impressive, janitor or building maintenance technician? Both titles suggest the same position, but one is a bit more impressive than the other. Just be careful not to go overboard; never underestimate the intelligence of your readers in any situation.

If you have a brand-new degree in electronics, but no experience other than two summers working for Radio Shack: make the indirect connection direct. Explain the duties and responsibilities, detail job related expertise obtained through this position; determine the reader's immediate needs and strive to meet those needs. It's not necessary to point out that these were summer positions. That's something that can be pointed out and discussed at the interview. Remember, don't give the reader any reason to reject your document.

1991–1992 Sales Associate, Radio Shack, Menlo Park, Ill.

Duties: Provided customers service and assistance in determining and selecting the appropriate electronic systems, devices and components.

When determining and constructing work histories, keep in mind the language you choose when detailing pertinent information. Always be prepared and ready to explain and provide additional detail supporting the data included on your résumé. Every choice made in the documentation process should have a clear, logical reason behind it.

In some respects, those who have a variety of career-related experiences may find this entry a bit easier to construct, but not always. First of all, the question one needs to address is how much to include on the résumé?

If you've been in the work force for a number of years, determining how much to include, how far to go back, is the issue at hand. There are a number of factors that should dictate how far you go back in work history on your résumé.

If you have over 15 years in the work force, it's probably best not to go back any further than 10 or 15 years. First of all, unless you've been doing basically the same thing for that period of time, chances are that whatever you did 10 to 15 years ago probably no longer applies. Time tends to diminish skills and knowledge unless we stay active in the field.

On the other hand, if going back 15 years shows a sequence of growth and success, you may want to consider including the entries. If you began as an entry level technician and currently hold the position of supervisor within the same field, indicate that positive kind of professional growth. Include the duties and responsibilities that most closely match the reader's requirements. Make an effort to discover what's currently favored in your field, what experiences are most in demand and emphasize accordingly. Always keep in mind the positive and negative ways your information may be regarded.

The Age Factor

For those of us who have been in the work force for more than a few years, the age factory should, at least initially, be considered. It's appreciated that the more experience an applicant has, the more potential they have for probable success on the job. Experience is one of the most important things your readers will be looking for as they scan your résumé, so point it out and emphasize the positive certainly. Generally, discipline-related experience will be regarded in a positive way. But could detailing 10 to 15 years of experience ever be regarded in a negative way?

When it gets right down to deciding who to interview, the reader will be asking a number of questions while involved in the selection process. Of course, they'll be determining whether education, skills and experience meets their needs. One question that they may ask when reviewing résumés, is if a particular applicant is eventually hired, how many years of commitment can they expect to get out of their investment? This has always been a matter of concern for older workers. Hopefully, our readers would never discriminate for any reason, but how sure can we be? It's generally not difficult to determine someone's age based on the chronological facts detailed on their résumés. Keep this factor in mind when deciding how far to go back in your work history. Remember, don't give your reader any reason to reject your document; and in this case, you.

General Experience

As indicated, use headings to benefit the purpose at hand. Work history and employment generally indicate traditional positions held in the work force. But what if your background consists of more than only positions held? Maybe you have limited work related experiences to include on your résumé but still need to show a diverse history.

The heading experience could indicate and encompass those things that wouldn't necessarily fall neatly under work history. Everyone's life is filled with more than just going to school and/or work. We may be involved in a variety of activities including volunteer work, clubs and organizations or social groups that require a certain amount of commitment and dedication. We may gain some valuable experience from these activities and want to indicate this to our readers.

If you've been involved in a number of volunteer experiences, give them their own section. Volunteer work indicates a number of different things about a potential candidate.

- Community involvement
- People person
- Altruistic
- Interests transcend monetary rewards
- Well rounded
- How would you, as the reader, regard this section?

Tutor, Project Literacy Plus, Cambridge, Mass.

Responsibilities: Assisted and guided adults through the process of learning to read and write.

I know I would be impressed by this entry and might want to learn more what it's all about. Remember the purpose, getting the interview.

Heading the section Experience also allows for a number of other possibilities in offering information to our readers. Just because you're not paid for a particular effort does not make it not valuable experience.

If your job history is somewhat limited, but you've participated in a variety of activities in school or in the community, title this section experience rather than work history.

Whatever you choose to title this section, Work History, Employment or Experience, allow the heading to work for you, serve your best interests and provide the reader with the information they need to make a positive decision. Emphasize and subordinate according to what the reader is looking for and how your background best fulfills this need.

If the title of the job you held is impressive or recognizable, begin with that. If the title is less than impressive, but the company is well known, begin with the company's name.

6/87–11/94 Lead Electrical Technician, Watts Electronics, Morgantown, PA.

6/87–11/94 IBM, Food Service, Rochester, NY.

When detailing the duties and responsibilities related to a particular job or experience always indicate those that would be of primary interest to a reader in your career area. Be straightforward and assertive with this portion of the entry. Begin each statement with an active verb and stress action in the statement. Make sure this portion of the entry is complete, clear and concise; encourage reader interest.

Suggestions for beginning detailed duties statement:

Accomplished	Applied	Broadened
Achieved	Arranged	Budgeted
Administered	Assembled	Built
Aided	Assisted	Calculated
Analyzed	Began	Centralized

Chaired
Charted
Checked
Cleaned
Collaborated
Collected
Communicated
Compiled
Composed
Computed
Conducted
Consulted
Controlled
Coordinated
Created
Decreased
Defined
Delivered
Designed
Developed
Directed
Disseminated
Distributed
Edited
Eliminated
Engineered
Ensured
Established
Evaluated
Executed
Expanded
Fabricated
Facilitated
Finalized
Focused
Formed
Formulated
Furnished
Gathered
Generated
Grouped
Guided
Handled
Headed

Held
Helped
Identified
Implemented
Improved
Increased
Initiated
Innovated
Inspired
Installed
Instituted
Instructed
Introduced
Invented
Investigated
Isolated
Judged
Kept
Launched
Led
Logged
Maintained
Managed
Marketed
Maximized
Met
Moderated
Monitored
Motivated
Narrowed
Negotiated
Obtained
Operated
Optimized
Organized
Originated
Oversaw
Participated
Performed
Persuaded
Planned
Prepared
Presented
Presided

Processed
Produced
Programmed
Proposed
Provided
Published
Ran
Realized
Recommended
Recorded
Redesigned
Reduced
Reorganized
Repaired
Researched
Resolved
Restructured
Revised
Saved
Scheduled
Secured
Selected
Served
Set-up
Shipped
Sold
Solved
Sorted
Spearheaded
Specified
Staged
Started
Steered
Streamlined
Strengthened
Stressed
Structured
Submitted
Suggested
Supervised
Supplied
Supported
Targeted
Taught

Tested	Uncovered	Widened
Tracked	Unified	Withdrew
Trained	Updated	Worked
Transformed	Upgraded	Wrote
Translated	Utilized	
Troubleshoot	Verified	

This list is certainly not inclusive, but it should get you started when detailing your duties and responsibilities on your résumé.

This section, like all sections of this document, should be regarded separately, at least initially, but keep the whole in mind. When constructing the work history/experience section you should decide what the reader may want, what the requirements for a particular position or career area are all about. What would the reader discover if they were to concentrate on this section? How might the entries be regarded positively and how could they be regarded negatively?

Additional Section Possibilities

As pointed out earlier in this chapter, name, address, phone number; education and work history/experience will be sections on most résumés. These three entries represent the heart of the document, what it's basically all about. But these entries certainly are not the only sections that might appear on a résumé. Individual background and specific position requirements will dictate what additional sections might go on your résumé. Here we'll take a look at some possibilities and maybe dispel some misconceptions.

Special Skills

Special skills can basically be defined as those talents, abilities, skills that can be directly associated in some way with a particular discipline. In other words, what else you may bring to a job that can enhance your chances at desired employment.

Remember, only establish a special skills section if you have more that one entry to include under the heading. If you determine you have but one special skill you think the reader may be interested in, include this under the heading it is most directly associated with.

If you acquired this skill through the educational process, include it under that heading. If you acquired this skill on the job, include under the work history section with the job it is directly associated with.

Maybe you specialized in a particular type of electronic repair during the course of your education. It's important, especially if this skill is not traditionally associated with your program. Point it out along with your education.

Maybe you learned how to operate and became proficient with the CAD on the job, but you possess no formal recognition. Include this along with that particular work history entry.

Caution

Initially, most of us could probably come up with quite an extensive list of skills we think we have and are special. Most people have a variety of talents in many different areas. So what do we list and when do we include them on the résumé? Again, keep the purpose of the document in mind and the reader's needs before determining whether or not to include a special skill.

As a technical writer, I acquired what I initially determined to be important, even special skills. I learned how to operate a computer directly tied into a publishing system. I must say I became quite good with the computer and its various peripherals. If pertinent, I wouldn't have any problem including this information on my résumé. I also took a basic course in sign language for the hearing impaired to better communicate with particular co-workers. The main difference between these particular skills is level of expertise.

I worked with the publishing system on a daily basis. Every document we produced went through this system; I had to understand it since it was a major part of my job. I was comfortable with this skill. I was not quite as comfortable with sign language. Sure, I could communicate with the hearing impaired, but in a very basic, rudimentary way. The conversations were slow and I'm sure somewhat frustrating for those who were proficient with this skill.

If I was to include this signing skill on my résumé, it would indicate to the reader that I considered myself a professional with this skill. If hired and, sometime in the future, I was called upon to use this skill, I would find myself in an embarrassing situation. I would be basically lost if called upon to translate for a hearing impaired individual. Translating in sign language requires extensive training and experience. It is not a skill that comes easily; it takes years to become good enough to be able to translate.

THE POINT IS, only include a special skill if you'd feel comfortable being called upon to practice this skill in any job related situation. Maybe you took four years of French in high school and think you're pretty good with the language. So you put this on your résumé. You're interviewed and hired. Six months into the job you receive a call from your boss. You run to his office and discover a business associate from France wants to take a tour of your facility but doesn't speak any English. Your boss remembers your résumé and asks you to put this special skill to use. Could you handle it? Does knowledge of high school French offer enough background to communicate with a native? It depends. Just consider the possibilities and include the skill only when appropriate.

Some Possible Special Skills

✔ Languages
✔ Computer Skills
✔ Machine Operation
✔ Communication
✔ Vehicle Operation

✔ Design
✔ Artistic Talents
✔ Mechanical Abilities
✔ Discipline Specialization

Hobbies

First of all, before we even get into it, what's the first thing that comes to mind when you hear the word, hobbies? Generally speaking, our first thoughts probably do not deal with something discipline-related or a highly skilled endeavor. The word itself indicates something frivolous and less than professional. That's not to suggest that a hobby can't be something that deals with commitment, knowledge and expertise. It's all a matter of semantics. The heading itself doesn't really belong on a document like a résumé.

Why not? The only information that should be included on this document has to be pertinent to the purpose; and we know the purpose here is to get an interview. Sure, maybe you do have a hobby that could be considered pertinent to purpose. So you're about to receive your degree in mechanical technology and you just love to repair small engines in your spare time. Okay, that can be considered pertinent to your purpose. Include it on your résumé, but don't call it a hobby, call it something else. Choose a heading that better serves the purpose here, better encourages reader interest and appreciation.

- Special Interests
- Related Interests
- Professional Activities
- Avocation
- Interests
- Call this section anything but hobbies.

WHAT IS A HOBBY?

There are probably a whole bunch of definitions that could serve the purpose here. Here, let's just say that a hobby is something you do to fill up your spare time while you're not working or taking care of your family or watching television. Oh yes, let's not forget the Human Factor here; the positive/negative reactions to our information.

Maybe you're in five bowling leagues and really dedicated to the pursuit of excellence in organized bowling. Maybe the whole family is involved and your philosophy is, the family that bowls together stays together. Well, when you really get down to it, who cares? Consider the reader's needs and possible point of view. How can you be sure of the reader's reaction to this information? Maybe they're lousy bowlers, or dropped a ball on their foot once.

Okay, maybe the bowling example is a bit exaggerated, but hopefully the point is clear. Whatever you do outside of the job is probably of no consequence to your reader. Suffice it to say, that as long as you're not an international jewel thief or ax murderer, a potential employer doesn't really care what you do after work. Your résumé should only include that information that demonstrates your ability to perform on the job. Okay, I can pretty much anticipate some points of disagreement.

Maybe the person slated to interview you loves bowling too. Well, good for them, but how can you be sure? Why take the chance? Don't clutter up your résumé with information that doesn't serve your purpose. If you walk into the interviewer's office and they have bowling trophies all over the place, bring it up then, not before. I hope I'm not alienating bowlers here; I just used that hobby as an example. The same issues should pertain to all hobbies. Unless it's directly pertinent to the purpose, don't include them on your résumé. If you love to repair VCRs and TVs in your spare time and have a degree in Electrical Technology and want to specialize in troubleshooting and repair, then include that information on your résumé. Again, use headings to your benefit, to serve the purpose at hand. Don't call these related activities hobbies, call them something that comes across as a bit more serious.

References

Another popular section for most résumés is the reference section. References are important; everyone needs references for many different reasons. We need references to rent an apartment, to borrow money, to be a roommate and to get a job. But when to provide references in the job search is a matter of timing.

We'll go out on a limb here and state, that the only information regarding references on the résumé should indicate, "available upon request." The primary reason for this, is the only name on your résumé should be your name, no one else's. When considering the length of time initially dedicated to a résumé, about 20 seconds, whose name will the reader remember? When included, references are traditionally offered at the end of the résumé. These names will probably be the last information your reader regards when scanning your résumé. Chances are they will recall the name of one of your references before they'll recall yours. Include only that which is pertinent to purpose and don't provide the reader with any reason to reject your document.

Another good reason for not including references on a résumé relates to the time factor. Most of us collect references for future use over a period of time. We may ask a former boss or teacher or someone who knew us when we were successful. There's probably even some serious thought behind who we choose to use as a reference. The point here is, shelf life.

When someone agrees to be a reference, it usually means they appreciated our efforts regarding the context of the situation. Maybe we were a good employee, did our work, operated as part of a team, or realized some success. So, based on what seems to have been a successful relationship, we ask the boss, and they say, sure, why not.

Now, armed with this person's name on our résumé, we begin the job hunting process. We target some positions and companies and begin sending out our résumés. Some time goes by as we try for the ideal job. The prospects turn out to be a bit more limited than we had anticipated and four or five months later we're still searching.

The question here is, how long can we expect a reference to serve our purposes positively? Consider the number of people a boss may deal with on a daily basis.

- Will they remember you?
- Will they still appreciate the job you did?
- Will you be blamed for past foul-ups now that you're gone?
- Is that boss still with the company or even still alive?
- Is the company regarded positively by your readers?

The point is not to take a chance with a professional reference. When you're sending out résumés with references included, you have no control over who calls or when they call. You can never be sure after a period of time elapses what kind of reference you may get. Again, don't give your reader any reason to reject your document, your résumé.

Generally, the same considerations apply to academic references. You can never be sure what kind of reference you'd receive after a certain amount of time goes by. College professors have hundreds of students on a yearly basis. Unless you were more than an exceptional student, chances are they won't remember you. When I have been used as a reference by former students, I generally have to rely on my grade book to recall their efforts if I don't personally recall the student. The problem here is, grades don't always indicate effort and ability. A student may have received a C in the class, but deserves an excellent reference because of commitment and effort. Unfortunately, if I don't remember the student, I can only rely on what the grade generally indicates. Make references available upon request. When they are requested, be prepared.

References are usually requested at the time of the interview. Call your references as close to the interview as possible; like the night before. Be sure they remember you and are still willing to provide a positive reference. You have the opportunity on the phone to jog their memories. The phone call gives you the time necessary to discuss your previous performance to ensure a positive recommendation.

Your résumé should be all that speaks for you until you have been offered the interview. Then it's up to you to speak for yourself. Give your references a voice only after the document has served its purpose.

References Available Upon Request

Excellent references Available Upon Request

Professional and Personal References Available Upon Request

Salary History

Most of us probably wouldn't consider putting salary history on our résumés. But why we wouldn't is worth some discussion here. We probably want to question whether or not we should even include this information on an application form even though it is usually requested. The rule here is, keep this information to yourself.

Even if you're searching for a job within the same disciplinary tract, what you may have made at a previous or current job has no bearing on what a prospective position may pay. Don't be prepared to accept what is offered, unless it works for you. The people who make the most money are the people who ask for the most money.

Every job has a salary range associated with it. It doesn't matter if you're flipping burgers or designing fixtures. The range is designed to take into account experience and education. The salary you begin with can play a very important part in how much you make while employed by a particular company.

You're in the market for a better job and have sent out some well focused résumés. Maybe you've decided to include your salary history on your résumé for who knows what reason. Let's say you're making about $29,000 a year at your current job and now a prospective employer knows it. Everything goes well at the interview and they decide to make you an offer, and that offer is $30,000 a year. Not too bad, you figure, $1,000 more than you're making now. So, you go for it. What you don't know is, the salary range for that particular job was $34,000 to $39,000 a year. Think about how long it will take you to even get to the bottom of their range. Probably more years than you'd like to think about. If you knew the range, you could be at least $4,000 a year richer than you would be without this information.

Find out what the salary range for a particular job is prior to the interview. It's not a government secret, call up and ask. If they won't give you that information over the phone, make that one of the first questions you ask at the interview. Request the salary you believe you're qualified to receive. Put N/A on the application form for Not Applicable and deal with the issue at the interview. Negotiate for the salary you want and deserve. Their job is to get you as cheaply as they can; your job is to get the most you can in salary.

Personal Information

This heading tends to associate information with the résumé beyond the name and address section. It could encompass a number of different things. Suffice it to say, that rarely do we include personal information of any kind on the résumé. The résumé, like many forms of documentation, has changed over the years regarding what is acceptable to include and what isn't. There was a time, believe it or not, when a small photograph of the applicant was included along with professional information. But times and attitudes have changed, and along with these changes has come a new attitude concerning résumé content. The need to divulge personal information should be left for the interview if it is required.

The types of information we're dealing with here could range from physical attributes to whether or not we're willing to relocate. If it's not pertinent to the purpose, don't include it on the résumé.

Forget about height and weight; who cares? The purpose of the résumé is to get the interview. Your audience will see how tall you are and how much you weigh when you walk into his office. If you believe you posses the personal attributes of kindness and responsibility, let the data on your résumé indicate that; don't be ambiguous with your language, be factual.

Leave any and all handicaps off of your résumé. Deal with them at the interview if they are pertinent. Remember the Human Factor; don't give your reader any reason to reject your document. If you're in a wheelchair, the interviewer will detect that when you wheel into the office. It's understood, you certainly wouldn't apply for a job that you're not physically capable of performing.

Forget about information like your social security number. You'd be amazed at the amount of information that can be discovered on an individual only from their social security number. Forget about including things like religious affiliations; it's not pertinent to purpose. Age or date of birth aren't factors; keep them off of your résumé. Requiring you to provide information like this is discriminatory anyway. I can certainly appreciate the debate that may arise over whether or not to include information like marital status.

Some may think that being married and indicating it on the résumé suggests a certain amount of responsibility and stability. It may, but I'm sure we all know lots of married people who are less than stable or responsible.

Maybe being single could indicate more of an open acceptance to travel or relocate. But being single, consider the Human Factor, could also indicate a lack of commitment or a frivolous life style. Sure, this may be somewhat exaggerated, but how can you be sure of the way your reader interprets your data? Forget the personal data, unless its's a job-related requirement. Only include that information that is pertinent to the purpose—getting the interview. Once you get the interview, anything regarding personal information can be discussed one-on-one if necessary.

Organization and Format

How you organize your résumé, like all documentation, depends on a number of different factors. The information included on the résumé should be emphasized and subordinated according to purpose and audience need. A targeted résumé, that which is constructed for a particular job, emphasizes that information that most closely matches the concrete needs of the audience. We plug into the requirements. A résumé constructed to serve the purposes of the general job search should emphasize that which indicates your ability to perform in a particular discipline.

If you lack professional experience, but have educational background relating to your discipline, you emphasize education over experience. If you do have experience suggesting an ability to apply yourself, a proven track record so-to-speak, emphasize experience over education. Education is certainly important, but does it indicate you can do the job? Not necessarily. Experience suggests that you have applied your knowledge and acquired skills.

Applicant without related experience:

✔ Name, Address, Phone Number
✔ Objective/Goal (Optional)
✔ Education
✔ Work History/Experience
✔ Special Skills (Optional)
✔ Interests (Optional)
✔ References

Applicant with related experience:

- ✔ Name, Address, Phone Number
- ✔ Goal/Objective
- ✔ Experience/Work History
- ✔ Education
- ✔ Additional background data

The most important thing to keep in mind when deciding the organizational structure of your résumé, is what order will best serve the purpose at hand and meet the needs of your audience?

Like any document, the most pertinent information should be emphasized. You can never be sure your reader will scan the entire document, so provide what counts first.

Format

All good résumés will emphasize the most important points dictated by a specific discipline consideration. Generally your goal or objective will encourage the most positive way to construct your résumé.

There are basically two ways to approach the style and organizational structure of your résumé: reverse chronological or functional formats.

Reverse Chronological

This organizational format lists, primarily, begins with the present or most recent job and provides work experience data going back in time. This is the most popular format because it shows an uninterrupted job history and rate of professional success. We use the reverse chronological format when we have an uninterrupted work history. Including the unbroken dates of employment indicates commitment to operating within and succeeding at your discipline.

Functional Format

Generally, use the functional format when job history is erratic. Use the functional format when you seek to change careers and that change requires that you depart form the chronological listing of past work history or experience.

There could be any number of reasons whey you have an erratic job history, a break in employment. You don't want to point out a break in employment on your résumé because it may cause the reader to question stability or reliability even though the reason was completely justifiable.

Maybe you took a year or so off to raise a child, but you're not going to indicate that on your résumé in order to fill in the reverse chronological format. That issue can be discussed at the interview if it comes up. Maybe you took some time off for health reasons. Your certainly don't want to point that out on your résumé, although your reasons for the break were justifiable. Use the functional format to indicate experience and skills, not unbroken work history.

There are many reasons for having a break in employment history. Early in my career I learned just how varied those reasons can be. I was working as an editor for a small, weekly newspaper. Because the newspaper had a limited budget, among my many responsibilities were interviewing and hiring for open positions.

At one point, the position for advertising manager was open and we were going through the search process. After receiving a number of résumés from possible candidates, we began considering the interviewing process and who we should interview.

One of the résumés we received was from a very viable applicant. He had the education and experience we were looking for and seemed to be a good possibility. His résumé was in the functional format, but it didn't seem to indicate anything that may have been regarded as less than positive. We called him in for an interview.

Everything his résumé indicated was true. His background nearly matched our needs perfectly. He presented himself well at the interview and satisfactorily answered all of our questions. When we were almost positive we had our new advertising manager, he indicated he had some additional information to divulge.

It turned out that he had employed the functional format because he had a seven year break in his employment history. He freely offered that he had spent seven years in prison for a crime he detailed and explained openly and honestly. His revelation was a shock, to say the least. The point is, he was honest about it. The fact that he had the opportunity to explain it during the interview gave him the chance to be personal and open about it. He dealt with it fine. He was hired.

He proved to be a quite capable and loyal employee, exceeding our expectations. Later on I wondered, had I known his past ahead of time would I have still called him in for an interview? To be honest, I'm not sure. His résumé was certainly no place to point out his prison experience; he left that for the interview. The functional format more than served his as well as our purposes. Okay, this example may represent the extreme, but it does serve to support the benefits of choosing the functional format.

Changing careers could also encourage the use of the functional format. Under these circumstances, the functional format allows you the opportunity to point out skills and talents, experiences without the dictates of dates requiring that you emphasize according to time rather than purpose.

Maybe you've changed careers a few times and desire to go back to a career related discipline from your past. The functional format allows you the opportunity to bring that information forward, emphasize it according to purpose rather than by dates.

The applicant has much more control over the information that might be included on a résumé with the functional format. This format doesn't require you to include any information you don't want to include for any reason. You certainly don't have to include dates, particularly if you've had a break in employment. Save it for the interview. You don't have to include the name of a particular company if that information might prove negative and not serve your purpose.

It can be debated, that using the functional format may cause your reader to question your reasoning for choosing this format. The question here is, will the information included in reverse chronological order be regarded as negatively as the use of the functional format? Again, consider the reader and the Human Factor. Use the format that will best serve the purpose of getting the interview.

The Personalized Résumé

There are certainly a variety of other sections that could be included on a résumé. It all depends on individual background as well as career objective. Besides those sections detailed here, a résumé could also include sections dealing with military experience, awards and recognitions, and whatever else may serve the purpose.

Everything that goes into your résumé should be focused on serving the purpose: getting the interview. Nothing else should be included unless you've determined it is pertinent to the purpose. Don't give your reader any reason to reject your résumé; keep them encouraged and interested. Focus on what you have and, as best you can determine, what they are looking for.

Remember, writing is a questioning process, and constructing the résumé is no exception. Evaluate and analyze what information seems pertinent to the purpose; select and reject and follow the writing process to success.

- What specific job are you seeking (type)?
- What information is most pertinent to that job?
- What details will meet the reader's needs?
- In what order should you present your information?
- How can you present your qualifications most effectively to get that interview?

Before you begin constructing this document, it is important that you ask yourself these questions and whatever other questions you may come up with. Answer the questions and determine whether or not the answers indicate additional questions. If they do, answer those also. Collect all the information that may serve the purpose, then decide what to use and what to reject. It's much easier to reject information than it is to discover you lack the necessary information and have to begin the process again.

See yourself through the eyes of potential readers and provide whatever information would be most helpful to them. Your résumé should contain brief but sufficient information to offer a prospective employer.

The way you write and organize your résumé should be businesslike and goal oriented like all professional documentation. Once you have collected your information, check your results.

Review your résumé with a neutral reader for honest responses and consider the following:

- Is your résumé to the point?
- Have you eliminated the unnecessary and repetitious?
- Is it logical?
- Is your résumé organized and in a format that is easy to read?
- Is all the information pertinent to purpose?
- Have you considered the Human Factor—positive and negative reactions?

Note: Take a look at the résumés following and then try some of the exercises to test your understanding.

Discipline Focused

Patrick W. Michael
266 Blackwell Lane
Henrietta, NY 14467
(716) 334-8758

WORK HISTORY

Monroe County Office of the Sheriff, Rochester, NY (February 1984 to present)
Deputy Sheriff–Police Bureau
- Enforce the laws of New York State.
- Investigate crimes, motor vehicle accidents and other incidents.
- Prepare reports, legal documents and other forms of written communication.
- Testify at trials, hearings and other legal proceedings.
- Mediate disputes.

Specialized Assignments
- Field Training Officer—responsible for supervising, training and evaluating recruit Deputies.
- D.A.R.E. (Drug Abuse Resistance Education) Instructor—presented a 17 week anti-drug course to fifth grade students teaching life skills that can be used to resist using drugs.
- Background Investigator—conducted extensive investigations into the background of applicants and prepared written reports.
- Case Analyst—analyzed crime patterns and developed proactive action plans. Acted as liaison between the Sheriff's Office and other police agencies, the District Attorney's Office, Probation Department and Division of Parole.

Accomplishments
- While Case Analyst developed new arrest warrant service procedure that resulted in a 50% increase in the number of warrants served at the zone level.
- In June of 1991 devised, organized and evaluated a special detail that addressed a large increase in the number of stolen vehicles. The detail led to the arrest of 5 suspects and cleared over 20 stolen vehicle cases and several other felonies.
- Member of accreditation committee that resulted in Monroe County becoming the first Sheriff's Office in New York to be nationally accredited.

EDUCATION

A.A.S. Accounting, Monroe Community College, Rochester, NY
(expected in May   )

A.A.S. Criminal Justice, Monroe Community College, Rochester, NY
May 19

REFERENCES

Available on request.

Tina M. Johnson
14 Geraldine St.
Rochester, N.Y. 14644
(716) 555-7915

EDUCATION: AS, Liberal Arts, Monroe Community College
Rochester, N.Y. (Anticipated Spring   )

SUNY College at Buffalo, Liberal Arts, 199

WORK
HISTORY: Bryan's Restaurant, Rochester, N.Y.

Server: Responsibilities include waiting tables, cashiering, hostessing, cocktail lounge service, and closing duties. Also responsible for completing daily cash and charge summaries.
May 199 – June 199

Department of Public Safety
Monroe Community College, Rochester, N.Y.

Campus Security Student Aid: Entrusted with the keys to entire campus. Responsibilities included routine building security checks, completing shift logs, securing vaults, and monitoring alarm systems.
April 199 – May 199

Department of Public Safety, SUNY, Buffalo, N.Y.

Student Dispatcher: Responsible for keeping daily logs and monitoring a six line phone. Also coordinated radio communications with Buffalo Police and Fire Department.
January 199 – May 199

Dixie's Pharmacy, Rochester, N.Y.

Cosmetics Sales Associate: Duties included cashiering, stocking shelves, inventory and customer assistance.
October 199 – December 199

SPECIAL
SKILLS: Computer Systems and Software
Macintosh SE, Microsoft Word – versions 3 & 4
Write Now version 2, Keyboarding 50 wpm

References Available Upon Request

Reverse Chronological – Targeted

Aaron L. Corrigan
27 Macintosh St.
Rochester, N.Y. 14622

OBJECTIVE

A writing position with a future-oriented company where experience in independent planning and execution will promote enthusiasm, goal achievement and effective, audience-directed communication.

SUMMARY OF QUALIFICATIONS

- Writing experience in professional research and promotional documentation
- General assignment investigation and reporting
- Project and account coordination
- Editing local and news service input
- Layout, design and research

PROFESSIONAL EXPERIENCE

Technical Writer, Eastman Kodak, Rochester, N.Y.
1989 – Present
Researched, wrote and coordinated the publication of marketing and technical documentation. Worked in conjunction with mechanical, material, electrical and manufacturing engineers in producing approved publications. Team leader for a group of six writers and illustrators.

Reporter, *Miami Herald*
Newspaper, Miami Florida
General assignment reporting covering the greater Miami area. Covered and wrote over 200 stories where more than half received front page and local front page coverage.

Reporter, *Democrat and Chronicle*
Newspaper, Rochester, N.Y.
1985 – 1987
General assignment reporting with a concentration on City Hall and the Courts. Covered and wrote a variety of stories including a number of series dealing with crime and local politics.

U.S. Army, Communications Specialist, Honorable Discharge, 1975 – 1979

EDUCATION

MA, English, SUNY College at Brockport, Brockport, N.Y., 1985
BA, Journalism, St. John Fisher College, Rochester, N.Y., 1983
Portfolio Available for Review Upon Request
References Available Upon Request

Functional

Rita Murphy
172 Magee Ave.
Rochester, N.Y. 14615
(716) 555-8849

SUMMARY

Six years experience in accounting including bookkeeping where balancing accounts was a primary responsibility. Fours years spreadsheet experience with IBM and Apple computers dealing with accounts receivable and payable.

EXPERIENCE

Cost Clerk   Edison Electric Corporation, Madison, Wis.

                  Responsible for the processing Field Service Technician's time, expenses and travel.

Time Clerk   Responsible for calculating and coordinating weekly payroll for 172 employees.

Accounts Clerk   Empire State Motor Service, Utica N.Y.

                  Responsible for the processing in- and out-going freight invoices.

Clerk/Typist   Responsible for coordinating purchases, inventory and shipments.

Clerk   Morgan National Bank, Utica, N.Y.

                  Responsible for all out-going correspondence and credit applications.

EDUCATION

AS   Accounting, Monroe Community College, Rochester, N.Y. 1996

AAS   Arts and Sciences—Liberal Arts, Geneseo Community College, Geneseo, N.Y. 1994

ADDITIONAL TRAINING

                  IBM Management Course
                  Micro Professional Communication Seminar
                  Atex Computer Training Course

EXERCISES

1. What's wrong with this résumé?

Michael C. Dobbs
174 Union St.
Samson Kentucky

OBJECTIVE

Entry level computer programming position offering challenge and experience.

EDUCATION

Associates Degree, Computer Information Systems, Haverford Community College, 1993

Courses: Computer Programming 102, 107, 210; Program Design 1 & 2;
Introduction to Sociology and Psychology; Business Writing

EMPLOYMENT EXPERIENCE

6/92 – present   Apex Marketing Group, Pittsburgh, PA

Telemarketer for a variety of products including music collections and charity solicitations

1/92 – 12/96   Computer Learning Center, Haverford Community College

Assisted Students with a variety of problems and questions relating to computers in the learning lab

1/91 – 12/96   Cashier, Fleecum Markets, Samson Kentucky

Front end cash register operator

HOBBIES

Enjoy a variety of activities including bowling (presently participating in 3 leagues), golf, collecting comic books, reading magazines and politics; also enjoy designing computer games

REFERENCES

More Than Excellent References will be furnished when needed

2. What's wrong with this résumé?

Albert Jones
201 Morning Glory Circle
Medina, N.Y. 14521
Tel: 555-8965

GOAL

Really interested in a job with a large company where there is opportunity to special-ize in electronics and advance.

EDUCATION

H.S. Diploma, Thomas Jefferson High School, 1987
Finger Lakes Community College, A.A.S., 1990
Major: Electrical Technology, GPA 3.00

Related Courses:

Instrumentation I & II	Technical Writing
Drafting Technology I	Sociology
Technical Math	Public Speaking
Electronics I & II	Health
Digital Circuits	Psychology I & II
Cinalog Electronics	Work History
Microcomputers Communication	

HOBBIES: Scuba Diving, Skiing, Little League, collecting vintage phonographs and radios.

MEMBERSHIPS

SME (Society of Manufacturing Engineers), Sons of the American Legion

WORK HISTORY

Summer 19 & — Rapidac, Medina, N.Y.
Machinists' Aide
Summer 19 – Medina Scholl District, Medina, N.Y.
Counselor and baseball instructor/coach
Summer 199 & '9 — McDonald's, Medina, N.Y.
Grill Person

References: To be furnished upon Request

3. Construct a résumé for the following individual to meet the requirements for the position indicated.

Jack Kasper
386 Ridgeway Ave
Rochester, N.Y. 14615

Education:

AS, Liberal Arts, Monroe Community College, 19. .
BA, English, University of Buffalo, 19
MA, English, SUNY College at Brockport, 19

Experience:

19 –'   Mechanic, Best Motors, Rochester, N.Y.
19 –'   Tool & Die Apprentice, Eastman Kodak, Rochester, N.Y.
19 –'   Tool & Die Maker, Eastman Kodak, Rochester, N.Y.
19 –Present Technical Writer, Eastman Kodak, Rochester, N.Y.
19 –'   Instructor, Photography, Continuing Ed. YMCA

Personal:

Married, 2 kids, 1 dog
Drive Volvo & Saab
Shade Tree Mechanic
Interested in Photography

Position Requirements:

RIT, Rochester Institute of Technology
Instructor in Mechanical Technology
2–3 years professional experience
2 years college level teaching experience
MS in Mechanical Engineering or combination of experience & Education

It's clear that Jack's background doesn't perfectly match the requirements for the position. But rather than limit his opportunities, Jack is going to apply and try and match what he does have with what they want. It's important to interest your reader in what you do have; don't emphasize what you don't have. Construct a résumé for Jack and help him get the job of his dreams.

4. Produce your own résumé; make it general unless you have a particular job or career area in mind. In addition to your résumé, produce an essay supporting your résumé choices. Explain and defend why you chose to include the information you include and why you chose a particular format and organization. This requires you to question all of your documentation choices. If you can explain your choices in a positive way, then you have probably made the right choices. If you find it difficult to explain your choices, you might want to reconsider.

Producing the Professional Letter

LETTER WRITING

With the many ways to communicate electronically today, writing letters may seem like a waste of time. If you need to get in touch with someone or provide information, you can call, leave a message on their answering machine and meet their needs. You can reach them in their cars or almost any place else considering the convenience of cellular phones. If the message requires more than a phone call, you can fax them. Whatever it takes, it doesn't seem difficult to get in touch. So why write letters? Writing letters can serve many purposes that electronic devices can't.

- You can't make notes in the margins of phone calls.
- Letters suggest a personal commitment to the receiver.
- You can't keep a file record of phone calls.
- You can't copy a phone call and share it with others.
- You can't refer back to the specifics of a phone call at a later date.
- Writing a letter allows you the time it takes to plan the message completely and ensure you meet the reader's needs.

Basic communication theory applies to letter writing more than we might expect.

SENDER—MESSAGE—RECEIVER

The effectiveness of the letter depends to a large degree on the sender.

- How well the sender understands the message.
- How well the sender understands why he is writing it.
- How well the sender understands who the receiver is.

The message is generally a set of facts being presented to a specific audience. The obstacles to avoid when presenting a set of facts to the receiver center around the breakdown of communication. Communication breaks down when there is a flaw in one or more of the three basic components of communication theory. It is the obligation of the sender to detail the set of facts necessary for the receiver to understand, appreciate and

75

act upon the information contained in the letter. Besides, generally, people appreciate receiving mail. Anyone who's ever spent some time away from home can certainly attest to that. Letters make us feel closer to the sender, yes, even in a professional environment. What else do letters accomplish and how?

Letters inform, solicit, demand, coax, invite, impress, thank, remind and many other functions that would be difficult to accomplish any other way. No matter what the letter's intent is, it is an extension of you, the writer; make a good impression.

Like any other document, the letter needs to be revised and edited for perfection. Remember to protect your credibility. As you edit, remember to be thorough, clear and correct. Remember the message is a set of facts; make sure they're accurate.

- Is your message clear?
- Have you created a favorable impression?
- Have you considered the reader's situation?
- Is your letter complete—addresses, date, clear purpose, reliable facts and necessary details?

The Personal Letter

Many of the same considerations and issues that relate to professional letters can also be applied to the personal letter, believe it or not. Taking a look at the personal letter is a good place to begin here, particularly for those of us who have little or no experience writing a professional letter.

First of all, why do we write personal letters? The individual reasons could be varied, but generally we write personal letters to keep in touch with friends and family. We write personal letters because we can take our time and put them together over a few days if we choose to. Personal letters are cheaper than long distance phone calls. Sometimes, personal letters allow the writer to say things that would be difficult to verbalize over the phone. Although we may not realize it, planning a personal letter encompasses many of the same considerations that go into constructing a professional letter.

Audience

A letter, like all professional documentation, requires that we analyze and determine the needs of our audience.

If you're writing to a friend you haven't seen in six months, determining the needs of that reader is probably quite clear. You're going to fill them in on what you've been doing since the last time you were in contact. You're going to provide information that they can relate to and appreciate without a lot of explanation.

You appreciate the needs of your reader and know what information will be pertinent to their needs. If they knew you were looking for a job when they left and you have since obtained one, you'll most likely detail the circumstances involving that

information. If you moved out on your own since they've been gone, then you'll probably inform them of that particular fact. In the personal letter, you'll offer information they can relate to and understand. What about providing information they may find obscure, won't immediately appreciate and understand?

Let's say you had an Uncle Joe who recently passed away and your friend wasn't aware of the fact that you even had an Uncle Joe. Do you offer this information? Probably, particularly if the relationship with this uncle was important enough to share with your friend. You certainly won't just come out with it and confuse your friend. What you can do is offer background, present the information within a context the reader can appreciate and understand.

"You may not have been aware, but I had an Uncle Joe who was very good to me when I was growing up. He used to take me fishing and to concerts and buy me candy when my parents wouldn't because they were worried about my teeth. He was very important to me and recently passed away. I'll miss him a lot, and that's the bad news for the past few months."

It's all about knowing your audience and reaching them with your message. Give them information they can relate to and appreciate, and give them background on information they may find obscure. Like all professional documentation, the audience for your letter should be researched and understood.

Planning Your Letter

One way to create a positive, sincere approach is to use simple, direct language. Don't try and impress your reader with your vocabulary; reach them with your message. Don't force your reader to interpret your information unless that is required according the letter's intent. Your readers are as busy as you are. They don't have the time to struggle through the formal, pompous phrasing some people use in a misguided attempt to heighten their image of competence.

Keep your message clear and concise; avoid trite phrases.

Trite	Better
attached please find	attached or enclosed
under separate cover	separately

Encourage Reader Interest

You attitude—substitute the "you attitude" for the "I" or "we" attitude whenever possible. Focus on and emphasize the reader. They'll appreciate the interest you take in them and will be that much more open to your letter's intent.

I or We	You
I appreciate your hard work on this matter	Your hard work on this matter is appreciated
We need your group to follow a new system	Your company will benefit from this new system

Your writing should be sincere. Using the you attitude helps achieve this tone by implying that you recognize the reader's point of view. No matter what the intent of your letter is, to some extent you're asking the reader to be fair, consider your information and possibly act on it. In order to solicit a positive response, you also have to display a certain amount of fairness in encouraging reader participation and interest.

Technique and Style

Everyone has a particular style of writing. We use the language and our understanding and ability to use that language based on a number of factors.

- Our vocabulary
- Our creative abilities
- Our knowledge of sentence structure
- Our knowledge of proper usage
- Our understanding of mechanics

With all of these, as well as other considerations in mind, we strive to produce effective documentation; a letter that serves the purpose and reaches the intended audience. Like with all documentation, one of the primary questions we need to address, is whether or not our language and how we use the language translates effectively to our readers.

Certain writing techniques can enhance letter writing strategies:

- Constructive tone—positive, goal oriented.
- Select appropriate, reader directed words.
- Vary syntax—be aware of the rhythm of sentence structure.

How effectively does our language and intent translate? Your choice of appropriate words as well as how you construct your sentences should present an effective tone and solicit a positive response. Don't use language that might be construed as aggressive or unfair in tone.

Aggressive	— We demand an immediate response.
Fair	— We would appreciate a prompt response.
Aggressive	— You should have tested the radio in the store or returned it within the warranty period.
Fair	— You were provided with the opportunity to check the radio at the store or for returning within the detailed warranty period.

Use Positive Language

It's like describing a less than full glass of water: it's either half full or half empty. Always stress the positive.

Negative—It will be another difficult year for the company financially, although the fourth quarter is forecasted as promising.

Positive—It should be another good year for the company, although there may be some early quarter downturns.

Remember, the skillful writer can always find a positive approach to the message, a positive point of view. Always choose language that emphasizes the positive and subordinates the negative.

In part, it's all about tone, your attitude and how you convey that attitude through your use of language. The importance of tone is obvious with conversation; and your listeners have little difficulty deciphering your attitude. They know whether or not you are being serious, positive, discouraging, negative or confused.

Be aware of tone when speaking, certainly, but also regard tone in your writing. Readers can generally sense your attitude by your choice of words and sentence structure. Use a positive tone and your message will be received in a positive way. The most effective time to consider the tone of your message is when revising. It's important to get your message down first and then go back and determine the tone, how your message might be regarded by your reader. Always keep the Human Factor in mind. Don't give the reader any reason to reject your document.

Thoughts on Organization

Whether you're writing a personal letter to touch base with an old friend, a business letter to get the attention of a desired contact or a persuasive letter requesting action, how you organize the letter will always be a factor relating to effective communication.

The letter, like any written document, has a beginning, a middle and an end. The pertinent content is plugged into one of these letter sections. And all of this is constructed within the boundaries of format.

The Opening

No matter what your intent is, the opening of your letter should accomplish one basic thing. Generally, a letter's opening should state concisely and clearly what has prompted you to write.

When the receiver is pondering your message, the first thing they want to know is why this person is writing. The opening should indicate to them whether or not they need to act immediately. The opening should point out whether or not they need to act at all.

Think about some of the mail you receive on the job or at home. Much of this mail could probably fall under the category of "junk mail." Still most of us probably spend a small amount of time at least scanning the first paragraph in an effort to find out exactly what the message is all about.

If a pitch is being made, it often takes place later on in the letter. The opening strives to gain our attention and, hopefully, hold our interest. One way this is accomplished is by making an offer of some positive return or express our good fortune at our being selected from a small group to receive some wonderful chance at remuneration. Most of the time, what we may stand to gain is overshadowed by what we need to expend. How many times have you been a finalist in some million dollar giveaway? I know I have, more times than I can recall. Consider when the sender points out this good fortune. It's usually right up front, in the beginning of the letter.

I remember receiving one of these notices one afternoon. The letter stated that I was a finalist in some ten million dollar giveaway. It even had my name printed next to my soon-to-be-sure winnings. The letter indicated that out of millions of participants, I was one of the four finalists. What luck, right? Wrong. The next day, I asked my students how many of them were finalists in this particular giveaway. Out of three classes, at least one third of the students in each class raised their hands. So much for our good luck. But the letter did get our attention. It offered their reasons for writing up front, even if those reasons were less than reliable.

Just the Facts

In our effort to detail exactly what has prompted us to write, we should certainly get the receiver's attention, but we also need to detail the specifics, the facts relating to our intent. Offer the receiver the information they need from the beginning to make a decision as to whether or not they need to read on.

Even when writing a personal letter, we offer our receiver the facts, although we may not give it as much thought as we would with a business letter.

Let's say you haven't been in touch with a good friend for six months and you decide to drop them a line and fill them in on what's been going on with you since you last talked or corresponded. You would detail those facts in the beginning when stating what has prompted you to write. "I figured it was about time I wrote to you. It's been six months since we were last in touch, so I decided to let you know what I've been up to." Those are the facts, what has prompted you to write.

If you were mailing in a payment to a local health club, the letter would detail exactly why you are writing in the beginning. "Please accept the enclosed check, No. 123, dated July 4, 1996 as dues payment for the month of August." It states exactly why you are writing and details all of the pertinent facts.

It's important to remember, while you're constructing the beginning of your letter, that you also keep in mind that you want the receiver to read this correspondence in its entirety. The beginning should only give the receiver what they need to determine what has prompted the sender to write. Leave the detail for the body of the letter. The facts relating to what has prompted you to write should be brief, clear and to the point. Once you have detailed the facts, offer one last point of encouragement, the transition, and move on to the body of the letter.

The final sentence in the introductory portion of your letter should generally encourage the reader to proceed to the body for additional, supporting detailed specifics. Encourage the receiver to want to go on.

Let's take the million dollar giveaway letter for example. The final sentence could state, "If you act within the prescribed time period, you could be our next lucky winner." That encourages the receiver to go on and discover what the prescribed time period is. The transition sentence in a personal letter should also encourage the receiver to want to go on. "You're not going to believe what's been happening to me lately." That sentence doesn't offer any specific information or discernible facts, but it does encourage the receiver to move to the body of the letter.

One thing to be careful of here is, don't make promises in the beginning that the body of the letter doesn't fulfill.

The Body

Following the opening, or introductory, paragraph detailing what has prompted us to write, comes the body of the letter. The number of paragraphs in the body will be determined, of course, by the letter's intent and the amount of information to be included.

The body of the letter will highlight and detail what the opening paragraph introduced. The body will include sufficient information for the receiver to act upon, make a decision or appreciate the message as directed by the sender.

Emphasize and Subordinate

How you organize the information in your letter depends on the letter's intent. Generally, emphasize the information the reader may be most interested in, and subordinate the information the reader may be least interested in. This is generally the way to organize most, but not all, letters.

If you're presenting the receiver with information that could be construed as bad, then that particular data would be subordinated. You probably want the receiver to read the entire letter. Giving them the bad news right up front certainly doesn't encourage them to absorb what follows.

If you're making a request of the receiver, you may decide to place that at the end of the letter also. You'd want to set up and support the eventual request to receive a favorable response.

Be True to Your Opening

Generally, the body of the letter would only detail and deal with information suggested by the opening paragraph. If your opening in a personal letter indicated that you were writing because you haven't seen the receiver for six months and wanted to fill them in on what you've been doing, then the body would fulfill that promise.

You would provide the receiver with information relating to your past activities; information they could relate to and appreciate. Or, as stated earlier, you would provide background and explanation on information that would be obscure without it.

Make sure the points you address, particularly those you emphasize in your letter, have detail sufficient for the receiver to appreciate and understand what you're striving to get across. Don't leave the message's content to the receiver's interpretation unless that's your specific intent.

Make Careful Choices

Choose the points you need to address in a letter carefully. Don't require the receiver to plow through information that has little or nothing to do with the message's intent. It's often a good idea to draft a letter prior to finalizing your message. It might be a good habit to get into outlining your letters prior to drafting. You want to be sure your message gets across, and careful planning is one way to ensure that.

Maybe the friend you haven't seen in a while is quite busy and you can't be sure they'll have the time to leisurely absorb 14 pages of your rambling. Plan the letter.

Why you're writing — haven't seen them in a while, want to fill them in.

Moved into a new apartment — "they thought I'd never move away from my parents."

Bought a new car — we used to wait for AAA together with the old car.

Broke up with boyfriend — they never liked each other anyway.

Uncle Joe died — explain who he was.

Got a new job — we both hated working there.

With this outline, it will take far less time to construct the letter. You'll be sure to provide all the information your receiver will probably be interested in and you'll be sure to accomplish the purpose of writing the letter completely and effectively.

Once you've introduced your message's intent in the opening, the body should meet the anticipated needs of the receiver and fulfill their expectations. Again, be sure to emphasize what you've determined to be most important and subordinate what is least important to the overall purpose of the letter. Be sure to include sufficient detail for the receiver to appreciate and understand your message. Don't leave anything open to interpretation unless that's your specific intent.

Take a look at some of the mail you receive at work or home. Pay attention to what the opening promises and how the body of those letters fulfills those promises. Make note of how the senders emphasize and subordinate information and provide detail appropriate to their intent. Of course, not every letter you receive is going to be well written. Figure out which ones work well and which ones don't, and why.

The Conclusion

The conclusion is often the most important part of your message. It wraps everything up neatly, calls for action, clarifies the message's overall intent. Like performing, entertainment, it's not always how you perform that counts, but how you finish. Leave the receiver with the thought that will prove most beneficial to your overall intent.

If you're providing bad news to the receiver, generally we save this for the conclusion. If you're making a request of the receiver, set it up in the body and ask for what you want in the conclusion. Always end on a note most appropriate to the message and its intent.

SOME POSSIBILITIES

- Thank the reader
- Provide your phone number
- Make your request
- Offer the bad news

- Call to action
- Take the initiative
- Refer to enclosed documents
- Reiterate your main point
- End on a positive note

The message's conclusion should clarify and verify, not leave the receiver wondering, perplexed or expecting more—unless, of course, that's your intent.

Your personal letter to a distant friend might end by asking some questions. The questions may relate to what they've been doing. This would encourage them to write back and provide you with that information, particularly considering you just provided them with like information. You would certainly end on a positive note, tell them to "take care," or "be happy." Maybe you would provide your phone number in case they felt like calling. What the conclusion would accomplish here is give the receiver options. They can either write or phone. It shows you're interested enough in not only the message and its intent, but also in the receiver and their reaction to your message.

Generally, the conclusion should be short and to the point. The body of the message already has provided the detail necessary for the receiver to appreciate your message. Make the conclusion memorable.

The Cover Letter

One of the most important letters you'll probably ever write is the cover letter. A cover letter is, basically, a letter written by you, the sender, that accompanies your résumé when submitted for consideration relating to a job. A cover letter can be general, not target a specific job, or it can be tailored to a particular company or for a single job.

The cover letter meets two basic requirements. It acts as an introduction to a prospective employer. It also allows you the opportunity to highlight specific points from your background that may prove most interesting to a prospective employer. Keep in mind, as stated in the chapter on résumés, the cover letter and résumé are not meant to get you the job. They should only be constructed with getting the interview in mind. You get the job.

The cover letter is a useful document in that in provides you with the opportunity to emphasize what you have determined the receiver will be most interested in. Unlike the application form where you basically have to fill in the blanks, the cover letter lets you make the most pertinent choices available.

In a general cover letter the information from your background to highlight should generally target those particulars you have determined are most in demand within your discipline.

The General Cover Letter

- Introduction (opening paragraph)
- Education highlights paragraph
- Experience highlights paragraph
- Conclusion (closing paragraph)

These are generally the four primary elements of the general cover letter. Of course, individual background and career goals may alter or eliminate some of these elements.

Every cover letter will begin with the introductory paragraph. What follows depends largely on individual background. Experience tends to be highly regarded within a given discipline and should usually be emphasized over education.

If you have little or no experience in your career area, education would most likely be the choice for emphasis. Again, this suggests the basic cover letter should have four paragraphs, particularly for those applicants just embarking on the career search.

The Opening

The opening paragraph in a general cover letter should accomplish exactly what was detailed earlier in this chapter. The first thing the reader should know, is what has prompted you to write? This is particularly important if you're unsure of an opening in the company you're applying to. The opening should state as clearly and concisely as possible why you're writing and why you should be considered for an interview with the company.

First of all, you have to determine why you're submitting your cover letter and résumé to a particular company.

- They employ people with your skills or educational background
  "It's well known that Datatrex is known for its sophisticated and innovative approach to computer design. I believe that my education and experience in the computer field could prove beneficial to your company. I would like to be considered for a current or future opening."

- You've heard a company may be hiring
  "I understand that Datatrex is currently considering interviewing for some key positions. I believe my experience and education could be useful to your company and would like to be considered as a candidate."

Keep the opening short and to the point. Only deal with the facts as you know them, or as you've determined them. An overly long introduction does little to encourage receiver interest. Most people will read a letter's opening, particularly if it isn't terribly long and involved. The longer it is, the fewer your chances are that the receiver will read the entire opening.

The General Body Paragraphs

It's difficult to determine what particular companies may be looking for in a prospective employee when you're conducting a mass, kind of blind marketing search for a job. The best way to approach what to highlight in your body paragraphs is to determine generally what might be required for employees within your career field. Check with practicing professionals and ask them what might prove interesting to the companies you're applying to.

Once you have discovered what might be attractive background information within your field, choose what highlights from your educational and experience background would most directly meet those requirements. Try and match your assets with their needs as best you can.

Conduct some preliminary research on the companies you're applying to. Check out what skills are most in demand within your career area at a given time. Identify your assets in the body paragraphs and include sufficient detail to draw attention to your background and how it could prove beneficial to their company. (More detail on this with the targeted cover letter.)

The Closing

Keep the conclusion short, positive and goal oriented. The closing is the only place in your cover letter where you should refer to your résumé. Any place else requires, at least in theory, the receiver to cross reference before they finish reading the letter. And we all know how much people love to cross reference. Just think about how heavy that dictionary gets after looking up that fourteenth word you're not sure how to spell.

Certainly be positive and thank them for their consideration and time. Reiterate your belief that you will fit in well with their mission.

Take the initiative. Indicate that you plan on contacting them on a specific day at a particular time to discuss the possibility of an interview. And provide your phone number. They may want to contact you before you make the effort. Even if they only call to tell you they are not interviewing, at least you've made direct contact.

The Targeted Cover Letter

There are a number of ways to discover specific job openings. Some are more reliable than others.

- The newspaper
- Trade journals & periodicals
- School coordinated placement services
- Commercial employment services
- Signs in windows
- State employment services
- Networking

These are the primary outlets for job openings and the ones that come to mind when conducting the job search. Certainly try all possibilities, but don't waste too much time looking for a professional job in windows, commercial employment services or even municipal services.

Networking and Advertisements

The majority of professional jobs are usually located through one of these two sources. The primary source is networking. Over 80% of professional openings are discovered through networking. Networking basically refers to hearing about a job opening through contacts through word of mouth. These highly sought after positions can be open anywhere from three weeks to three months before they are advertised. Getting the word early is the key to success.

That's why it's important to make contacts within your field. Find out what professional organizations are active in your area and join. Make some contacts with practicing professionals; keep in touch and be in the right place at the right time to hear about that opening.

Generally if a position isn't filled through networking, most companies will conduct an ad campaign to fill the position. Most companies will advertise the opening locally, but many will also solicit applicants in a wider format such as in trade journals and professional publications. Once the word is out, the applications come flooding in. So it's important to do the best job you can with your cover letter and résumé—get noticed.

Once you learn about a particular opening, whether it was through networking or advertising, you need to act as quickly as possible.

The Receiver

To whom do you address your job package once you discover there's an opening? Generally, those soliciting applications will request that the cover letter and résumé be forwarded to personnel or human resources. But who's the person? Who will be receiving this information?

Always address a letter to an individual. Never address a letter to "Dear Sirs." What if they're not? Never address a letter to "Whom it May Concern." Who's that? A letter addressed to an individual will always reach that person. What they do with it is another matter. But at least they've had the opportunity to see the message and mentally record the sender's name. You've made contact and that's a very important first step.

Identifying the Receiver

How do you find out who to send your package to if that information wasn't included with the opening? It's not all that difficult. Call the company; it's generally not a government secret who heads up the personnel office or human resources. Ask who's in charge of the group seeking to fill the position within the company.

Okay, so you call and their policy is not to give that information out over the phone. Don't give up. If it's local, go to the company and stop in. Ask the receptionist who's in charge of personnel and the group hiring. Okay, what if that doesn't work either? Just say the heck with it and send the package out addressed without an individual identified? No. Keep searching; ask the right people. Who are the right people? The people who work for the company, of course. Who better knows the names of supervisors and directors?

Stand outside the main entrance when a shift is ending. Ask people as they come out. Keep asking until you receive a positive response. Someone is bound to know and tell you who's running personnel and the group looking to fill a position. If there is a bar or restaurant across the street, stop in an have a beer or cup of coffee. There's sure to be an employee or two unwinding after work. Ask them.

Meeting the Receiver's and Sender's Needs

Once you've discovered individuals' names, you can send out your job package. But don't just send out the one package to personnel, if that's what's requested. Certainly meet their requirements, and forward your cover letter and résumé to the appropriate source. But also send a package to the individual who heads up the group looking to fill a position. If it's addressed to an individual, they'll receive it.

Personnel will probably collect and compile the applications as they come in. They might even do a quick, initial screening for minimum requirements. Then they'll most likely wait until the predetermined deadline for applications before they get further involved in the screening process.

You also send a package to the person in charge of the group looking to fill a position; they will probably be quite involved in the decision-making process concerning who will be interviewed and eventually hired. So, what will this group leader do with your cover letter and résumé once they receive them?

Chances are, they'll forward them to personnel because they are initially in charge of collecting applications. That's fine, but you've accomplished something very important. You've made contact with the person who'll probably have a large say in who is to be interviewed and hired. They know your name and general background. You can be fairly sure, that if the package was addressed to them personally, they opened and read at least part of your cover letter and résumé.

When personnel sends them a stack of cover letters and résumés for review, your name should stand out. When considering that most of these applicants have similar professional backgrounds, who's interviewed is often based on other factors. Maybe recalling your name and initiative will be one of those factors.

Targeted Opening

Once you've discovered a job opening worth the effort, make the cover letter work for you. The opening should include that information discussed earlier in general terms. The receiver should be able to determine from the first paragraph what has prompted you to write. The first paragraph must deal with the facts, the information relevant to the job opening. The first paragraph should also encourage interest in the remainder of the letter, prompt the receiver to go on.

Deal with the specifics relating to how you became aware of the particular opening. If the job was advertised, relate the facts associated with the ad. Detail the name of the publication, the date and the position title as it appeared in the ad. Also, make your intent clear; don't leave it to the receiver to determine exactly why you are writing.

If you're applying for the position, make it clear. Don't just say you're interested in the position, or recently came across the ad. State directly that you want to be considered for the opening.

"I would like to be considered for the position of Electronic Technician advertised in the May 22nd edition of the Rochester *Democrat and Chronicle*. I believe my education and experience closely match the requirements for this position."

It's important to identify all of the relevant facts associated with an advertisement because a given company may have more than one opening available to fill. Identify the name of the publication so the receiver can determine when they placed the ad and how long it's been running. Give the receiver information that's pertinent to their needs as well as yours. Point out the date the ad appeared for the same reasons. Don't require the receiver to figure out facts that you can supply. Detail the specific position exactly as it appeared in the ad. Again, a company may, probably has, more than one opening available.

One you've given the reader all of the facts pertinent to your intent, including stating exactly what it is you want, encourage interest beyond the opening. Supply an appropriate transition to the remainder of the letter. After all, you are writing because you believe you can do the job based on certain elements from your background. Let them know you believe this and state it clearly, but generally. The remainder of the letter will support, with detail, your general belief.

"I believe my three years of experience in the electronics field qualifies me for this position."

"My education and experience, I believe, closely match the requirements for the position of Electronic Technician."

We generally state our belief relating to how well what we have matches what they want. It suggests allowing them to make the ultimate decision to interview us.

Discovery Through Networking

The same considerations apply if we discover an opening through networking as with advertisements. We detail all the pertinent facts for the receiver. But rather than point out the name of the newspaper and date, we point out how we learned about the opening. If we made the discovery based on information supplied by an individual, we offer those facts. We supply the date of the conversation along with their name and position. If they don't work for the company, we detail the context of how the information was offered.

"In my May 12th conversation with John Wiggins, Associate Engineer with Captron, I learned of an opening for an Entry Level Accountant. I would like to be considered for this position. I find the requirements for the position, as offered by John Wiggins, closely match my background."

Here, we are giving the receiver the information they require to make a clear decision. In a cover letter, like any professional letter, it's important to give the reader something, particularly when we are making a request. If you're asking the receiver for something, an interview here, give them something in return: the facts relating to how you discovered that there was an opening.

Background Highlighting

Once you've obtained the receiver's attention, move on to pointing out what from your background qualifies you for the position. Try and match, as best you can, what you have with what they want.

Determining your employable assets is an important step in the cover letter writing process. Begin by making a list of your most important employable assets. Take a look at the requirements for the job and match those assets that work best, most pertinent to the purpose.

If the requirements for the position are stated in the advertisement or offered by your contact, determining what to highlight won't be terribly difficult. But what if the requirements for a particular position aren't made obvious in one form or another? How do you match what you have with what you don't know?

You do a little homework; we all remember what that is. That's where you take that extra step, put in the effort to succeed. Do some research on what's generally required for the position you're interested in. Call the company and ask. Talk to some professional already employed in your particular field. Consult with a professor in your discipline. Make an effort to discover what sort of education and skills are most in demand when applying for a position.

Organizing the Cover Letter

Like with any other document, we generally emphasize that which is most pertinent to the purpose. Most of us will probably have a detailed education and a detailed experience section in our cover letters. What comes first, following our opening, depends on what we have the most, and what the requirements for the position are.

If experience in a particular area seems to be what our receiver is most interested in and we have that experience, then we would emphasize our experience. But if we have little or no experience in a particular field or area of concern, then we would point out and highlight our educational background. Organize your cover letter according to their needs first, backed up by your education and experience.

Highlighting Experience

Experience in your field is one of the most important assets you can offer a company. It states that you can apply your knowledge and can operate successfully within your discipline. Point out what you have and how it could prove beneficial to their needs. Offer the facts and state the context relating to those elements of your professional background that the receiver might be most interested in. Detail the name of the company or companies you've worked for, length of time and what your duties and responsibilities were. Don't go overboard here; only detail what you've determined they would be most encouraged by.

Introduce a point before you address and support it. State the name of the company, time frame and position first.

> "I have over three years experience with Ziptron Industries as an Electrical Technician."

This sets up the context before you go on to offer supporting detail. These are more of those facts the receiver requires before they can make a determination about interviewing you. Once you've set-up the context you can go on to support and point out the probable benefits the receiver might derive from your professional experience.

> "My experience at Ziptron includes trouble shooting and designing a variety of electronic circuits. The majority of the circuits I worked on involved computer mainframes, such as Comtrec I & II advanced data retrievers. This experience can be quite applicable to your circuit design efforts."

Be sure to point out the specifics relating to the generalities of your experience. Don't leave the receiver guessing about the extent of your experience. Offer the facts supporting the extent of your professional background and how they might prove useful.

The main consideration to keep in mind when highlighting experience, is to match as closely as you can what you have with what they are looking for.

- Introduce the point—facts and context relating to experience.
- Support the point—detail specific duties and responsibilities.
- Clarify extent—offer specific examples regarding efforts.
- Point out benefits—suggest how experience might apply.

A cover letter should generally not be longer than one page. Any longer and it might discourage the receiver from reading it in its entirety. It's not necessary to offer in detail your entire professional experience; that's what the résumé is for. The cover letter should only point out the primary elements of your background and how they might apply to the opening. Ideally, we want to keep our experience limited to one paragraph unless diversity dictates otherwise.

Highlighting Education

Whether or not you have experience in your field, it's important, practically required, that you detail educational background. Experience is certainly very important, but so is education. It states a theoretical background in your discipline, an ability to understand and appreciate the basics, the fundamental elements relating to your field. Highlighting education is even more important if you have little or no experience to offer a potential employer. Again, look at what you have and match it with what they want.

You offered the same kind of facts and detail with education that you would with experience. Give the receiver concrete details to base a decision on. First, point out the facts and context relating to your educational background. Point out the institution, degree, major and time frame or year of graduation.

"In May of 199 I received a B.S. in Accounting from Nazareth College in Rochester N.Y."

This introduces the point and sets up your opportunity to offer the supporting detail that will interest the receiver. It's not necessary here to state the obvious. Unless you've determined it's pertinent, don't include educational detail that's obviously connected to a particular degree.

When offering support regarding your educational entry, consider the receiver's needs and what skills might be highly regarded not only in your field, but also generally as a professional.

Consider detailing extracurricular activities here. Including information regarding club memberships, particularly discipline related, indicates a commitment beyond minimum requirements.

"As president of the Accounting Club, I gained practical experience in organization and group budgeting."

This indicates practical effort beyond the classroom and chosen responsibility, not required. What else might interest the receiver depends, of course, on their needs. But there are some educational efforts that will generally be appreciated.

Detailing certain educational efforts outside of traditional discipline requirements can prove interesting to the receiver. If you have a minor, you may want to briefly explain the specifics and how they could prove useful. Certain courses not traditionally associated with a degree program could also point out particular skills that are beneficial and real world related.

"In addition to my degree in accounting, I have also taken a variety of courses to improve my abilities to communicate with people. I have successfully completed courses in professional communications, technical writing and public speaking."

Including this additional course work points out employable assets beyond those that are strictly discipline related.

It's probably best to avoid such things as GPA and class standing here. Don't forget the Human Factor. How might certain information be regarded positively and how might it be regarded negatively? If, for some reason, you're set on detailing this kind of information, leave it for the résumé. Remember, the cover letter's intent is to introduce you and highlight those elements of your background that most closely match the requirements for a position.

- Introduce the point—facts and context of education.
- Support the point—detail specific course work and academic activities.
- Clarify benefits—point out how education could prove beneficial.
- Encourage interest—be enthusiastic regarding your education.

Targeted Conclusion

The conclusion for the targeted cover is not unlike the conclusion for the general cover letter. You basically want to accomplish the same thing.

Once you've highlighted those points from your background that most closely match the requirements for an opening, you want to be sure to finish on a positive note.

Thank the receiver for taking the time to read your cover letter and résumé and for whatever consideration they may give your application package.

"Thank you for your time and consideration."

Keep it short and to the point. Generally your receiver will appreciate brevity. Your concluding paragraph is where you refer to your résumé. Don't reference it earlier; allow your cover letter to serve its purpose.

"Please take a moment to review the enclosed résumé."

Again, keep it short. Allow the résumé to serve the purpose it was meant to serve. If the cover letter does its job, the résumé will too. Take the initiative in your cover letter. The receiver will appreciate a sincere, assertive approach.

"I will be contacting your office on July 7th at approximately 10:00 A.M. to discuss the possibility of an interview."

This indicates your seriousness concerning the opening and your desire to be considered as a viable candidate. Be specific with the date and time in case the receiver wants to get in touch with you prior to the indicated date.

You might consider reiterating your belief in your ability to do the job. Remember, in the body of the letter, you've pointed out those elements from your background that most closely match their requirements.

"I believe you'll agree that my experience and education closely match the opening's requirement."

Finally, it's important to provide a way for them to get in touch with you. Don't rely solely upon your address. It's somewhat presumptuous to assume that they will take the time to write you a letter and request you come in for an interview. Generally, an interview is set-up over the phone. They also may want to contact you prior to your calling their office. Any contact is positive when it comes marketing yourself.

"Please call anytime at (716) 555-7912."
"I may be reached, or leave a message at (716) 555-7912."
"I may be contacted at (716) 555-7912."
And sign your letter; always remember to sign your letter.

Mr. Lewis Clapton
213 Monroe Ave.
Rochester, N.Y. 14618

May 22,

Henry Gibson
Department Head
Turtle, Inc.
111 Colgate St.
Potsville, N.Y. 13253

Dear Henry Gibson:

I am writing in response to your advertisement for a computer programmer appearing in the Rochester *Democrat and Chronicle*, May 17, 1993. I would like to be considered as candidate for this position. I believe my education and experience closely match your requirements.

I received an Associate in Science degree from Monroe Community College, May 1992. My program at Monroe Community College has included a considerable amount of individual work and independent study, experience that would particularly suit me to the advertised opening. I have taken a variety of courses in software development. In conjunction with my course work, I designed a personnel record system for staff and management at Heath National Bank as a requirement for my fieldwork. I have also successfully completed courses in professional communications and public speaking to enhance my abilities to better communicate on a professional level.

I have been employed by Datadesign in Rochester N.Y. for over four years now. Among my various duties, I am responsible for dealing with customer questions and concerns regarding Datadesign's innovative software programs. This position has given me the opportunity to apply my academic training and knowledge to practical, real world inquiries.

Please take a moment to review the enclosed résumé. I'm sure you'll agree, my education and experience closely match your requirements. I will be contacting your office on Monday, June 1st at approximately 10:00 A.M. to discuss the possibility of an interview. Thank you for your time and consideration. I look forward to meeting with you soon. I may be contacted at (716) 555-8316.

Sincerely,

Lewis Clapton

73 Wyndham Road
Rochester, NY 14612
February 19,

SONY Theatres Pittsford
Mr. Colin M. Davey
3400 Monroe Avenue
Rochester, NY 14618

Dear Mr. Davey:

I'm faxing you this letter in reference to the secretarial position you have advertised in the Sunday, February 18, 1996, *Democrat & Chronicle*. With my educational background and work history, I believe I am a qualified candidate for this position.

I am a graduate from the State University of New York at Canton with an A.A.S. Degree in Secretarial Science. For the past six years I have been employed at Eastman Kodak Company. I currently provide secretarial support to the Director of Finance. In this position I've become proficient with Microsoft Word and Excel, creating numerous spread sheets and financial reports. One of my responsibilities, in addition to travel arrangements, correspondence, and daily secretarial duties is the department budget. I am responsible for submission, maintenance and tracking of the budget which I review with the Director on a quarterly basis. This has given me the opportunity to take on some financial responsibilities and to work in several on-line accounting systems.

In addition to my work experience at Kodak, I am a Core Team member of KNECT (Kodak-News-Education-Communication-Team). KNECT is being honored with a Special Recognition Award for the 1995 Team Achievement Award due to their accomplishments over the years. Association with this team has given me strong communication and organizational skills as well as teamwork skills.

Enclosed is a copy of my resume. I thank you for taking the time to look it over. I will be contacting you at 10:00 A.M. on Wednesday, February 21, to discuss scheduling an interview. Should you wish to speak with me sooner, I can be reached at work at (716) 722-4537 between the hours of 7:00 A.M.–3:30 P.M. Or you can call me at home at (716) 581-0843 after 4:00 P.M.

Sincerely,

Laurie Alianell
Enclosure

Letters That Persuade

Most of the letters we produce strive, to a certain extent, to persuade. Whether we're writing a cover letter trying to encourage an interview, or a letter to friend requesting a response, persuasion is part of the effort.

Effective communication requires an assertive approach. It's important to understand that in order to be effectively assertive, we also need to be fair in our correspondence, fair and convincing, ultimately persuasive. What it comes down to is getting what we want.

We've all been in situations where we needed to request something from someone, or to make a claim of some kind or point out a difference in opinion or understanding. To be aggressive, or non-assertive in these types of situations usually will get us little in return.

The Difference

You're in an elevator going up to the top of the World Trade Center in New York City with one other person. Around floor ten, the other person proceeds to light up a big smelly cigar in spite of the "no smoking" warnings posted in the elevator. The last thing you want is to be asphyxiated for nearly 100 floors. So what do you do to correct the situation?

> **Non-assertive:** You move as far away as you can from the individual and cover your face with your hanky and say nothing.
> **Aggressive:** You shout at the offending party, "Hey, idiot, put out the cigar before I make you eat it."
> **Assertive:** You address the possibly uninformed person in a reasonable, calm voice, "Maybe you're not aware of it, but there is no smoking in this elevator. Besides, this is quite a confined space and the smoke is annoying. Could you please put your cigar out until we reach our destination?"

Being non-assertive gets you nothing except a miserable ride. The aggressive approach may get you something, like a punch in the nose, but little else. The assertive approach points out the facts involved supporting your request. You're showing a certain amount of fairness and understanding because that's what you're asking from the other individual. Hopefully, they would see the reasonableness in your request and comply.

Anyway, backing away from a situation serves no one's purpose. Getting angry settles nothing, and is generally counter productive. Showing fairness with a reasonable attitude will at least get the receiver to pay attention.

Persuasive Technique

When motivated to produce a persuasive letter, we need to understand first, what our objective is. If our objective is non-monetary in nature, such as saving time or effort, the message needs to support that objective exclusively. If our objective is monetary, such as making or saving money, that objective must be met and supported.

We can meet our objectives if we keep a couple of points in mind when involved in the process. Our letter should promote good feelings, such as prestige, esteem, and self satisfaction. Strive to encourage the receiver to feel positive about your request and open to what you are proposing. Construct your letter with this in mind.

- The opening—secure interest.
- The body—explain and justify benefits of request.
- The close—press, fairly, for action.

There is certainly more than one possible approach to the art of persuasion, particularly considering the many situations that may require persuasion. But there are a number of considerations that generally apply to the persuasive message.

Generally we begin with a description of the problem our message will deal with. This supports letting the receiver know what has prompted you to write. The introduction of the situation should be brief and contain only the facts pertinent to the problem. The clarification and support come in the body of our message.

We could then follow with a proposed solution to the problem, dealing with possible ways to resolve and satisfy all involved. In conjunction with the proposed solution, we could also indicate the possible benefits derived from this solution.

Hopefully, by this point in our message, we have the receiver's attention because we've detailed the facts and displayed fairness relating to our proposed solution. Once this is accomplished, we can move on to explain the specific details that support and clarify the situation for the receiver.

Once the situation has been adequately explained, the next step could involve detailing the tasks required to reach the proposed solution. Here we could also summarize the specific benefits provided by the detailed solution and satisfy all involved. Detailing the benefits ends the message on somewhat of a positive note, because we've also pointed out the benefits for the receiver.

Persuasive Specifics

Everybody wants something. Most of the time, everybody believes their point. But that's not enough to convince someone else to respond favorably. Consider the many situations where effective persuasion is required.

- Incorrect charges
- Faulty instructions
- Lousy merchandise
- Unsatisfactory service
- We want a day off, a promotion, a raise
- Countless situations on the job

The specifics of persuasion should be as detailed and goal oriented as the situation requires. Those communicators who receive satisfaction generally appreciate the Human Factor and how important it is when considering persuasion. We need to give the receiver something, provide the detail necessary for them to make a decision and understand our request. Again, we need to show fairness, because we're asking them to be fair in return. The sender needs as best they can, to put themselves in the receiver's situation; try and understand from their point of view.

Specifics of the Persuasive Message

- Focus on the point of concern, disagreement by detailing the facts.
- Support the appeal by offering statistics and examples.
- Consider and refute possible objections or conflicting opinions.
- Use a positive tone and stick with the main point; don't stray.
- Use logic by conceding a point or two; show understanding.
- Make sure the request is fair and based on the facts.
- Overall, strive to be goal directed and fair.

How all of these persuasive specifics might work when addressed in a message depends on the point of the message, the sender and receiver. Let's say you want to ask your boss for an unscheduled day off so you decide a memo is the best way to approach this request.

You want the day off to attend a motivational seminar that isn't necessarily supported by the company you work for. You begin by focusing on the point of the request.

> "On Monday, September 7th there will be a motivational seminar, 'Succeeding at Work and Home,' from 8:00 A.M. to 4:00 P.M. that I would like to attend. I understand that I would need a day off in order to attend this seminar, but believe it will prove valuable to my efforts as an employee."

Once you've detailed the facts of the situation, move on to support your appeal.

> "This specific series of seminars has received publicity, and positive responses from a number of national publications, including *Time* magazine and *Business Weekly*. It was reported that these seminars have been directly linked to increased productivity for the companies that have encouraged employee participation."

What you're doing is building a case for a positive response. In order to be sure of the response, it's important to consider the possible objections your boss may have.

> "I understand that we are currently involved in a project that must be completed by the end of the month and my involvement is essential to its completion. I've rescheduled my time and with some over-time I'm sure I can make up the lost day by staying one hour later for a week."

Deal with all possible objections at the same point in your message and refute any negative thoughts the receiver may be considering regarding your request. Always remember to stick with the point of the message: your desire to attend the seminar.

"These types of seminars have been highly regarded for some time now. I'd be happy to provide a report and discuss how we might implement some of the suggestions that are offered."

As you stick with the main point, keep logic and understanding in mind. Remember, you're requesting fairness, so show fairness and concede a point or two.

"I understand that this is an unscheduled day off, but the seminar was just recently announced in the local press. I also appreciate the effort we're currently involved in, but I believe this day off will not cause difficulty because we are ahead of schedule."

End the memo by reiterating your belief that this is a fair request, and showing your understanding and fairness.

"Allowing me this day to attend the seminar should prove more valuable in the long run when considering how some of what I come away from the seminar with can be implemented within our company and help increase productivity. Making up the time should not be difficult, and I look forward to the successful completion of our project."

The Claim Letter

The most direct and positive way to point out and clarify the specifics of persuasion is probably through detailing the elements of the claim letter. The claim letter encompasses all of what persuasion deals with.

There are many situations in business, industry, and life today that may require you to write or respond to a claim letter. Because we are all subject to human error, we must expect others to make mistakes. Here we should appreciate and deal with the Human Factor. We may be required to deal with incorrect charges on invoices, incomplete shipments, inaccurately priced tickets, poorly written instructions, poor service, faulty products and many other possibilities.

To correct such mistakes, it is often necessary to write claim letters requesting satisfaction. And, depending on the situation, it is often necessary to respond to such messages.

Claim letters can easily create unpleasant situations. Think about any letters you may have received making what you believed was an unreasonable request. Whether it was on the job or at home, receiving a poorly constructed claim letter probably wasn't welcomed. They can often be regarded as unjustified. Letters of this nature that relate to our professional lives could possibly lend themselves to negative publicity and damage to reputations. The question of credibility could be addressed here. And we know that once our credibility is questioned, it's difficult to get it back. That's why claim letters are more often than not construed negatively. What we as communicators want to do, is to avoid negative feelings regarding our messages.

- Claim letters require special sensitivity and diplomacy if they are to prevent a hostile reaction and encourage a satisfactory reply.
- Call attention politely and calmly to the problem—you increase the chances of having the grievance handled quickly, with satisfaction.
- Don't be aggressive and use an angry tone—this could irritate the receiver.
- Anger, ridicule, name calling and threats could make the sender seem irrational. This approach is counter-productive.

"I recently purchased a six pack of your beer and found some strange sediment in three of the bottles. It was a disgusting discovery and I almost got sick. Your brewery has to be one of the worst operating in the area, if not the worst. I have no idea how you can remain in business when you produce such a terrible product. I will never again buy anything made by your company. I will also encourage my friends not to purchase your crappy beer. Your company stinks."

Think about how you would react if you were to receive a letter like this, probably not very favorably. In fact, letters that come across in an angry and accusatory tone tend to quickly find their way into the round file and are rarely answered.

The claim letter should strive to receive a satisfactory response. Just like persuasion, appeal to the receiver's sense of fairness by demonstrating fairness.

The claim letter should:

- Explain the situation that has prompted you to write.
- Describe the loss or inconvenience.
- Appeal to the receiver's sense of fairness to right the wrong.
- Concede a point or two and refute objections when appropriate.

"On November 4,   I purchased a six pack of Webster's beer at Kopple's Market, 11 West Avenue at approximately 1:00 P.M. I discovered that three of the bottles had some foreign substance floating in them when I got them home.

I have been a faithful customer of your product for some time now, and found this recent discovery disturbing and surprising. I do understand that with the volume your company produces on a daily basis that mistakes such as this might occasionally happen.

Although the $3.89 purchase price of the six pack is not a large amount of money, I feel justified in requesting a refund as I am reluctant to consume the beer. Again, I do understand that quality control is not infallible and occasionally a less than perfect product may escape your scrutiny. Maybe a reevaluation of your quality control standards would discover the source of this problem.

I would appreciate a refund of my $3.89 and I look forward to continued enjoyment of your product. I would be happy to provide the contaminated six pack for your analysis."

This letter would probably receive a much more favorable response than the first one. It completely details the situation regarding the purchase. This provides information to the receiver that might prove useful to their efforts in resolving the problem. The letter also demonstrates a sense of understanding and fairness by not requesting anything beyond the purchase price. More often than not, when the situation is handled this way, the sender receives more than they request.

An actual situation similar to the one detailed here produced more than positive results. Not only did the company honor the request, they went beyond what they were required to do. Two cases of beer were delivered along with a thank you note.

Responding to Claim Letters

Writing the persuasive claim letter may seem to be an involved, complicated process but if you have the facts and believe in a legitimate judgement, the difficulty may only be in finding the time to successfully construct the message. Understand and follow the process and you should meet your goals. Consider the receiver and how they might respond based on the information you provide.

Responding to a persuasive request such as a claim letter offers a different set of challenges.

- Person writing believes he or she has a legitimate claim.
- Address each issue, point expressed in the letter.
- When refusing a request, give the impression your decision is based on a clear and fair judgement.

Responding favorably to a request is not, usually, a difficult task. It's when the response is one of refusal that the sender should consider tact and diplomacy.

The Refusal Pattern

The general refusal pattern applies to many disagreeable business messages; specific patterns exist for a number of these messages. Typical of these specific patterns are those for request refusals, credit refusals and order refusals. Mastering these patterns will help in writing all disagreeable messages.

Your position, as you consider responding to the request or claim letter, is one of responsibility. Answer the letter based on its content and justification. The decision is yours, but whatever that decision is, be sure to address each point in the letter. That will demonstrate your sense of fairness and professionalism.

- Relate—display understanding; begin by putting the receiver at ease.
- Reason—offer specifics leading to and relating to subsequent refusal.

- Refuse—be specific and state exactly what you are refusing.
- Reconcile—conclude by expressing regret or confidence or both relating to letter writer and claim or request.

You work for an electronics store, and one of your many duties is to answer customer correspondence. The first letter you open Monday morning requests a refund for a voice activated mini-tape recorder purchased at your store some nine months prior. The voice activation, according to the writer, no longer works. The warranty was for six months.

Of course, follow correct letter format.

"Dear Mr. Finglenut:

Thank you for your recent letter. We always appreciate hearing from our many valued customers. We at Circuit Shack believe the customer comes first, and strive to satisfy their needs.

According to your letter, you purchased one of our mini-tape recorders nine months ago. The Zip mini recorder's voice activation element no longer works. They are quite sensitive, and this occasionally happens. Unfortunately, your recorder is no longer under warranty and can't be replaced or repaired at our expense. Had you contacted Circuit Shack prior to the warranty running out, we would have been more than happy to oblige.

Again, we regret not being able to positively honor your request and trust you'll understand. We'd be happy to repair your recorder at your expense any time you'd like to bring it in. We have an excellent repair shop, and hope you'll make use of our services. We understand the problem here and trust you can appreciate our position. We look forward to your continued business with Circuit Shack."

Hopefully, that refusal not only informed the receiver that their request was denied, but did it in such a way that they won't be terribly disappointed and will understand.

Agreeing to a Request or Claim

Responding favorably to a request or claim is far less difficult and complicated than the refusal. After all, you're giving the sender what he wants. You're going to make them happy and make their day.

Refusing a request requires that you offer bad news to the sender. It's important to set up for the refusal; don't refuse at the beginning of your message. When you're granting a request, it's generally acceptable to state that positive response at the beginning of the message.

- Grant request or claim.
- Express regret if you are at fault.

- Explain cause, reason for problem.
- Assure error will not happen again.
- Always end courteously.

Like with the prior example, if you have determined with certainty that you, or your company are not at fault for the problem, your request refusal should follow a particular pattern.

- Begin with a statement of appreciation for the letter.
- Agree with the writer about some aspect of the situation.
- Explain your investigation of the request.
- Politely refuse request.
- Build goodwill by granting any possible concession or by appealing to the writer's sense of fairness.

Stamping the Envelope

These are just a few examples of professional or business letters. The cover letter was persuasive, but also informational. The claim or letter of request dealt with the primary elements of persuasion. Again, when we write a letter, we are generally looking for something in return. Most letter writing is somewhat persuasive by nature, and following the patterns and suggestions detailed here should help lead to success.

There are a variety of other letters you may be faced with writing either on or off the job, but if you understand letter writing's purpose and intent, you should have little difficulty meeting those challenges. Always remember the Human Factor and keep the receiver in mind when constructing those important letters.

EXERCISES

1. What's wrong with this cover letter?

Mr. John Lyons
657 East Ave.
Rochester, N.Y. 14522

August 5,

Ms. Beverly Plimpton
Personnel Director
Heath National Bank
17 Corrigan St.
Lurchville, N.Y. 123744

Dear Ms. Plimpton:

I recently read about a job you have opened in your company. I'm very much interested in this position. I have always desired to be involved in the banking industry.

I have a BS degree in accounting from a prestigious institution. I have successfully completed all of the necessary course work for this degree while maintaining a 3.00 average. I was active in the Accounting Club and the Chess Club throughout my college career.

My experience includes 2 years as the part-time assistant night manager for Dewey's Market here in Rochester. I also have some experience keeping their books and balancing certain budgets.

Thank you for taking the time to read this and think about me as a possible candidate. As you can see from my résumé, I have a varied background that should prove interesting. I look forward to hearing from you soon.

Sincerely,

John Lyons

2. Go back to exercise 3 in the preceding chapter. Construct a cover letter for Jack Kasper to apply for the following position.

Ad in the *Democrat and Chronicle* Newspaper. Position–Rochester Institute of Technology, Instructor in Mechanical Technology. Requirements–MS in Engineering, 2 years college level teaching experience, 2 years professional experience. Address–Personnel Director, RIT, 1 Lomb Memorial Drive, Rochester, N.Y. 14623.

3. Construct your own cover letter.

Go to the campus library and locate a job in a published source. Take a look at newspapers, and don't forget periodicals and professional, discipline-specific publications. Try to find an opening within your field and match, as best you can, what you have with what they want. It doesn't have to be a recent opening, just an opening you can focus on. Another possibility might be the campus job placement office.

4. Construct a claim letter for the following situation.

Mrs. Anthony, eight months pregnant, and her 1 year old son, Joseph, stop in Citywide Market Monday, October 12 at approximately 1:00 P.M. to do some shopping. She places Joseph in the child's seat in the cart and proceeds to shop. While stopped at the meat counter, Mrs. Anthony momentarily diverts her attention from Joseph as she chooses some fresh pork butt. She hears a thud and a scream. Joseph has fallen out of the cart.

She quickly picks him up and notices a large bump forming on his head. She asks the man behind the meat counter, Ian Platz, for some ice and a towel. He refuses, stating it is against store policy. She asks again; he refuses again. He does direct her to the drinking fountain. She discovers it is out of order. She returns and once again asks Mr. Platz for some ice. He, again, states store policy. She asks if there is a phone available. He offers, only in the manager's office.

She hurries, screaming Joseph in tow, to the manager's office. The Asst. Manager, Mr. Snipes, states it is against store policy to allow customers to use the phone. All she wants is to call the child's doctor to see if she should bring him to emergency or not. Angry, Mrs. Anthony retrieves her purse, with Joseph still screaming, and leaves the store. She brings him to his doctor. The child is fine. The unscheduled visit is $35.00.

You are a good friend of Mrs. Anthony's and believe the store is somehow at fault and she deserves some kind of retribution. One thing you discover is that Citywide's shopping carts are not up to code. Write a letter to Citywide's Corporate Office requesting what you believe to be a fair judgement.

5. Once those letters are completed, exchange them with your classmates and write a response based on the content of their request.

6. Design a scenario, either from experience or imagination, where it would be necessary for you to write a claim or request letter. Make sure it is realistic and believable.

EXERCISE

Claim/Request Letter

You have a one o'clock appointment with a new dentist, Dr. Scwartz. You believe you have a cavity, and would like to have it checked and possibly filled.

Your old dentist, Dr. Yankem, recently retired; that's why you had to locate a new dentist.

So, on October 18th you show up at Dr. Scwartz's office at 1000 Dewey Ave. in Rochester, N.Y. at 10 minutes to 1. You proceed to check in with Joanne Fleece, the receptionist. She gives you some "new patient" forms to fill out—it takes you approximately 15 minutes.

You have taken an hour off from work to meet your appointment. Because you had to take off from work—manager of PayLess Shoes in Northgate Plaza—you are docked $18.00.

You finally get into the chair at 1:20 P.M. Dr. Scwartz discovers your cavity and assures you that he can have it filled in plenty of time for you to get back to work by 2. Because you are allergic to novicane, you must have gas (nitrous oxide) which puts you to sleep.

While asleep, the dentist discovers at least 8 additional cavities.

Although they are relatively small, he decides to fill them while he has you in the chair, It takes him an additional hour and a half. And by the time you are done, it's after 3 P.M. You, of course, wake up angry and refuse to pay the bill. The bill came to $263. You will also be docked $36 pay.

You finally do pay the bill, and as you storm out of his office you find that the parking meter you parked at has expired and you have a $20 parking ticket on you window.

When you arrive back at work, you discover the district manager has arrived unannounced (Joyce VanStringy) and she is extremely angry because you left your lead sales clerk in charge of the store (Gino Benevenutti).

Now, write a claim letter to your new dentist seeking what you believe to be equitable compensation for this situation.

C h a p t e r   F i v e

Writing Descriptions and Analysis

Why Description?

As a working professional writer, I was given an assignment to write a product description on an about-to-be-introduced copier. I began by thinking about what I knew about copiers and how I could relate that knowledge in the description.

I observed, went to where the copier was and studied its characteristics and subtle nuances lending to the whole. I considered the audience, salespeople, and what they needed to know to help them do their job.

I considered language and how the way I used certain words would influence their understanding and approach to the product, and how well the description translated to the intended audience. As this was one of the first descriptions I was charged with writing, I began to better understand how words, usage and audience depend on organization and reader appreciation to create a product that works. I was encouraged to consider how my language, word choices, translated to a specific audience.

I was encouraged to ask questions as I went through the process of description.

- How detailed is the description and what does it lack?

- Will the audience receive the message intended?

- Is the descriptive detail accurate?

- Do the descriptive elements support the whole?

- Did I create an accurate picture?

One of the things I discovered while involved in the descriptive process, was how well it lent itself to the opportunity to be creative. Certainly not creative in the sense of being solely entertaining, but plausibly informative with genuine concern for the reader.

Innovation can be one of the primary tools for the industrial communicator today. Professional information is often regarded as dry and boring. But, of course, that's in part its nature; it's meant primarily to inform, not impress. But, considerations can be offered to the reader beyond simply offering the information in logical order.

It's important to always remain aware of the readers and their needs. Putting them to sleep does not encourage utilization of a professional document. Through description, we can use our creative sense to cultivate and hold the reader's interest.

Description and Metaphor

The term "metaphor" is a figure of speech where something is referred to or spoken of in terms of what it resembles. Basically, a direct or implied comparison suggesting that one thing is another. The use of metaphors can prove quite useful in description.

Actually, the use of metaphor in communication is far more popular than we might initially believe. In professional documentation, metaphor is not necessarily considered in its strictest sense as it might relate to creative literature, but as a tool to enhance and clarify professional description.

Metaphor is often required in documentation to clarify, although figuratively, and describe something it relates to, compares with, or accentuates. Metaphor is helpful in the clarification of complicated professional description. Parts of the body are often described not by their scientific names but by the shape they resemble. For example, we call the bones of the inner ear the hammer, the anvil and the stirrup.

It is often easier to use metaphorical names, they offer universal understanding and rarely get confused with other, more detailed specifics. A specific, concrete image can offer detailed recognition of complicated material.

Metaphor is often used to differentiate one bit of information from another. With the advent of computers into the area of communication, new terminology was established for clarification. A "hard copy" of a document, for example, refers to an actual paper copy. This term is used to separate the documentation copy from the documentation appearing on the screen. The term "hard copy" is now accepted and understood by those involved with publications and industrial communication. The terms "hard disk" and "floppy disk" do not accurately describe their functions, but more aptly refer to the form. Using metaphor is a practical way to convey certain kinds of descriptive information.

As a task or device is described, you may encounter functional detail requiring the turning of an element clockwise or counterclockwise. Obviously, turning a screw, a chuck, a plug or filter has nothing to do with a clock. Metaphor not only provides adequate description, but also ensures reliable instruction.

Without the use of figurative language, or metaphor, many professional documents would suffer from lack of clarity. How better to describe the elements of gears than with the incorporation of the term "gear teeth"? A gear certainly does not have teeth in the strictest sense, but the term does provide concrete detail.

The use of metaphor in documentation is not the central issue; purity of meaning is. Metaphor does have a place in documentation and its use is to be established in the need for clarity. How better to describe difficult spatial concepts like shape, size, texture and so on?

The Basics of Description

To some extent, description is required for many different forms of documentation. We need to describe devices and mechanisms for product and process design, instructions, procedures, reports, manuals and a variety of other reasons.

Creating an initial impression is primary to the descriptive process. Once we understand the basics of what we are required to describe, we can move on to the complexities and detail that requires understanding and appreciation in order to adequately offer this information to our intended audience.

Descriptions are characterized by objective information responding to specific considerations.

- What is it?—definition
- What is its purpose?—function
- What elements make up the whole?—parts
- What does it look like?—appearance
- What are its features?—material, size, color, texture, etc.

There are basically two primary approaches to the process of describing something: physical characteristics and functional elements.

Physical

This general element relates to what something looks like and the parts that make up the whole.

- What does it look like?
- What are its dimensions?
- How many parts does it have?
- What is it made from?
- What color or colors are visible?
- What are its prominent textures?

Everything requiring description has physical characteristics. What particulars are emphasized and how important they are to the description depends on the task.

Functional

This primarily deals with what you're describing does, and how it accomplishes what it does.

- What is its primary function?

- What, if any, are its secondary functions?

- How does the whole accomplish its primary function?

- How do the parts assist in accomplishing the primary function?

- How does it accomplish its secondary functions?

Everything requiring description has a function; it does something. What particular functional elements are emphasized, again, depends on what is being described.

Creating a Complete Description

In order to describe something sufficiently and completely, both physical and functional elements need to be considered and addressed. What you are trying to accomplish with description is to create a picture in words.

Let's begin by taking something we encounter every day and see how simple or complicated the process of description can be. What if, for some reason, we were faced with the task of describing a person. This is a good place to begin considering description. People have physical as well as functional characteristics—personalities.

Maybe we have been required to describe a person in the past for some reason. Think about those situations and the language you may have used when describing what they look like and what kind of person they were. Maybe you used words like tall, beautiful, funny, well built or goofy. Unless the person you were describing this individual to was extremely familiar with you and your particular use of words, they probably didn't get a very clear picture of this individual.

Ambiguous words offer little if any relatable detail required for accurate description. Adjectives, or descriptive language leaves far too much room for interpretation. Generally, when we're required to describe something, the picture we are trying to create is not open to interpretation.

It's not to say that we can't utilize descriptive language when striving to create an accurate image of what we're describing. We just need to go beyond the general and

support with specific, relatable detail. We need to compare what we're describing with something our audience will appreciate, and offer examples in an effort to meet the audience's visual needs.

The specific process of description is like the process of writing in general. It requires determining and asking the right questions, and determining what detail is pertinent to the purpose.

When describing a person, like anything else, we need to determine the appropriate questions to ask. We establish descriptive priorities and consider primary and secondary questions.

- What stands out about this person—what's most important?

- What is their primary function?

These primary elements are often regarded as features relating to the most important aspects of what we're describing. In the case of an individual, we can probably all agree that's what's most important is who they are, not necessarily what they look like. This relates to their function. What's primary, translates as a benefit to the audience?

Do we describe them in professional or personal terms? Maybe this person is a doctor and a family man. Would we separate one from the other as primary? Of course, it depends on the purpose of the description.

When we consider what stands out, could physical elements be considered as primary characteristics? Again, these are questions all worth asking and answering. What we choose to describe and emphasize depends on the purpose of the description.

Informational Description

Let's take an individual we'll call Jim. We want to describe a complete picture of him for someone who doesn't know Jim.

We can begin with general descriptive language by stating that Jim is big. This is certainly not enough, so we need to go further and offer dimensional detail. Jim is 6' 5" and weighs about 280 pounds. Okay, but that's still not enough detail. We also need to deal with body type and describe his appearance: what he looks like physically. Jim is well proportioned with the body of a well-toned boxer. Now we have more of a detailed, reader-directed description.

We began by offering an overall, general description—big.

We followed with dimensional detail—6' 5", 280 pounds.

We followed that with clarifying detail—comparison.

Combining all of these descriptive elements will eventually create a concise, detailed picture of what Jim looks like.

✔ General appearance

✔ Dimensional detail

✔ Comparative detail

In order for our description of Jim to be complete, we need to add functional detail to the physical characteristics we described. We certainly haven't created a complete physical description of Jim, only his overall physical makeup. In other words, we described the whole. The next step would be to describe Jim's individual parts, such as his face, hair, extremities and so on. As we described his various parts, we would keep the whole in mind and show how everything interacts.

In conjunction with describing his whole and parts, we could include functional elements. In order to create a clear picture of him, we might detail how he walks, runs and moves. How the various parts of what we're describing function is the first step in detailing how what we're describing works.

Let's say that Jim's primary, professional functional element is that he is an industrial illustrator. With this information, we're beginning to clarify what Jim is all about. We could then move on to what he does outside of his profession and describe his personal life. If we were to determine that he is a husband, father, and loves fishing, we are establishing additional concrete details that help to establish a clear visual and mental image of Jim.

In order to solidify our description, we might move on to offering examples of how Jim might operate in a given situation. The key to this descriptive approach is example.

We could detail particular comparisons relating to his physical appearance as well as his behavior. We might begin by establishing a point of view, in other words, describe Jim from a preestablished perspective. Jim will be described as though facing the receiver of the information. It might help to establish a point of reference. In other words, we begin our description by detailing what is prominent or stands out, such as, Jim has a terrific smile, or his size is, at first, overwhelming. In short, consider whatever it takes to create a clear and complete visual description of Jim, or anything else we may be required to describe.

- Physical characteristics
  - ✔ Dimensions
  - ✔ Material
  - ✔ Color
  - ✔ Shape
- Functional elements
  - ✔ Various parts
  - ✔ How each part works
  - ✔ Methods of attachment
- Comparison
  - ✔ What it looks like
  - ✔ Metaphor
- Examples
- Point of view
- Primary point of reference

These are some of the considerations we need to deal with when describing something. To what extent we consider each of these points depends on our purpose.

Terminology

In describing a device, be sure to use very precise and accurate terminology. It might be easier to use ambiguous language, but your description won't be very clear. That's why it's important to use precise, specific language. Rather than say the rod is narrow, for example, express the dimensions, such as $1/18$ inch wide.

Also be sure to detail variances. Again, be specific by stating the gears vary in size from 2 to 16 inches.

Purpose

Determining the purpose of your description should be one of the first steps in the process. What type of document is required and how will it be used? Be sure to study similar documents to discover what might work for your current project. Consider what format will work best with the purpose and audience in mind.

Audience

Once you've determined the purpose of your description, concentrate on the needs of your audience. Determine how they will use the document, and what their experience level is. For example, an electronic description for a general audience should probably include some definitions to meet their needs. The same description for a group of electronic technicians would probably require less in terms of definitions and explanations.

Observation

Even if you are familiar with what you're required to describe, it's a good idea to spend some time observing the device. Get to know the device better, how it works, and what its purpose is.

If you're basically unfamiliar with the device, the observation period is even more essential. It might help to interview someone who is familiar with the device: get their ideas. Determine how the device works, and how each part relates to and interacts with the whole. The key here is to observe and learn.

Process Description

Describing a process is somewhat different than describing a device or mechanism. Basically, describing a process is explaining how something is done. It is somewhat instructive in nature, but rather than give orders or commands, you would provide statements of fact.

Instructions	Describing a Process
Buckle the center clip.	The center clip is buckled.

An audience comes to an understanding regarding a process once they read the description. Although a process could be construed as somewhat instructive, there are some types of processes that can't be explained with the goal of performance as the outcome.

The processes carried out by nature can certainly be understood, but can't be performed. For example, no one can perform the process of the cardiovascular system, but it can be understood through description. The more simple process of driving a car can be explained, but that explanation can only go so far when it comes to performance. This type of process needs to be experienced in addition to being described in order to be performed.

Process Description Audience

When it comes to describing a process, the communicator should make few assumptions about the level of knowledge or experience an audience may possess. The complexities of any process should be detailed and fully explained for a given audience to completely understand iot. This would entail defining terms and fully supporting all process details.

Illustrations

With a process or device description, illustrations can certainly add to the audience's understanding. But, generally, illustrations should only be used to enhance the descriptive text, the language. Readers tend to retain or form a more concrete understanding through language. Illustrations can certainly enhance description but can

be relied on to achieve retention alone. Illustrations are the final step when it comes to all types of description. If describing appearance, size, dimensions, material, color, function, utilizing comparison and examples don't quite serve the purpose of description, we then rely on illustrations.

Plan for the Process Description

- What is the process to be described?
- Who is the intended audience?
- How will the audience use the process description?
- How should the process description be organized?

Once these questions are fully considered and answered, outline an organizational plan leading to meeting the goal of the description.

- Why is this process description important?
- What are the major steps, or elements of the process?

Device/Mechanism Description

Device—A device is generally something used in the process of performing a function or a task, to meet a goal.

- A hand-held can opener is a device used to meet the goal of opening a can or a bottle.
- A ratchet is a device used to meet the goal of tightening or loosening various sizes of bolts.
- Fingernail clippers are a device used to meet the goal of clipping your fingernails.

Mechanism—basically describes the working parts of a machine where the operation itself is the goal.

- A television is a mechanism where the goal is the operation itself.
- A bicycle is a mechanism where the operation is the goal, not transportation; that's the result.

- A mechanical pencil is a mechanism where the operation is the goal; graphite on paper is the result.

These terms are often used interchangeably. To keep it simple, and for the sake of consistency, we will use the term "device" throughout this discussion.

The Task

Once we've been presented with the task of describing something, we begin to plan our strategy. Consider the process.

- It begins with questioning; determining what we know about the device, or product and what we don't know and need to find out.
- Observation follows; we familiarize ourselves with the device we are required to describe.
- At the beginning stages of the process, we also determine who the audience is. Is the audience general, or discipline specific?

Let's say a particular segment of our audience is made up of package designers. What do they need to know and why, in order to do their jobs? Consider their needs in a logical manner. Their responsibility is to design a package for the device. The package has to be attractive as well as serviceable.

The package designer would need to know general as well as particular details. How to begin, of course, depends on the device. Keep in mind that one of the goals of our descriptions should be to promote, to some extent, enthusiasm for what we're describing.

They would need to know overall size and weight in order to design a proper package. They would need to know what it is made out of, the material to determine how sturdy the package should be. They would certainly need to know function, what the device does, in order to decide whether or not to design a clear view or closed package. In short, they would need to know everything for their particular needs.

Organization

Once we've become familiar with the device we're required to describe, the purpose, and who our audience is, the next step is deciding what to do with all of this information.

We want our audience to understand and appreciate what the device is all about. In our efforts to accomplish this task, we need to create as clear a visual picture as we can. Before we even get into the actual part-by-part description, it's important to place our device into a general category, giving a context for understanding.

General Category

In the introduction to our device description, we need to define what it is we're describing, state what it does (function), offer an overall description (size and shape), and identify the category the device fits into.

What we are doing as we establish the general category is to define the subject. One way to determine the general category is by asking some specific questions.

- What function does this device perform?

- What else also performs the same or a similar function?

We establish the general category in order to place our device into a particular context for audience understanding. Without the general category, we can't be sure our audience will appreciate the specifics of our device, what makes it unique, how it stands out and apart from the general category.

What we're doing here is going from the general to the specific. Sound familiar?

Our audience will better be able to understand and appreciate our specific device when we show how the differentia of the device sets it apart form the general category.

Specific Device	**General Category**
Tape Measure	Measuring Devices
Crescent Wrench	Wrenches
Gumball Machine	Candy Dispensers
Floor Lamp	Household Illumination Devices
Zippo Lighter	Flame Producing Devices
Mechanical Pencil	Writing Instruments or Pencils

If the task was to describe a disposable, mechanical pencil, the general category could be writing instruments or pencils. The way to determine which general category works best is to ask the questions. What does the device we're describing do? It basically deposits graphite makings on paper. What else can perform the same function? Wooden pencils, as well as a variety of mechanical pencils perform the same function. If you'd feel more comfortable having a broader general category, you could include all writing devices in this category. Establish the general category considering how distinctly the specifics of the description can establish the differentia that sets the particular device apart from the general category.

Specific Device

Once we've established a clear, detailed general category with examples of the variety of devices that perform the same or a similar function as our device, we can move on to describe our device overall. Here we will detail the specific features that set our device apart from the general category.

As we move on to describe the specifics of our device, we consider those features that make it special or can translate as benefits for the audience and the user. For certain audiences, such as customers, we may want to begin pointing out the specifics of our device by dealing with function. Overall, what we're trying to accomplish here is a complete device description. We're going to describe the overall characteristics of our device and what makes it unique.

- Function—what it does.
- Dimensions—overall size.
- Shape—what it looks like.
- Material—what it's made from.
- Color(s).

The organization of the specifics depends on the audience and the device. All of this detail is necessary even before we get into the part-by-part description. The second part of our introduction points out the specifics of our device.

The disposable, mechanical pencil is used to deposit graphite makings on paper, generally in the form of words, numbers and drawings. It is 5 ½ inches in length and ¼ inch at its widest point and $^1/_{16}$ inch at its narrowest point. It's made out of plastic, rubber compound for erasing graphite, and graphite. Its primary colors are black and purple. Its overall shape is octagonal.

Those are the basic specifics or features that set our device apart from the general category. This is the stage where we begin to construct a visual picture for our audience. We're still dealing with the general, overall elements of our device, but those elements are getting more specific as we get closer to describing the individual parts that make up our device.

List Parts

As we continue in the introductory portion of our description, we move on to list the various parts of our device. By this stage, we should have determined what parts we need to describe in order to create as clear a visual picture as possible. It's at this point that we should consider the spatial design of the device. What is the logical order in which to list and describe the parts? If you can recall back to Jim, we might describe him from head to toe. That's the logical order of description with a person. That takes into account the spatial design. With the pencil, it is probably logical to begin with the eraser and proceed to the point.

Point of View

Prior to listing the parts, it is often a good idea to establish a point of view. Point of view indicates to the audience how we will be describing the device. It establishes our vantage point so the reader will understand our particular order of description. Point of view allows us to limit the angles of description to one view that is predetermined.

The disposable, mechanical pencil will be described as though it was lying on a flat surface with the pocket clip facing the viewer, the eraser to the left and the point to the right.

This will assist the reader in understanding the location of the parts as we describe them. It establishes angle and takes into account spatial design.

Listing—Remember, when you have the opportunity to list in professional documentation, always list. Listing the parts of our device establishes the final portion of the introduction. Listing the parts in a particular order accomplishes more than pointing out what parts will be described. Listing the parts also indicates to the audience the order in which the parts will be described in the body of the description. It's important to number the parts in your list for future document reference.

1. Eraser

2. Eraser Head Holder

3. Body or Shaft

4. Pocket Clip

5. Graphite Inserts

The disposable pencil is a rather simple device to describe. It has few parts, and those parts are less than complicated. If you were required to describe a more complicated device, the parts list could consist of principal parts and the related assemblies.

For example, if we were describing a pocket knife, one of the principal parts could be the body of the knife and the sub-assembly could consist of what makes up the body.

1. Body: composed of plastic enclosure sizes (2), metal separation pieces (3), and blade retaining hinges (2)

Naming Parts

If the particular part you're listing has a universally accepted, recognized name, use it. But if the part doesn't have an accepted name, or you've determined that what it's called doesn't serve the purpose of your description, give it a new name. There are two things to consider when establishing the name of a part.

- What does it do?

- What does it look like?

Often a combination of these two can clearly define a part. For example, when determining the names of parts of the disposable pencil, most have logical names. But when it came to listing the part that holds the eraser, the name seemed elusive.

- What does it do—holds the eraser.

- What does it look like—not unlike a head.
  "eraser head holder" establishes and clarifies the part.

With description, like all documentation, it's necessary to have a clear, detailed introduction. The introduction gets the audience involved in the document, and hopefully, interests them in the process.

Introductions provide the best opportunity to be creative. Again, getting the audience's interest is essential if we're going to expect them to continue through the document.

Create enthusiasm for the device you are describing in the introduction of the description. Remember, you're trying to create interest in the device as well as the document. Use language that suits the purpose and intent of the document. With the disposable, mechanical pencil, we could use words like, "innovative," "lightweight," "comfortable," "handy," to create interest and enthusiasm for the device.

The body of the description will flow clearly and accurately from a well-detailed, audience-directed introduction.

- The introduction should begin with a clear, general category definition with examples of the variety of other devices that perform the same or similar task.

- The introduction should also describe the specific device's overall appearance, including size and function. Point out what makes the device you're describing unique and sets it apart form the general category.

- The introduction should establish a point of view so the audience appreciates the logic of the description as it relates to the spatial design of the device.

- The introduction should number and list the parts in the order in which they will be described.

Describing the Parts

Once you've provide the audience with a clear, detailed introduction you can now verbally take the device apart, take it apart and describe each part. Remember to follow the list of parts provided in the introduction as a transition to the body of the document.

You're going to basically accomplish the same thing with each part in the body that you did with the whole in the introduction. The only thing that generally isn't necessary with the parts description is establishing a general category.

Take one part at a time and define what it is and what it does. Here we're going to describe size, weight, shape, material, color, and method of attachment to the whole and subsequent parts.

In most cases, it is probably appropriate to begin the part description by detailing the function of the part and how it interacts with the whole. For example, the eraser is a rubber-like compound used to remove undesired graphite makings deposited by the mechanical pencil. This deals with the specific function of the part and relates to the whole.

In detailing the size of the part, provide the dimensions and overall shape. For example, the shaft of the mechanical pencil is 5 ½ inches long, ¼ inch wide at its widest point where it connects to the eraser head holder, and tapers down to $1/16$ inch at its narrowest point where the graphite protrudes. The shaft resembles a standard pencil or an Apollo rocket ship in shape. This provides the dimensions, location of varying dimensions and overall appearance. Note where comparison was used.

Material, color and any other descriptive elements should be incorporated into the part description. For example, the shaft is black and made from plastic. Be more specific with the material if the information is available. Basically, provide the same detail with each part as you did with the whole device.

Method of Attachment

Describing how one part is associated with and attaches to the next part supplies some important data leading to visualization and creating a clear picture of the device. It encourages the audience to appreciate how each part acts independently, but also operates and relates to the whole device. Detailing the method of attachment clarifies points of spatial design and part location. Describing how one part is attached to the next part also acts as a transition to describing the next part of the device.

For example, the eraser is fitted and glued into the eraser head holder. This describes how one part is attached to the next and acts as a transition to describing the next part, the eraser head holder.

Remember what you're trying to accomplish with the part by part description. Your task is to create as clear a visual picture of each part as possible and how it attaches to each subsequent part. Once this is accomplished, and each part is fully described, the audience should have a clear, detailed picture of the device. Creating a picture with words requires attention to detail and use of effective, audience-directed language.

Vague Description

There are a couple of things to be careful of when describing a device in order to avoid overallcreating an inaccurate picture. Dimensions, function, material and color are the least difficult characteristics to provide. Where you might run into difficulty when describing the parts is when detailing shape and appearance. Just be sure to always describe what it looks like by utilizing comparison and examples. Also, be sure to detail part location in reference to preestablished point of view.

Before you can move on to the conclusion of the device description, it's important to verify that each part has been fully described with sufficient detail allowing for the creation of a clear, visual picture for the audience.

- The description of each part should, generally, begin with a clear, detailed definition of the part's function—what it does—and how each part's operation relates to the operation of the whole device.

- The description of each part should clearly detail the size and appearance, utilizing comparison when necessary.

- The description of each part should indicate material or materials and color or colors.

- The description of each part should take spatial design into account when clarifying part location.

- The description of each part should adhere to the preestablished point of view.

- The description of each part should detail all necessary dimensions using consistent format when expressing important measurements. Be sure to indicate variances and clarify dimensions's reference, i.e. width, height, length, etc.

- The description of each part also should point out how each part is attached to each subsequent part to clearly indicate location and relationship to the whole device.

Once each part has been fully described, you can move on to the conclusion. An effective conclusion is certainly important to any document, but particularly to a document of a professional nature. It's essential the audience knows, without question, when they've come to the end of the document. They need to understand that nothing follows, no pages have been misplaced, no other information is to be provided at a later date.

Wrapping It All Up

In the introduction you established the general category, pointed out the specifics that make the device unique and listed the parts in the order in which they were to be described. The body or individual parts description detailed each part and how it related to the whole by verbally taking the device apart. So now that the audience knows what each part looks like separately, the logical conclusive step is to put the device back together.

In the conclusion, you will put the device back together by describing how each part is attached to each subsequent part. You will take the parts, by name, and explain how each is attached to the next. What you're doing is recreating the whole minus all the descriptive detail provided in the body of the description.

The conclusion should of course use language that continues to encourage interest in the document as well as the device being described. As we reassemble the device, in this case the mechanical pencil, we could again refer to it as innovative or lightweight.

The eraser to the lightweight mechanical pencil is conveniently located at the end of the pencil, opposite the point, and is glued into the eraser head holder. The eraser head holder is fitted and snapped into the shaft of the pencil forming a sturdy bond between the two parts. The handy pocket clip is inserted and glued into the upper portion of the shaft of the pencil. The three graphite leads are housed inside the shaft of the pencil and are extracted by pushing down on the plunger assembly of the eraser.

Granted, this particular conclusion may be somewhat exaggerated, but the point is clear. Put the device back together and retain enthusiasm for the device as well as the document.

Internal Mechanisms

When it is necessary to describe the internal parts of the device you're describing, be sure to clarify the location of these internal parts and their relationship to other, more than the visible parts. This is important, because the primary difficulty with describing internal parts is noting their exact location. Outside, visible parts should be used for orientation.

Verifying Effectiveness

- Can the audience produce a reasonable drawing of the device based solely on the description?

- Is the point of view, spatial design considered, clear and consistent through the description?

- Does the part-by-part description verbally take the device apart, and does the conclusion reassemble the device?

When there are identical parts to the device being described, it's not necessary to repeat the part description. Just be sure to clearly indicate the number of parts that are the same and their specific location.

- Always keep direction and location in mind when describing the various parts of the device, particularly internal parts.

- When using illustrations to enhance description, be sure to accurately label the parts of the device.

- Once you've established a point, only repeat when necessary. For example, if the entire device is made from plastic and you have pointed this out in the introduction, don't repeat it with the part-by-part description.

- One thing does not necessarily define another; consider naming parts effectively.

- Choose descriptive language carefully. Remember to question how accurately your language translates to the audience.

- Remember to combine observation, experience, understanding and comparison in your efforts to reach the audience. Effective questions produce reliable answers.

Format

The format for your description should have a logical sequence and be audience conscious. Title your description. Follow with the general category separate from the specific overall device description. Number and list the parts in the order they will be described.

Number and label each part being described. As each part is described, separate with white space but indicate connection by stating method of attachment. Always consider the use of bold facing, headings, underlining, white space and whatever else it takes to encourage audience participation in your document. Illustrations, as indicated, are used to enhance the language of your message but they can also be used to break up text and encourage reader interest in your document.

Make your document look good and your audience will make use of your document.

Description is used constantly when communicating in industry today. Whether you're faced with describing a process, a device or a situation you need to reach your audience with the detail necessary for them to draw conclusions or create a picture that's relatable and clear. Take a look at the sample description and try some of the exercises that follow.

Sample Descriptions

1. Description of a Service

SURFACE MOUNT TECHNOLOGY
BY ELECTRICAL ASSEMBLY

Surface mount technology is up and running at Buildrite. Our knowledge and expertise are supported by over five years of concentrated experience. Our organization is firmly established and eager to serve your surface mount assembly needs. Electronic Assembly's 5600 foot production facility is equipped with the automation and flexibility required to deliver your job professionally and at a competitive cost.

Buildrite Electronic Assembly is a consolidation of experienced personnel committed to the application of surface mount technology, as an organization, our goals include maintaining the highest quality service available. As these efforts are directed toward a positive conclusion. The entire process is monitored by a hose computer system. Our organization is devoted to close customer service and that service is supported by the considerable talents of Buildrite Company.

Services Offered Include:

Computer-aided design layout
Worldwide component sourcing
Low, medium and high volume production
Automated testing

A Sample of our SMT Production Equipment:

- A.M.I. 1505—Printer
- DYNAPERT MPS500—Placement
- SANYO TCM40—Placement
- VITRONICS SMD718—IR Oven
- CORPANE VP18—Inline Vaport Phase
- DETREX—Solvent Cleaner
- HOLLIS GBS II—Dual Wave Solder
- HEWLETT PACKARD—Host Computer

For more information call or write:
Ted Wally
Buildrite Company
231 Main St.
Rochester, N.Y. 14677
(716) 555-0987

This service description is obviously aimed at the discipline-specific audience. If the audience was more general in nature, some of this information would require explanation and definition.

2. Description of a Device

DESCRIPTION OF THE
MINILIGHT FLASHLIGHT

A hand-held illumination device is generally called a flashlight, but is not the only hand-held device that illuminates an area on command. There are glow sticks and a variety of hand-held lights that are powered by DC current such as the mechanic's chaser light. There are many different kinds of battery operated hand-held flashlights available for private use. What distinguishes one from the other is, generally, their size and reliability. Hand-held illumination devices range in size from the very small keychain variety to the large kind policeman are known to carry. Some are fragile and some are durable.

The Minilight flashlight is a reliable hand-held illumination device that can provide hours of service and can fit comfortably in the glove compartment of your car. The Minilight is 6 inches in length, 3 inches at its widest point and 1 inch wide at its narrowest point. The Minilight is made from high impact plastic and is black overall. It requires a 9 volt battery for power.

The Minilight will be described as though lying on a flat service with the illuminating end to the left of the viewer.

Primary Parts

1. Head Assembly

2. Illuminating Lamp

3. Battery Housing

4. Threaded End Cap

1. HEAD ASSEMBLY

The head assembly houses the lens, reflector, securing cap that operates the light by twisting on and off, and the lamp housing. All components, except for the lamp, are made from high impact plastic. The lens is clear allowing for illumination and the reflector is silver for projecting light. The entire assembly is 3 inches in length and tapers in width from 1 ½ inch to 2 inches where it connects to the battery housing.

The securing cap screws on to the main portion of the head assembly and holds the lens in place. The reflector is conical in shape and is secured within the assembly by means of heat resistant glue. The illuminating lamp is screwed into the reflector base and the portion of the head assembly that meets the battery housing.

2. ILLUMINATING LAMP

The lamp is a unique, vacuum sealed gas lamp that promises longevity and reliability. It is cylindrical in shape, of durable glass construction and 1 ¼ inches long, 1 inch around, and ¼ inch in diameter. Threads and two male prongs secure it to the battery housing.

3. BATTERY HOUSING

The battery housing acts as the body to the minilight and houses the 9 volt battery. It is the gripping portion of the minilight. It is shaped like a hollow tube and made of the same durable plastic as the rest of the minilight. It is 3 inches in length and 1 inch wide from the head assembly to the threaded end cap. The internal mechanism consists of the 9 volt battery plug located at the threaded end cap and two wires that run from the plug to the illuminating lamp. The threaded end cap secures the internal mechanism as it is threaded on to the battery housing.

4. THREADED END CAP

The cap not only secures the internal mechanism of the minilight, it provides an outside elements resistant seal for protection and completion of the minilight. It is 2 inches in circumference and $\frac{1}{6}$ of an inch in width, and has standard threads where it is secured to the battery housing.

The Minilight flashlight is a very reliable hand-held illumination device. Its construction is durable and is easy to assemble. The head assembly is screwed into the battery housing providing a secure connection where the illuminating lamp is threaded inside the assembly where it is connected to the main housing. The threaded end cap is screwed into the opposite end of the battery housing securing the internal mechanism.

This device description is more for the general audience than the previous service description. The minilight flashlight description strives to assist the audience in not only creating a visual picture of the device, but also in clarifying what the device is all about functionally.

The format seems to serve the purpose as do a number of the other elements of the description, but could it be improved?

Classification and Division

A means of organization of information for presentation.

When communicating, we are often faced with the task of analyzing a jumble of information in an effort to put it into some sensible order. Depending on our purposes, figuring out how to organize information can be one of the primary steps in the process of communication.

Generally, information we are required to classify and divide has some similarities. For example, if we were faced with classifying and dividing a diverse group of animals, the fact that they're animals would be the similarity.

In this case, we might put all fowl into a category, cats into another, reptiles into yet another and so on. Maybe we're designing a new zoo and classifying and dividing the animals would help us come up with the best design available. Once we can come to terms, and make sense of the information we can better inform our audience.

A simple, yet informative way to consider classification and division, and its value might be to look at a regular toy store. Most of us could make some pretty decent guesses as to what most toy stores offer. That's not difficult, but how many of us realize what toy stores say about our culture?

Let's say you were putting together a report about the recreational pursuits of children in our society.

> Most of the toys, not all, are generally classified by gender and displayed accordingly in the various aisles.

> Toys for boys generally consist of items that often require some kind of aggressive behavior: guns, action figures, race cars, war toys, footballs, baseball bats and so on.

> Toys for girls tend to be more domestically oriented: baby dolls, appliances, board games, doll houses and so on.

The differences tend to suggest that girls are being taught, even in play, that they have to learn early how to be mothers and housewives. Believe it or not go to a toy store and check it out. Boys are being taught to get ready to be a fighter of some kind, to get ready for competition in the big, bad world.

There are certainly toys available that cross gender boundaries but there always have been. Classifying and dividing what's available in your average toy store would help the communicator draw a particular conclusion about the recreational activities of children today and what those activities might suggest about the culture.

Magazines

Just like toys, magazines could also be classified and divided according to preestablished criteria. For example, let's say we were going to look at a particular magazine to see whether or not it was meeting the needs of a particular audience.

Some of the elements to consider as your analyzing the magazine could include:

✔ Effectiveness

✔ Audience

✔ Attitude

✔ Truth/Fantasy

✔ Soft sell/Hard sell

✔ Articles

✔ Departments

✔ Advertisements

✔ Format

Understanding how these elements work independently as well as together, can lead to determining how effective the magazine is in relation to its purpose and audience. This is particularly true of trade, discipline specific, magazines. The value in a magazine is directly associated with how well it meets the needs of the intended audience; does it live up to expectations and how well?

PUBLICATION ANALYSIS

Example

Financial Banking & Trust Company
Interoffice Memo

To: Kenneth Ryan
          Senior Vice President Retail Administration

From: Susan Gilliland
          Kuhn Road Office

Subject: Acquiring Subscription to *ABA Banking Journal*

Date: March 24, 1996

Statement of Problem

We are fast approaching the end of our first quarter for the fiscal year, 1996. It is apparent, at this time, that we are not on target with our projected goals for this first quarter. Our projected goal was 1.5 million in new money, and we are now just reaching 1 million. Although we are still ahead of last year's mark for the same period, we always want to increase our market base. We are a banking institution that places high emphasis on customer service, as well as offering a wide variety of services. Therefore, we have to ask ourselves if we are doing everything within our power to increase our new investments.

Proposed Solution

My solution to help increase our new accounts and to consistently meet our goals—if not exceed them—is to stay well-informed of the trends in banking. We need to pay attention to what other banking institutions are offering. We need to learn how to implement the ideas that will work. How do we do this? We can keep a focus on what the economy is doing by subscribing to *American Banking Association Banking Journal*.

Support

The *ABA Banking Journal* offers several regular departments that can keep us on top of the banking industry as a whole, not just our area of jurisdiction. Some of the regular departments deal with Credit Card trends, Mortgage Lending, Asset Liability Management, and Investment Products, to name just a few.

By keeping up to date on Credit Card trends we can evaluate whether we should strive to increase our "Credit Card" base or our "Debit Card" base. We have to keep in mind, funds we generate from credit cards come from annual fees and finance charges. Where as debit cards are always connected to a checking account and customers use their own money, therefore they always keep balances in their accounts to do this.

This magazine also contains another department pertaining to Mortgage Lending. This department can help us learn how to attract these customers to our institution. Studies have shown people usually have their checking accounts as well as savings, or certificates of deposit with the bank that has their mortgage.

The *ABA Banking Journal* also has a regular department pertaining to Investment Products. This department can help educate us on what to offer customers in annuities as well as mutual funds, which in turn will increase our new money.

As well as the regular departments, there are several special features each month that deal with various Banking issues. For example, in the February, 1996 issue, there is a article about keeping customers. This particular article states keeping customers well informed and educated about how to invest their money will develop much more loyal customers, customers who will continually bring their accounts to your institution as well as their children's. In doing this we will increase our new money as well increase our customer base. As a financial institution, we know it is practically impossible not to lose customers and their accounts, but through this magazine we can find suggestions on how to decrease this loss.

In this issue, you will find another article detailing the top twenty-five banks and several common features found among them that may help them achieve this status. Through this magazine, we can gain an understanding of what our competition is achieving, as well as how well they are achieving it.

This magazine can also help us learn how to diversify. We can learn how to increase our Credit Card base, and our Mortgage Portfolio, just as two examples.

Recommendation

My recommendation is to subscribe to *ABA Banking Journal*. Therefore, let me break down the cost for you. Since we have twenty-six branches, we can receive a group rate of $9.50 per subscription per year. The cost to implement this with all our branches would be $247.00 per year. I recommend we subscribe for one year for all of our branches. The cost to experiment is minimal compared to the results we can achieve with this product. Enclosed you will find a copy of this magazine. If you would like to discuss this further, please contact me at extension 3925.

KR/SG
Enclosure:

Example

To: General Managers & Lab Technicians

From: Liz Hayes, Lab Technician

Proposal: Recommendation to subscribe to
            Modern Printing Inks & Coatings

Date: March 20, 1996

STATEMENT OF PROBLEM

Flint Inks's annual report shows that our competitors are taking 4% of our accounts due to the fact that we are not up to date with the new technology in the printing ink industry and we are not up to date with the new raw materials available to produce a better quality ink.

PROPOSED SOLUTION

I would like to recommend that our company subscribe to the publication, *Modern Printing Inks & Coatings*. This publication has been on the market for eighty-five years and has been highly recommended by other ink companies.

SUPPORT

I have done research on other publications such as: *Processing, Industry Week* and *Chemical Week*, where I found they would be of no benefit to our company.

I had the opportunity to discuss *Modern Printing Inks & Coatings* with other lab technicians from Sun Chemical and Inks International; both gentlemen highly recommend this publication to help our company to keep up to date with technology and raw materials.

While reviewing this publication, I have found that their departments and columns would benefit our company in many aspects.

Their Department section includes:

"Advertisers Index"

In this section they have distributors for raw materials advertised. I called a few of these distributors to make a comparison in prices for raw materials with our present distributors. In my findings I found that we could save:

$7,400.00   yearly on Organic Yellow Pigments
$1,900.00   yearly on Polyethylene Waxes
  $800.00   yearly on Mineral Filters

This would give us a total savings of $10,100.00 yearly.

As you can see this section can help us purchase new and present raw materials at lower prices. We could also use this section to advertise our company products to increase our sales and to inform printing companies of our business too. This will help increase our profits yearly and acquire new accounts.

"Equipment Section"

In this section, they had advertised the CVS-1/M multi-source viewing station. This would be a benefit to our company. It will make it possible to evaluate color samples under three different types of lighting. It will help us develop a better quality ink and it would also improve our quality control department. This section will also give us knowledge of the new technology available and where to purchase it. It will help us acquire new and up-to-date equipment that we are badly in need of. It will help us increase our production at a faster rate and produce a better quality of ink.

"Industry Update Section"

This section will inform us about new industries opening up and present industries opening at different locations. This would benefit our company in the future when we decide to open another branch. It will help give our company's name recognition to other printing companies.

"Meeting Section"

While reviewing this section I found that "The Detroit Society for Coatings Technology is holding its 21st annual all-day scientific and technical conference at the MSU Conference Center in Troy, Mich. Featured topics include raw materials, regulations, pre-treatments test methods, formulations strategies, end-user updates, substrates, troubleshooting, and application and curing techniques." This will let us speak directly to distributors about their raw materials and ask any questions concerning their materials. It will also keep us up to date about new raw materials available on the market that will help us produce a better quality ink and help us get acquainted with other ink companies.

Their Columns Section include:

"International Review"

This section discusses the use of Diatech inks and how they have increased steadily internationally and in the United States. As we all know, Diatech is a fast seller to printers all over the world because of its "Stayopen" qualities. As you can see this section will inform us of what products are being used world wide and user reactions. This will help us determine if the user is satisfied with different products and it will help us determine what is in demand or not in demand.

"Raw Material"

In this section it explains what the material is used for, such as Micro Wax Product, "Code PC-8125 reduces gloss in powder coatings. At 2%, it can reportedly drop 60 degree glossmeter readings below 10%. It is especially effective in clears where it will not show yellowing." As you can see, this section can be used as a reference to what the product capabilities are and it could also help us answer questions our customers may have concerning the raw materials we use.

BUDGET

One year (13 issues) $52.00
Two years (26 issues) $82.00

RECOMMENDATION

I highly recommend *Modern Printing Inks & Coatings*, published monthly with thirteen issues yearly. Larry Anderson, the editor, does an excellent job preparing this magazine to help ink companies stay up to date with the ink business. I feel this magazine would benefit our company by increasing our profits, and production, helping us keep up to date with new technology and raw materials, helping safeguard our current accounts, acquiring new accounts, and helping us to be more competitive in the ink business. Don't you feel its time for our company to be rated as a '90s ink business, instead of '60s ink business?

EXERCISES

1. For a product announcement introducing a new device your company is soon to market, write a description of a device that will meet the needs of a package designer, wholesalers and retailers.

   Choose your own device, but keep it relatively simple. Choose something that will allow you to write a thorough, effective description.

2. Describe a service you're familiar with. Remember to choose language that is not only accurate, but also encourages audience interest.

   Follow this sequence: Definition of Operation
   Principle of Operation
   Sequence of Operation

3. Choose a person you can spend time observing without them thinking you're weird. Describe the person for someone who doesn't know them. Create as complete a picture as language will allow.

4. What's wrong with this description of a disposable lighter?

A lighter is a handheld, flame producing device used for lighting cigarettes.

The Micro Disposable Lighter is about the size of most hand held lighters. They come in a variety of colors, and last at least a month.

Plunger Assembly

Lighter Body

Fuel

Plunger Assembly—The assembly is composed of the thumb plunger, flint and flint wheel. You engage the flint wheel and hold down on the plunger at the same time to produce a flame. It is made of plastic, metal and flint. Altogether, it is about the size of the normal thumbnail.

Lighter Body—It is approximately the size of your thumb, 2 ½ inches and oval shaped. It is made almost entirely of plastic and is red in color. It holds the lighter's fuel.

Fuel—It is a gas-like substance that is flammable. It escapes the lighter when the thumb plunger is pressed to produce a flame.

The handy Micro Disposable Lighter is made up of the Thumb Plunger assembly that is attached to the body which contains the lighter's fuel.

EXERCISE

PUBLICATION ANALYSIS (Classification & Division—a means of organizing information for presentation.)

You work for a company that manufactures a product or provides a service. (Which service is up to you.)

Your boss has come to you and indicated there is a real need to increase production. You're up for the challenge.

There are many avenues to explore, but your particular assignment is to explore and research publications (periodicals) the company might possibly subscribe to.

GOAL
To discover a magazine that will assist in increasing production by ensuring everyone in the company will be familiar with the latest news in your particular industry; will be aware of the latest innovations; will be familiar with industry projections to be better prepared for competition and the future.

Examples   Travel and Tourism magazines — You work for a travel agency.
                 News and journalism Magazines — you work for a T.V. news show.
                 Business and Accounting Magazines — you work for a bank.
                 Literary Magazines — you work for a publisher.
                 Education journals — you are a teacher/administrator.

OUTCOME
Submit a proposal recommending that your company subscribe to the magazine you believe will serve the intended purpose.

Proposal Format: Statement of the problem
                      Proposed solution
                      Support (Evidence from magazine detailing why.)
                      Recommendation

In addition to the written proposal, you will verbally report on your findings during a managers' meeting. You will have a maximum of 8 minutes to make your verbal recommendation.

Professor Brooks will play the role of your boss—go to him for advice and additional project clarification.

C h a p t e r   S i x

Instructions, Procedures and Manuals

Including instructions, procedures and manuals in the same chapter is a logical choice. A manual is, generally, a collection of instructions and procedures with some illustrations thrown in when necessary. Before you can appreciate the subtleties and complexities of manual writing, you need to understand what instructions and procedures are all about. Manuals are certainly a part of high-tech industry today, as are instructions and procedures.

INSTRUCTIONS

How many times have we confronted a set of instructions and the only thing we got out of them was confusion? Probably more times than we care to remember.

Instructions seem to be almost always poorly written. And when they're poorly written, they fail to serve the purpose they were intended for. Instructions can be presented in a less-than-audience-conscious manner for a number of different reasons.

- The primary reason is the writer is too close to the task, too familiar, and makes too many assumptions on the audience's behalf.
- Instructions, particularly those that come with electronic hardware, are translated from the parent language into English and the translator fails to take into account such things as cultural differences.
- Instructions are written by people who have few, if any language skills. They simply don't know how to effectively communicate with people; maybe it's not their primary responsibility.
- The introduction to instructions is not as detailed as it should be.

The introduction to a document, as we all know, is very important. It needs not only to create enthusiasm for the task, but also for the document itself. The introduction should fully prepare the individual for completing the task at hand.

I recall purchasing a ceiling fan that I could assemble and install myself. At least the outside of the package indicated the simplicity of the task. When I got it home I proceeded to unpack and assemble the fan. I followed the instructions, and in the matter of a couple hours I had the fan assembled and ready, I thought, for installation.

What I discovered when I began reading the installation instructions, was that a certain part of the fan, the base unit, should not be assembled until installation. This was pointed out halfway through the instructions, not in the introduction where it should have been. Poorly written instructions can cause more than a few problems for the audience, as well as for the company producing the instructions.

- The audience has little or no faith in the document, therefore doesn't rely on it.
- The audience has little regard for the product or task.
- The audience questions the professionalism of the group or company who produced the document.
- The audience doesn't rely on subsequent documents coming from the same source.
- The audience is not encouraged to follow reliable instructions when coming from the same source. This can cost time and money in industry.

Types of Instructions

Whether we make a mental note of it or not, we are faced with instructions on a daily basis. They're all around us, even outside of the work place.

- Road signs
- Building evacuation procedures
- Directions in buildings—enter, exit and no smoking
- Recipes
- Programming VCRs—getting that "12:00" to stop flashing
- Shampoo in your shower—"Squeeze a small amount into the palm of your hand, apply to hair, massage in, and so on."
- Toys—As a parent, Christmas Eve was often like putting in a full shift for me.
- Computers—we usually end up asking the resident expert for help.

Granted, these are just a few of the simpler examples of instructions we come in contact with almost every day. We probably pay little attention to most of them because of their simplicity, and because we're usually quite familiar with the task involved. We know what to do. But what about those tasks that are not as simple or familiar? How can we produce a set of instructions that reaches our intended audience with clarity and reliable detail?

The Basics

The purpose of a set of instructions is quite simple—to describe how to successfully complete a specific task. What makes instructions unique is that the task is generally intended to be performed one time and one time only. The intent is not to necessarily create an expert, but to get the individual successfully through the task.

When discussing the audience in industry for a set of instructions, the key to its knowledge and ability was usually indicated by the term "idiot proof." Sure, it sounds nasty, but the phrase was never intended in a negative way. Making the document idiot proof was just an accurate way to portray how much detail would be necessary for the document. With instructions, we make few, if any, assumptions about our audience.

- The audience has the ability to read.
- The audience has basic analytical abilities.
- The audience has basic handtool knowledge.

Any assumptions beyond these would negate the purpose of instructions. Again, instructions are generally meant to be performed one time and one time only.

With instructions we explain how to perform a specific task based on clear thinking and careful planning. It's important the writer is familiar with the task in order to effectively instruct in how to successfully complete the task.

If the writer isn't familiar with the task, he or she should get familiar. Go back to the process of communicating. Think about what you do know about the task and what you don't know. Research what you don't know.

Observation and practice support understanding a specific task. Watch someone perform the task over a period of time and then try it yourself. The more familiar you are with the task, the better you'll be able to instruct in how to perform the task. But be aware of assumptions. Don't assume your audience knows as much about the task as you do. Remember, you're trying to reach an audience that is made up of people who have little or no knowledge relating to the task. Make it "Idiot Proof."

General Principles

- The audience dictates the level of detail for a specific set of instructions. Make few, if any assumptions.
- Know what you're writing about—be familiar with the task and its purpose. Consult the necessary sources to understand what the task requires.
- Reliable instructions are accurate and effective. Meet all the instructive needs of your audience.
- Complete instructions have no gaps—step-by-step detail doesn't require the audience to second guess what to do.
- Instructions are simple and direct—use as few words as possible; define unfamiliar terms.
- Instructions should be carefully formatted—encourage audience interest and participation.
- Instructions can benefit from well chosen and designed illustrations and graphics, particularly detailing location.

Directions

Directions are similar to instructions for a number of reasons.

Whether verbally offered or written down, the purpose of giving directions is to inform the uninformed and encourage them to successfully complete a task—get to where they need to be.

Have you ever asked someone for directions and discovered even after they explained how to get someplace, you still ended up lost? Well if you have, join the club. It's not that the people we asked directions from were being nasty or we were too stupid to understand; the giver of directions probably made the same kind of mistake that can be made with instructions. They assumed too much to provide clear and reliable detail. We might have even made the same mistake when someone asked us for directions. We need to provide complete, goal-directed detail.

When instructing in a task or giving directions, the intent or purpose is to ensure the audience completes the task or journey in a timely, successful manner. We need to appreciate and consider what's required for our audience to meet the intended goal.

When giving directions, we certainly need to explain what roads to take, distances and time frame. But we should also consider those things that might get in the way of successfully completing a journey on time and what might impede the audience's progress. If a particular road is under construction, indicate it. Point out particulars along the route so our audience can check their progress. Indicate traffic patterns at any given time of the day, or speed traps. Provide whatever detail is necessary to ensure success. Don't include too much detail with each step of the directions. Take the audience from one point to the next clearly.

Think about giving directions to your own home from a specified point. It might not be as easy as it initially seems. Driving to our own home is something we do on a regular basis, something we take for granted. I would bet that some of us might not even know the names of all the streets and highways we travel on a regular basis. Again, even with directions, we shouldn't make any assumptions. Just because we can travel a route with little thought or complete a task as easily, doesn't mean our audience can.

Introduction to Instructions

When composing the introduction to your set of instructions you probably want to avoid announcing your intent. Don't begin by stating, "This set of instructions will instruct in how to peel a grape effectively." Forget about the grape part, just don't point out your intent; it's obvious what the document's intent is, even if only from the title. Don't refer to the document as though it's a separate entity, let it speak for itself.

As with other industrial/professional documents, the introduction not only has to introduce the content and intent, it has to encourage reader interest and participation.

Title The Instructions

Choose a title that accurately reflects the intent and purpose of the set of instructions. The title can also indicate what audience the document may be aimed towards.

"General Operational Steps For the Whatzit Extractor"

"Helicopter Assembly Instructions"

Choose a title that does the job and suggests something about what is to follow in the introduction and throughout the entire document.

Define Purpose

In defining the purpose of the task, you're indicating to the audience what's to be expected; what will follow. You're providing a certain amount of background clarifying the purpose of the task. Defining the purpose of the task is not unlike establishing a general category in a description document. We need to give the audience information that will effectively prepare them to carry out the task. You're answering the question, why should the audience want to perform this task, or why does the audience need to perform this task?

Defining the purpose of the task requires the audience to consider what they do and don't know about the task at hand. Indicating the purpose explains the general reasons for performing and successfully completing the task.

For example: In defining the purpose for changing the oil in a specific make of car, you would begin by explaining why it is necessary to change a car's oil.

"The purpose of changing the oil in a car is to improve its performance and extend its longevity. Dirty motor oil in the crankcase contains particles that can harm the engine. Introducing clean motor oil every 3,000 or 3 months, whichever comes first, will prolong the life of the car."

Expected Results

Once you have detailed the general purpose for performing a task, you address the specifics regarding the tasks by indicating the expected results. This part of the introduction introduces the specifics that make this particular task unique by explaining what will happen once the task has been completed. Point out to the audience what carrying out this specific task will accomplish.

For Example:

"Changing the motor oil in a 1972 Ford, Grand Torino Station Wagon will improve the car's overall performance as well as extend its operational reliability. Changing the oil in your Torino is a relatively simple task requiring limited mechanical knowledge."

You're going from the general to the specific as you prepare your audience for carrying out the tasks. You're explaining why this task is essential and how it relates to the specifics of your set of instructions.

Keep the introduction brief and to the point. Use language the audience can relate to and understand.

- Encourage audience interest and participation.
- Define the general purpose of the task.
- Detail the expected results.
- Address the specifics of the task's intent.
- Be as clear and concise as introducing the task allows.

What the introductory portion of the instructions should accomplish is to fully prepare the operator, technician or individual to begin and complete the indicated task without interruption. Defining the purpose and detailing the expected results informs the audience and puts them in a frame of mind that directly relates to the task. But they're still not prepared to begin the task. Remember, you don't want your audience to stop at some point in the task before it's completed because they weren't fully prepared to successfully see the task through to its conclusion.

Think about what's required for completing everyday tasks for a moment. You wouldn't go to school without the necessities required to be successful. You'd be sure you had your books, folders, pencils, money for lunch, gum to chew, walkman or whatever else was required to successfully see you through the task of completing your day at school. The same kind of preparation applies to a set of instructions.

Preparatory Information

Once the definition of the purpose of the task has been detailed in conjunction with the expected results, the next step is to list the preparatory information for the intended audience. Remember, in professional communication we list data when the situation allows.

Listing the preparatory information indicates to the audience what is specifically required to begin and complete the task without interruption. We want to be sure our operator is fully prepared for the task at hand. We need to ensure the task will not be interrupted for any reason.

What might be required to complete a particular task depends on what the task is; what we need to instruct in. But there are some general considerations, questions that should be addressed with all tasks requiring instruction. Again, we need to be sure the operator is fully prepared to carry out the task successfully. Consider the general possibilities.

- Tools
- Equipment conditions
- Parts
- Materials

- Time
- Environment
- Personnel
- Safety precautions
- Whatever else is required to complete a task successfully

Tools

Depending on the complexity of the task, we list those tools specifically required for the task. It's okay to assume basic handtool knowledge when determining what's required for the task. Under certain circumstances, tools may not be listed. They wouldn't be listed if the operator was designated with particular skills, and we could assume they would have particular tools available to them as part of their job. An electrical technician, for example, would have tools available on a regular basis without having to list them. But when we're not making this assumption, list the necessary tools. Changing a light switch might require:

Tools
Standard size screwdriver
Wire cutters

Equipment Conditions

Equipment conditions generally refers to any equipment that has to be prepared prior to beginning the task. Anything that has to be turned on, heated up, switched off, or kicked in should be listed before the steps of the task are detailed. If you were writing a set of instructions for some kind of electrical task that required a soldering iron, you would indicate in the preparatory information that the iron should be plugged in ten minutes prior to beginning the task. Fully prepare the operator to begin and complete task without interruption.

Equipment Conditions
Soldering Iron—Plug in 10 minutes before beginning
Coffee—Brew 15 minutes before beginning

Parts and Materials

Parts and materials are generally those things required for inclusion with the task; what is necessary for the successful completion of the task. A part is usually something that can't be used up, or dissipated; something that becomes a physical part of what the instructions are detailing the assembly of, like a screw. A part is something that can be, in theory, used again if we were to remove it from the assembly.

A material is generally something that can be used up, or dissipated. Something that, in theory, can't be used again. Something like wire, or oil or grease.

Parts
¼ inch rubber
patches (3)

Materials
Tube of patching
glue (1)

Time

We list time, just like all preparatory information, when it directly relates to and is essential for the task we are instructing in. Time is listed when it is a factor for successfully completing the task. We indicate the amount of time the task takes in order to point out to the operator how long the task will take. We may want to ensure that they don't begin the task too late in the day for completion if it is a particularly long task. We indicate time as a check factor also. If a task takes two hours, and the operator is still struggling with the task after four hours, they will probably need to go back and check on what they might be doing wrong. Indicating time keeps the reader aware and informed, and allows them to monitor their efforts.

Time
3 ½ hours to completion

Environmental Conditions

We indicate the condition of the environment when a particular kind of environment is essential to the successful completion of the task. If the task required some type of liquid that produced toxic fumes, we would indicate a well-ventilated environment. We might require a dust-free environment if we were instructing in a task that dealt with highly sensitive hardware. Testing particular kinds of hardware and equipment requires specific environmental conditions.

Environment
Dust free
72 degrees F

Personnel

When it's pertinent, we indicate how many people are required to successfully complete a task. We not only list the number of people required, we also indicate skill areas. If an electrical technician and a plumber are required to successfully complete the task, we indicate the required skills.

Personnel
1 Computer Programmer
1 CAD Operator

Safety

Safety considerations should always be factors in detailing how to successfully complete a task. Safety factors are rarely unimportant when detailing a set of instructions. It's important to consider the operator as well as tools and equipment when instructing in a particular task. There are basically two designations for a safety precautions: warnings and cautions.

A "warning" generally refers to that which could cause injury to an individual involved in the completion of the task. A "caution" generally refers to something that could possibly cause damage to tools or equipment. Cautions and warnings are detailed prior to the step of the task they most directly relate to, or effect. If the caution or warning is important enough, of considerable concern, they can be detailed in the introductory portion of the instructions as well as in conjunction with the related step. When detailing safety precautions for changing the oil in a car, we might issue a warning in the introduction that the motor oil may be hot. We would also reiterate that warning when instructing on how to remove the drain plug and drain the oil.

Cautions	*Warnings*
Don't engage engine once motor oil has been drained	Draining motor oil may be hot

Before moving on to the body, or the steps for instructions, verify that the introduction serves the purpose of the task and meets the needs of the audience.

- Define task (purpose)
- Detail expected results
- List preparatory information
- Consider overall cautions and warnings
- Is the individual fully prepared to begin and complete the task uninterrupted?

Steps

Once the task has been introduced, and the audience is ready to get right to work, we prepare the steps to the task.

Each step should be numbered and clearly separated from each subsequent step. This is accomplished through numbering and effectively utilizing white space.

Consider the logical chronology of the task: What needs to be detailed first and what would logically follow? Remember, if you are unfamiliar with the task, become familiar with it prior to writing the instructions. Also, remember not to make any assumptions. Your audience is basically unfamiliar with the task, and the amount of instructive detail should meet their needs. What information should be supplied with each step depends, in part, on the task, but there are some general considerations that dictate what type of information should be included in each step.

WHAT

The first thing that should be included with each step in your instructions is the "what" information. The "what" information basically announces what the step is. It acts as a kind of title to the step. The "what" information doesn't instruct, it only announces what the step is.

1. Engage engine
   This obviously does little by way of instruction, but it does point out to the operator what the step is all about.
   Let's say we were charged with writing a simple set of instructions on how to turn on a light switch. Ridiculous, yes, but it should clarify the point.

1. Turn on light
   This doesn't instruct; it only points out what has to be done, not how to do it. The instructive detail is the How information.

HOW

Once the step has been clearly announced, given a title, the "how" information is provided to instruct how to carry out and successfully complete the step. This is where difficulties may arise; where we might be encouraged to make certain assumptions. Generally, we leave little to chance. Be sure to completely detail the "how" information and effectively instruct in how to complete the step.

1. Turn on light

   Place finger under black switch. Push in an upward motion.
   Now we have a complete step; it goes beyond only announcing what needs to be accomplished, it explains how to do it. The primary trouble with instructions today is they don't fully instruct in how to complete the step. The difficulty with writing instructions arises when we don't provide the instructive detail necessary for our audience to carry out the task.
   When constructing the step that points out how to remove the drain plug from a car for removing old motor oil, we would first announce and then instruct.

1. Remove drain plug

   Warning: Motor oil may be hot.
   Secure ¼ inch ratchet to drain plug. Exercise the necessary force to break the seal and turn counterclockwise until sufficiently loose to remove by fingers. Slowly turn by finger until plug is free of oil pan.
   This not only announces, titles the step, it also instructs in how to carry out and successfully complete the step. We included the warning prior to instructing in how to complete the step to ensure safety precautions are observed before the fact, not after, when it may be too late.

Are we getting the point here? For each step in our instructions we first detail the "what" information followed by the "how" information. The first announces what is to be done, the second part instructs in how to complete the step.

Additional information that may be included at this point is the "why" information. But not for a set of instructions. We will save the explanatory detail for procedures.

Certainly include cautions and warnings when appropriate to the step as well as notes. Notes are generally those points we need to make that don't fall under a preestablished category. Also be sure to use the name of tools, parts, etc. as they were established in the introduction.

Instructive Detail

1. Operation For Each Step

Each step should only instruct in one operation. One operation is generally defined as a single physical motion, like removing the drain plug from a car. The operation only requires the single motion of turning the drain plug with the ratchet and then with the fingers. The operator is concentrating on one particular area, one operation. Instructing in how to turn on a light requires just one physical motion, concentrating all effort on the switch itself.

Be careful not to include too much instructive, or how-to detail with each step. Too much detail could confuse the operator, and encourage taking shortcuts to complete the step.

Operator is Assumed

It's not necessary to constantly refer to the operator, the individual required to carry out the steps of the instructions. Rather than say: The mechanic will now remove the drain plug, we would suggest: Remove the drain plug. The operator is assumed so as not to clutter up the instructive elements of the task with unnecessary information.

Use Command Language

With each step, use the imperative form of the verb, or command language. Limit the detail to that which is solely instructive. Rather than say: Now the drain plug can be removed, we would say: Remove the drain plug.

BAD

The operator should now raise the compartment lid.

GOOD

Raise the compartment lid.

This clearly points out what is required for this particular step without cluttering it up with excessive, unrequired words. Use language that announces and instructs. Balance the detail by keeping each step clear and brief—to the point.

Illustrations

Illustrations can come in handy with instructions because they allow you to limit the number of words, particularly when it is necessary to indicate the location of parts. Illustrations can allow the writer to focus on the steps, rather than on the description of parts, or what a step may be concentrating on regarding the subject of the instructions.

Conclusion

Once you've successfully instructed the operator through the steps of the task, you need to clearly indicate that the task is now complete. Don't leave the audience wondering; be clear about the conclusion to the task.

It's often a good idea, depending on the task, to separate the conclusion from the steps. There will certainly be a conclusive or final step, but it might not always clearly point out that the task has been completed.

Part of what the introduction required was to detail the expected results. In order to wrap up the task, the conclusion should verify the expected results. Explain to the audience what should now exist if all the steps were followed successfully.

FOR EXAMPLE

> Now that the fan has been assembled and installed, it can be engaged.
> The new oil and filter now introduced into your car should provide three months or 3,000 miles of worry-free friction wear on your car's engine.

Verifying expected results gives the audience the opportunity to double check the task and their efforts. They're encouraged to verify what was expected. Occasionally, a troubleshooting guide may be included as part of the conclusion. Of course, it depends on the complexity of the task and the chances for something going wrong with the instructive steps.

The numbered steps are the most important part of the instructions. Each step needs to be clear, balanced and appropriately detailed.

- Don't make assumptions about your audience's knowledge.
- Organize the steps in a logical chronology.
- Number the steps.
- Announce the step—what does the step deal with?
- Instruct in how to complete the step.
- Include one operation for each step.
- Use imperative language (commands).

- Balance instructive information—what & how.
- Verify expected results as conclusion.

Sample Set of Instructions

REPLACING A 120 VOLT ELECTRICAL WALL OUTLET

The purpose of changing a damaged 120 volt electrical household wall outlet is to ensure the safe, reliable flow of electricity from the power source to the power receiver. Once the replacement has been completed, a new, operational outlet will be ready for use.

WARNING: Working with any source of electricity can prove dangerous; use extreme caution at all times.

Preparatory Requirements
1. New UL Approved Wall outlet
2. Standard Voltage Tester
3. Wire Strippers
4. Long Nosed Pliers
5. Flat-Head Screwdriver

STEPS

1. Disengage power to outlet
   Proceed to the main breaker panel, generally located in the basement, and push the main breaker down until it reads OFF. (See figure 1.)

2. Remove cover plate
   Take the flat end of the screwdriver and place it into the screw at the center of the cover plate. Turn screwdriver counterclockwise until the screw is fully out. (See figure 2.)

3. Test power flow
   With the voltage tester, grasp the two lead wires with the prongs. Place one prong on the gold screw attached to the black wire, and the other prong on the silver screw attached to the white wire. You can be sure the power is off when the light on the tester doesn't light. (See figure 3.)

4. Remove damaged outlet
   With the screwdriver, unscrew the two screws holding the outlet in place. They are located at the top and the bottom of the outlet. (See figure 3.) Pull outlet out towards you about 2 inches to access the wires.

5. Detach wires
   Remove the black and white wires from the screw terminals. Discard damaged outlet.
   NOTE: The wires must be replaced in the same order on the new outlet.
   NOTE: Check to be sure at least 1/2 inch of the wire's insulation has been removed. If not, employ wire strippers and pliers to remove. (See figure 4.)

6. Attach wires to new outlet
   Position new outlet with ground opening facing down, silver screws to the left. Wrap the black wire around the gold screw and the white wire around the silver screw. Tighten all screws. (See figure 3.)

7. Install new outlet
   Insert reattached outlet into the box by pushing gently in. See step for 4.
   CAUTION: Check to be sure no wires are pinched around the outlet.

8. Secure new outlet
   Secure the outlet to the box by screwing in the two screws, until snug, provided with the outlet.

9. Reattach cover plate
   Attach cover plate by screwing in center screw until snug.

10. Turn power on
    Proceed to location of the breaker panel and flip main switch to the ON position.
    You can now verify the task has been successfully completed by introducing an electrical plug into the new outlet and verifying device operation.

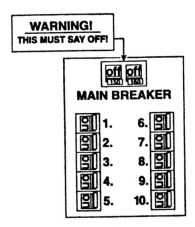

FIGURE 1. BREAKER PANEL

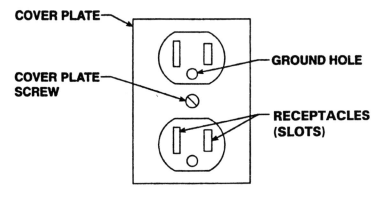

FIGURE 2. COVERED OUTLET

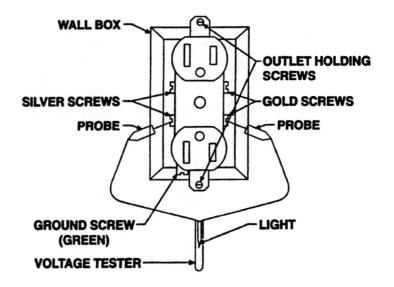

FIGURE 3. UNCOVERED OUTLET

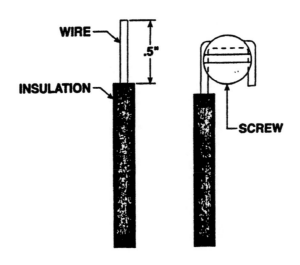

FIGURE 4. WIRE

PROCEDURES

With instructions clearly understood, procedures are the next step, and follow what instructions are all about with some additions.

Procedures are quite important to industry. Most, if not all, actions carried out in industry have a procedure associated with the action that clearly details how to effectively carry out the action and complete the task successfully.

Procedures are produced, based on careful experimentation on how best to do the job. It takes time to put an effective procedure together; trial and error is a part of the process. When a procedure is completed, it should accurately and clearly detail the best way to perform an industry-related task.

The criteria involved in designing a procedure are dictated by purpose and audience. The most important element to consider when constructing a procedure is that it be in chronological order, not unlike instructions, with each action clearly detailed and defined.

It's important to note that, again like instructions, a procedure generally covers a task from set-up to completion. It can cover a single work shift or as many shifts as necessary to complete a particular task. A procedure has a definite audience as well as a definite purpose. A procedure is rarely, if ever, general. The communicator should strive to present detail appropriate to match the level of the operator's experience. We begin by considering what a detailed procedure should accomplish.

- Be completely accurate and reliable.
- Reflect the real-world job which needs to be carried out.
- Contain all necessary information.
- Reflect the most efficient way to perform the task.

These general thoughts are where we begin when faced with writing or rewriting a procedure. As with instructions, we also determine what we know about the task and decide what it is we need to discover in order to effectively reflect what the task is all about for our audience. The next step is to consider what requirements should be basically filled by the procedure.

- Define the purpose of the task as well as the expected results.
- Provide a complete listing of the preparatory detail—what the operator will need in order to complete the task.
- Ensure that all information is easy to locate.
- Organize all information in a logical, chronological manner for the most efficient use by the operator.
- Provide a checklist for the experienced technician as well as detail for the inexperienced.
- Number all steps and assign figure designations to illustrations.
- Construct format that encourages interest and participation.

Audience

Generally, the audience for a procedure has some prior knowledge relating to the task that needs to be performed. That experience is what, in part, makes the document a procedure. That level of experience or knowledge, of course, varies. A procedure not only has to meet the needs of the audience, it also has to serve the purpose of the particular task.

Unlike instructions, a procedure's purpose is to detail information relating to a task that has to be performed often by the technician; certain requirements can be expected.

Qualifier

A qualifier indicates that level of experience or knowledge the technician must possess in order to successfully complete the task. There are many tasks in industry today that are highly complex and professional. The qualifier ensures that the technician performing the task has the necessary experience. If they don't have the experience, they shouldn't begin the task. It would be unproductive for the technician to get part way involved in a task and find out they don't have the skills to complete the task.

The qualifier should clearly and accurately detail what requirements the technician should meet. The requirements indicated can be basic or complex:

- The technician should have basic handtool knowledge

- The technician should have a minimum of two years electronic troubleshooting experience.

The qualifier is included in the introductory portion of the procedure in order to be sure the technician performing the task has the experience or knowledge to successfully complete the task. After detailing the purpose of the task and defining the expected results, the qualifier is stated. The addition of the qualifier is what makes a procedure a procedure initially. The rest of the introductory portion of the procedure follows the same requirements as for instructions.

Introduction to a Procedure

Remember, the same general requirements for a set of instructions fulfill the basic requirements when introducing a procedure. The primary difference is the addition of the qualifier.

- Define purpose of the task.
- Detail expected results.
- Indicate qualifier—required level of experience.
- List preparatory information.

Format

Almost any format variation may be used when designing a procedure. The criteria involved in the design is partly based on purpose and audience, and particular industry requirements. But the discussion of a particular format should help define the specific requirements for the procedure. The format that will be detailed here follows particular industry standards and can easily accept variations.

It's generally referred to as the columned format, and serves to accommodate the experienced as well as the less experienced technician. The Step column details the steps in a chronological sequence, acting as a checklist for the experienced technician. The action column offers the additional detail for the less experienced technician. The remarks column details all other considerations relating to the task, such as cautions and warnings.

STEP	ACTION	REMARKS

Step Column

The step column basically details the what information as discussed with instructions. This column announces what is to be done. Each step is numbered and announced. This column also serves the purposes of the experienced technician; it serves as a checklist to ensure he doesn't skip a step when performing the task over a period of time.

1. Remove Filter

Action Column

The action column includes the detail necessary for the less experienced technician to successfully complete the task. It includes the what, or instructive detail; it also includes information required of a procedure. It includes why information, or that detail that explains the action taken with each step. The why information serves to educate the less experienced technician so he or she will eventually become an experienced technician.

STEP	ACTION	REMARKS
1. Remove Filter	Secure oil wrench around outside of filter—turn counterclockwise until loose. Remove filter by hand, allow oil to drain in order to attach new filter.	

Step 2 of the procedure would not begin until all the necessary data for step 1 had been completely detailed. This allows the format to keep all step-associated data directly in line with the pertinent step. Remember, the step column acts as a checklist for the experienced technician, while the action column details the instructive and explanatory data for the less experienced technician. Understanding the step of the task promotes expertise.

Remarks Column

All additional information associated with a particular step is included under the remarks column. The remarks column serves to include data that might clutter up the instructions and explanation.

The remarks column could include cautions, warnings, notes, references and illustrations. Of course, if the illustration is too large or complicated to fit under the remarks column, then its location would be referenced.

STEP	ACTION	REMARKS
1. Remove Filter		Warning: Oil may be hot. Caution: Filter retains oil. Note: Be sure drain pan is beneath filter. Ref: See figure 2, page 3.

Just like with the action column, once all of the detail included under remarks has been completed, the next step can begin.

All of the associated information for each step would be included across the page. Remember, no matter how lengthy a particular step maybe , no matter how much detail is included, the next step doesn't begin until all the data from the previous step has been completed.

Remember, there can certainly be variations on this format depending on the task at hand and the specific needs of the audience. But the three column format does serve the purpose of what a procedure is all about; it meets the needs of the experienced as well as the needs of the less experienced technician. The three column format is designed to meet the requirements of a professional audience—those who will be required to perform a particular task on a regular basis.

- Number each step.
- Include headings: step, action, remarks.
- Indicate What is to be done under action—instruct.
- Indicate why it is done under action—explain and educate.
- Include all additional step related data under remarks.
- Label each remark.
- Do not begin the next step until the previous step has been completed.
- Refer to qualifier when determining extent and depth of step detail.
- Ensure the format encourages interest and participation.

Conclusion

The conclusion to a procedure can be just like that of set instructions: simply verify expected results. But a procedure can go beyond only detailing results. A procedure can also include a troubleshooting guide to check problems encountered in the steps of the task. A procedure can also include post-preparatory information along with the conclusion indicating proper clean-up direction and tool and machine maintenance and care.

It's important that the conclusion clearly indicates to the technician that the task has been completed and doesn't require any further task-oriented action, only concluding elements.

- Verify expected results.
- Provide trouble shooting guide.
- Detail clean-up information.

Clearly indicate task has been completed.

Sample Procedure

Changing the Oil and Filter in a 4-Cylinder Automobile

General Description—This procedure covers the changing of the oil and filter in a 4-cylinder automobile. Frequency of action is determined according to various driving conditions—consult Owner's Manual. It is suggested that the oil and filter be changed every 3000 miles or 3 months, whichever comes first. Changing the oil and filter on a regular basis improves performance and prolongs the engine's life.

Caution—Oil should never be changed without also changing the filter; fouled oil is retained in the filter.

References—According to make and year of auto, current Owner's Manual (OM).

Note—Many automobiles have relatively easy access to oil drain plug; raising the car is not necessary.

Mechanic should have basic handtool and auto parts location knowledge.

Tools	*Materials*
Standard wrench or Socket wrench, ¼"	4 quarts of oil—consult OM for type
Oil drain pan	Oil filter—consult OM
Filter wrench	Rags (2)

STEP	ACTION	REMARKS
1. Drain Oil	Place oil drain pan beneath oil drain plug. Remove drain plug with wrench—turn counter-clockwise until loose, finger turn remainder of turns. Allow fouled oil to drain in order to introduce new oil.	Note: Consult OM for exact location. Warning: Oil may be hot. Caution: Avoid dropping plug in pan.
2. Remove Filter	Secure filter wrench around filter—turn counterclockwise until loose and remove used filter.	Note: Be sure drain pan is beneath filter. Caution: Filter retains oil.

3. Replace Filter	Coat new filter rubber gasket with fresh oil to ensure reliable seal. Insert filter on threaded post. Turn clockwise by hand until secure.	Note: Be sure old gasket was removed with discarded filter to form adequate seal.
4. Replace Plug	With wrench, turn oil drain plug until secure so new oil will not run out.	
5. Replace Oil	Remove oil cap and introduce 4 quarts of new oil into the engine's crankcase to replace fouled oil.	Note: Consult OM for exact location Caution: Replace oil cap.
6. Remove Pan	Remove drain pan from beneath car to discard fouled oil.	
7. Cleanup	Properly dispose of fouled motor oil.	Note: Consult OM for proper disposal. Warning: Refined motor oil is hazardous to the environment. Check with EPA for disposal locations.
	Clean tools with dry cloth and put properly away. Dispose of used filter.	Caution: Dispose of filter according to local regulations.

With 4 quarts of new oil properly introduced into the 4-cylinder engine, along with the replaced oil filter, harmful engine contaminants have been eliminated for another 3000 highway miles or 3 months of reliable motoring.

Note: Oil and filter replacement does not guarantee complete engine mechanical reliability.

MANUALS

Everything in professional documentation can lead to or find its way into a manual. A manual is basically a collection of descriptions, instructions, procedures and, when appropriate, illustrations. In everyday life, as well as in industry, manuals are constantly a part of our lives.

How would the machinist get the mill operating without the set-up manual?
How could the administrative assistant incorporate the new computer and software into the existing system without the operation manual?
How would any of us get our VCRs up and operating without the owner's manual?

The intent of a manual is generally not singularly focused. It rarely covers a single process or a particular operation. A manual is heterogeneous in that it covers everything necessary that relates to the subject matter.

A manual not only covers operation, it also covers set-up, care and maintenance, usage as well as whatever background data may be required for reader usability

Writing a manual for industry today can be one of the most difficult and time consuming tasks facing the professional communicator. There are many variables to be considered. It would be difficult, maybe even counterproductive, to include a specific example here, but we will detail the requirements of the manual.

All of the process elements of technical communication are important when putting a manual together.

- Thinking—what do you know, what do you need to discover?
- Research
- Interviewing
- Compiling data
- Coordination
- Sharing with appropriate professionals
- Design
- Revision
- Proofing and editing

Manual Organization

The specific organization of a manual, of course, depends on the intent, or purpose and the intended audience. But there are some basics, or general manual elements, worth considering here. They should assist in pointing out and clarifying how to effectively construct a complex, in-depth document like a manual.

Professional manuals are generally organized into divisions and subdivisions to make the information easy to understand, access and use.

- Front Matter
  - ✔ Introduction
  - ✔ Table of contents
- Parts
  - ✔ Chapters
  - ✔ Paragraphs
  - ✔ Illustrations
  - ✔ Tables
  - ✔ Charts
  - ✔ Subparagraphs
- Appendices
- Glossaries
- Indexes

It's equally important to consider particular detail relating to audience access such as titles and headings when constructing a manual.

- Placement
- Capitalization
- Style

It is also essential, as with all documentation, that the reader feel comfortable when using the manual.

- Explain unusual aspects of the manual—Usage section.
- Get user involved with the manual—Organization.
- Offer practice to solve real problems—Content.

When faced with a manual writing task, it is always suggested that the communicator study previously published manuals for organization, style, content, design, etc. And don't forget to research and meet the needs of your audience.

Consider the standard organization of a car owner's manual. Most are organized the same way to meet the logical, sequential needs of the owner of the vehicle.

They all begin with an introduction to create enthusiasm for the product as well as for the manual. It's important to keep the user involved immediately and in the future.

Most car owner's manuals begin with broad, general content listings for quick reference, then specify particulars.

- Before Starting your vehicle section
  Generally deals with those considerations that are necessary to know before hitting the road: child restraint, gasoline requirements, seat belts, license information, safety tips and so on.

The car owner's manual deals with the typical required necessities as means of introduction.

- Starting and operating

  This section generally deals with those elements that relate to set-up and usage in a manual. Here the user begins to understand how to operate the various features of the vehicle, like lights, shifting, wipers, speed control, air conditioning and whatever else may be pertinent to the majority of manuals. It's important to indicate how to care for the subject properly for long term reliability and use.

The manual then could be broken down further, addressing more specific details relating to intent and audience need. Ensure that readers are comfortable with the manual even before they get actively involved with the specifics.

When planning the organization of the manual, be consistent and audience aware. There should be at least two of each subdivision incorporated into the manual. If you title a section Part 1, make sure there is a Part 2. If there is a Chapter 1, make sure there is a Chapter 2. Don't confuse the audience and have them searching through the manual for something that doesn't exist. Remember to always check out preexisting manuals for guidance.

Team Effort

Manuals are rarely a solo effort. Because there are so many considerations involved with producing a manual, a team is generally employed to produce the product. The team is usually made up of particular industry professionals encompassing whatever disciplines are required for the manual.

The team charged with producing the manual has to begin thinking in terms of purpose and content, and how the team can achieve its goals.

- Team management—someone to coordinate the effort.
- Time management—set reasonable time limits.
- Document management—work with a predetermined design and style.
- Task analysis—determine how to meet the requirements of the task.
- Conflict management—be prepared to deal with differences of opinion.

In a team effort, just like all professional documentation efforts, everyone must come together and envision a mutual unity of focus.

- Plan project—equal participation.
- Assign responsibilities—gather information.
- Collect and review, as a team, gathered data—use only that which is pertinent to purpose.

Audience Focused Format

One way to be sure of audience interest and participation in your manual is to design it with their best interests in mind. Make the manual easy to use; don't require the reader to search for particular information; make it easy to find. Use graphics and illustrations to enhance the document; make it look good. Use headings and various type styles to enhance the manual's appearance.

PRIMARY HEADING

RUN-IN HEADING Text flows from heading

Untitled text—used to break information into short, easy to read and find segments. These segments should deal with one idea/one point.

Organizing and Formatting Content

Content material should be organized in integrated sections of text and related graphics and illustrations. Each section should begin with the appropriate heading and, when possible, begin on a new page.

For example, if you were constructing an owner's manual for a bicycle, an integrated section could deal with assembly, and everything associated with assembly would be included in this section.

If a particular section requires two pages, it should generally begin on the left page and conclude on the right page. This allows the reader to have the entire section visible at one time without having to turn pages. Particularly short sections can appear on the same, or facing pages.

If a section is rather lengthy, requiring more than two pages, it should be subdivided by using secondary headings. Remember, keep the reader interested and ensure information is easy to locate.

When incorporating illustrations, graphics, statistics, charts or other types of data that don't fit into the text, they should be assigned a title and integrated into the section it relates to.

If these other types of data are to be collected in one specific place in the manual, they should be assigned figure numbers. They should also be referred to in the text and identified by the assigned number.

Work to ensure the format for your manual complements the material and encourages reader participation.

Know the manual's purpose and the audience's needs. Grab and hold their attention right away in the introduction. Make them feel good about the product, or series of tasks, by pointing out benefits and features. A clear and well organized format should keep them interested as they proceed through the manual.

- Quick access to information—lowers performance time.
- Finding information quickly reduces problems.
- Encourages manual use.
- Supports purpose participation.
- Consider innovative format possibilities—different colored stock for each section, tabs protruding for quick section access, dividers between sections or whatever else might serve the purpose.

Remember, a manual is a collection of descriptions of parts, machinery and products; instructions on how to assemble, clean or maintain; and procedures on how to use and complete. There are so many different kinds and styles of manuals, including one as example wouldn't serve the purpose.

To gain a better understanding of what manuals are all about, take a look in the junk drawer in your kitchen; that's where I keep my appliance manuals. Go out to your car, open the glove compartment and pull the owner's manual out from underneath the gloves. Does anybody really keep gloves in there? Look around on the job for operation, or machine set-up manuals. Do they differ from product manuals? Oh yes, don't forget all of those computer manuals that seem to multiply. Take a look at the general elements these different manuals have in common.

- Introduction
- Parts illustrations
- Organization—logically, most manuals are organized similarly.
    ✔ Introduction
    ✔ Part identification
    ✔ Assembly
    ✔ How to use
    ✔ Care and maintenance
    ✔ Recommended additional uses
    ✔ Warranty
    ✔ Parts replacement

Pay attention to what works best in these manuals; how well they encourage use. Check out how the information is presented, and how illustrations are incorporated into the text.

Now that we've taken a look at instructions, procedures and manuals, we should be ready to test our understanding. Try some of the exercises that follow. Remember, bring whatever is required to produce your document together to satisfy the purpose and meet the needs of your audience.

EXERCISES

1. What's the matter with the following set of instructions?

Repairing a Bicycle Tire

When a tire on your bicycle gets a hole in it allowing air to escape, it is necessary to repair or replace it.

Tools   *Materials*
Screwdriver   Patch kit
Wrench   New tube or tire

Warning: Sniffing the patch adhesive could be hazardous to your health.

1. *Tip bicycle upside down*

   Grasp bike and invert to rest on handlebars and seat

2. *Remove tire*

   With wrench, unbolt tire from rim and pull off.

3. *Remove rim*

   With wrench, unbolt tire from rim and pull off.

4. *Remove tube*

   Slowly remove damaged tube from rim
   Caution: Be careful of air intake valve when removing.

5. *Locate hole*

   Inflate tire with air and immerse in water—note escaping air bubbles. Place finger over hole to identify location.

6. *Patch hole*

   Prepare patch according to instructions on kit and place over hole.

7. *Replace tube*

   Replace tube in the opposite direction it was removed.

8. *Replace tire*

   Replace tire on rim and rim on bike forks securing with wrench. Flip it over and you are done.

2. Select a task you are familiar with and produce a set of instructions that meet the requirements of instructions.

3. Write a set of instructions/directions for a foreign exchange student to get from the main entrance of your school to your home to tutor you in physics. He has a license, knows how to drive and is familiar with the rules of the road, but not the area. You really need his help, but you can't go to him because the cable guy is coming.

4. Locate a set of instructions that came with a product you have purchased and determine if they could be improved.

5. Remember that foreign exchange student? Well, he really helped you ace your test. Now you want to return the favor. He's about to begin the job hunting process and wants to look good for interviews. The only problem is, he doesn't know how to tie a tie. Write a set of instructions on tying a tie for this new found friend.

6. What's the matter with this step from a procedure on planting a tree?

STEP	ACTION	REMARKS
1. Prepare hole	Dig approximately 1 and ½ feet into the soil. Add peat moss.	Note: Depth of hole should accommodate existing roots.

7. Choose a job you've held, or currently hold, and write a procedure for your duties or a portion of your duties for new employees to study and learn.

8. Take the set of instructions you've written and turn it into a procedure. Remember, the audience needs to be determined from a professional standpoint.

9. Take a product, or device that's available and write an owner's manual without considering the existing one.

10. Bring in some manuals you may have around and determine how they could be improved and better meet the needs of the intended audience.

Proposals and Reports

PROPOSALS

A proposal is basically a document a writer puts forward, proposing and soliciting certain things from the intended audience. There are many different reasons for developing a proposal in industry today.

- To request permission to conduct a research project—could be private sector or academic related.
- To encourage new business—in or out of plant.
- To request capital, financial backing for a project, product or service.
- To place a bid for a contract—private or public.

Of course there are many other reasons to present a proposal, but the main intent is that the writer, through the document, is *requesting something*. Remember the persuasive elements discussed in Chapter 4? Much of what was pertinent in terms of the persuasive, or claim letter is pertinent here.

A proposal basically combines the accepted aspects of a document with the persuasive. The writer is asking for something by presenting all of the pertinent facts that should assist the reader in making a decision along with persuasive techniques. The basics of proposal writing follow a logical organization focusing on the point of the request.

- Detail the problem or situation that requires solving.
- Support your credibility as the right person to carry out the proposed task.
- Present the benefits of granting the proposal with the reader's point of view in mind.
- Detail, specifically, facts and related data, how the solution can be realized.
- A proposal can have one of several purposes, or combinations of those purposes.
  - ✔ To solve a problem
  - ✔ To investigate a subject
  - ✔ To sell a product or service

Investigative Proposals

Investigative proposals are exactly what the term suggests. They can range from lengthy, formal presentations and inquiries to brief, informal documents possibly handled by a memo.

To write effective proposals, it's important the communicator understand and appreciate persuasive techniques. Effective use of persuasive techniques helps to convince those you are submitting the proposal to, to approve or accept what you're asking for.

To write an effective proposal, be persuasive; the writer should always approach the subject with a positive attitude. This does not suggest manipulation; rather, it applies credible, logical arguments to convince the reader that the writer's views are correct.

For example:

> Allowing our entire group to have the day off on Tuesday, April 3rd to attend the Zycom Industrial Seminar will not only enhance our effectiveness on the job, it will also encourage on-line innovation. What the presenters have planned directly relates to our unique mission within the company.

This example not only makes a credible pitch for what's being proposed, it clearly indicates the reasons what is requested will prove beneficial.

There are basically four factors that influence the success of a proposal.

- The needs of the reader—understand what they will appreciate.
- The credibility of the writer—clearly indicate that you have done your homework.
- The logic of the message—don't require the reader to interpret.
- Achievable limits—don't request more than can be logically accomplished.

Whatever the purpose of the proposal, your chances of getting it approved are much greater if you follow some general guidelines.

- Discover the content, information necessary to win acceptance of your plan—remember, outlines always help.
- Research and understand the subject.
- Make note of deadlines—submit promptly.
- Find out the review and evaluation process.
- Determine possible objections and refute in proposal.
- Always support your general points with specific information.
- Present a logical, achievable schedule.
- The writer's attitude should be audience directed when possible.

When constructing a proposal, address those issues that are expected from a proposal. Format and organize this document, like all professional documents, to encourage reader interest and participation.

SUBJECT SUMMARY

INTRODUCTION OR BACKGROUND—Identify the subject in more detail.

GOAL OR SOLUTION—Explain the importance or benefits that will result.

INQUIRY OR RESEARCH PLAN—Establish the limits.

SCHEDULE—Indicate time requirements to complete inquiry.

Format and organization requirements can vary according to intent of proposal and the audience's particular needs.

As the proposal writing process begins, it is often a good idea to *consider why a proposal can be turned down*. This supports the persuasive technique of refuting possible objections prior to submitting the document. Keep the reasons a proposal can be turned down in mind.

- Lack of new or original ideas.
- Vague research plan.
- Unfamiliar with resource material available.
- Little regard for future ramifications.
- Illogical reasoning with approach.
- Amount of work required seems unrealistic.
- Lack of preliminary work indicating success.
- Approach lacks specific commitment to goal.

These are just some of the possible reasons a proposal can be turned down. Being aware of them can help to eliminate reasons for rejection while involved in the process of constructing and submitting your proposal. Remember the Human Factor—don't give your audience any reason to reject your document or its content.

Sample Proposal

The following example is a proposal requesting permission to research a topic in an academic environment that will culminate in a report submitted for a grade. The same point and considerations the proposal addresses could also apply to industry.

TO:	Dr. Bryan Douglas
FROM:	Erin Leigh
SUBJECT:	Proposal for a Study of Pedagogical Theory and Approach to Technical Writing.

BACKGROUND

With the increasing recognition of the growing importance of effective communication in the private sector, industry, institutions of higher learning are incorporating professional writing courses into established curriculums. The various elements involved generally relate to the singular process of professional writing and interpersonal communications, ultimately defined as product or message. These elements, although influenced by product, are heterogeneous in nature and should be considered independent concerns within the pedagogical approach and concept of professional writing.

Information needs to be collected, interpreted and presented as the data relates to pedagogical theory and approach in a cohesive study.

GOAL

The primary elements of professional writing to be concentrated on in this study include:

1. Theoretical Foundations
2. Current Issues
3. Curricular Directions
4. Varied Disciplinary Approaches

The above mentioned elements will be researched as independent concentrations, although accepting their interrelationship to pedagogical theory and approach.

The inherent, although not necessarily inclusive, elements which dictate the linear aspects of professional writing need to be considered from the proposed research direction.

RESEARCH PLAN

The information presented in the study will be gathered from current (1990–96) periodicals, publications, journals, books and other sources that may be located during the course of the research.

This information will adequately support and serve the proposed study. An abundance of material has been discovered through a preliminary search. The majority of this material is available locally.

The limits of the inquiry will be dictated to by concentrating solely on the aforementioned elements.

SCHEDULE

Preliminary draft—1st week of May
Final Document—July 1st

COST

The cost of conducting the research and producing the study will be minimal. The overall expenditure will cover the cost of copying and paper, and will not exceed $25.00.

The minimum length of the proposed study should be at least 100 pages typed according to MLA standards.

cc: Dr. D. Albert

The content language of this proposal serves to meet the needs of the audience. The proposal is being submitted to the individual's professor for approval.

All of the information contained in the proposal is directed at the audience's needs to understand exactly what is being proposed. They will make a decision based solely on the proposal; so it is important to include all of the pertinent detail. Don't require your audience to interpret or guess at that which wasn't included.

Remember, there are many situations in which you must submit a proposal in order to obtain the go-ahead for a project. They range from suggestion systems many companies employ, to major changes in the organizational structure of a company or business.

Be assertive in your approach to proposals; take a chance. If the document is taken seriously, and includes all of the necessary data, the chances of it being approved are increased.

To better understand what proposals are all about, think about the verbal proposals we submit on a daily basis. Very simply, we're asking permission to do something for specific reasons. PLAN AND SUBMIT

Alternate Proposal Format

Because there can be many reasons for submitting a proposal, there can and should be variations in format. Choose the format that best serves the particular purpose. The following format offers some slight variation to the previous proposal. It can meet many general situations requiring proposals in industry.

TITLE

Remember to always title your documents.

SUMMARY

Offer sufficient background on your topic to allow your audience the opportunity to place the situation into proper context.

INTRODUCTION

Problem: Clearly explain the problem this proposal will address and why it should.

Objectives: Explain what you hope to accomplish and how the audience will benefit.

Advantages: Indicate the importance of reaching these goals.

BODY

Professional Plan: Explain exactly what you plan to do; how you will reach your goals. Indicate, specifically, the gains to be realized such as, monetary, safety, morale, company image, and so on. Explain in detail the steps you will take to achieve your prescribed goals.

MANAGEMENT PLAN

Clearly explain why you should be approved for carrying out the task detailed in the proposal; why you are the right individual for the job. Address the involvement of others and the extent of shared responsibilities. Indicate the time plan, how long the task should take. In short, what it will take to get the job done.

BUDGET PLAN

Indicate exactly what this task will cost. Point out where the expenditures will be made and the significance of each.

CONCLUSION

Here you want to reiterate what you hope to accomplish and the benefits that will be derived.

REPORTS

Reports follow the same organizational logic as all documentation. It is a document meant to accomplish a variety of things. It basically reports information to an interested audience. It reports and encourages interest in the uninformed audience. Reports can often be persuasive in nature. They can require the audience to make a decision based on the information it contains.

With reports, you begin with general or background information; detail the main point or points. You detail the importance of the main points before providing the clarifying detail. Reports are not unlike proposals, except they don't always require some kind of approval before the writer can proceed with a plan.

Types of Reports

There are as many reasons for writing reports as there probably are varying situations in industry. A report could be required to analyze. This report would take the parts of something, a meeting for example, and provide an analysis. A professional report generally requires the writer to report on some kind of direct observation. A new assembly line has been dedicated in your company and your job is to observe and report on its progress. A trip report would require the writer to detail particular elements of a company sponsored trip. The elements could relate to cost or information gathered during the course of the trip. Informational reports present information on a professional subject that would include conclusions. And the variety goes on, including feasibility reports, regulatory reports, troubleshooting reports and so on.

What to include in a Report

Let's say your boss wants you to go to an important meeting and write a report detailing the results of that meeting. Like all documentation tasks, you begin by doing your homework.

- What's the subject of the meeting?
- Who will attend the meeting?
- Why is the meeting being held now?
- Why do you need to go to the meeting?
- How could the meeting influence your particular group's mission?

Always be prepared when faced with collecting and reporting on information. The better prepared you are, the more you'll get from the situation.

So you do your background homework on the upcoming meeting and are ready to get all you can out of it. But there are still a few details that you would like to be more sure of. How long will the meeting take? How important is the meeting to the overall scheme of things where you work? Well, you can certainly ask the right questions to discover the answers. If that doesn't work, consider the time of day the meeting was scheduled for.

Rarely are important meetings scheduled first thing in the morning. People are just getting to work, having some coffee and getting settled down for the day. Besides, early morning meetings tend to suggest bad news. Few important meetings take place the hour prior to lunch. Lunch is on people's minds, and their efforts may not be as substantial as they should be. And after lunch is not always a good time for a meeting; we all know how we feel right after lunch. Towards the end of the day is not a good time either; people are getting ready to go home—this all relates to the Human Factor. Look around where you work when the hour to quit approaches. What are most of your fellow employees doing?

The best time to schedule an important meeting is about 9:00 or 10:00 A.M. Everybody is generally eager and rolling along by this time; the peak energy hours.

So you know what time the meeting is, who's going and basically what it's all about. Fourteen separate reports will be given relating to some area of quality control. The dilemma seems to be accurately reporting on these fourteen different reports. It would seem impossible to accurately describe everything that occurs. Don't worry about it. Take copious notes only on those areas that most directly relate to your group's particular interests. It's all about emphasizing and subordinating. Certainly include detail on the areas of less interest, but not in as much depth. Consider your audience—your boss—and what is essential to meet its needs.

Primary Characteristics

- Attractive—invites a favorable reading
- Well organized—clear and detailed—easily understood
- Reliable—accurate and well documented—credible

Organization

Depending on the complexity of the report and what kind of report you are writing, the organization can follow three basic sequences.

Informal, Short Report

- Statement of the problem
- Discussion of possible solutions
- Conclusions

Semi-Formal

- Statement of the problem
- Proposed solution
- Advantages
- Disadvantages
- Conclusions

Formal

- Statement of the problem
- Detailed information obtained
- Discussion of information related to problem
- Possible results
- Conclusion
- Recommendations

These are just some possible ways to approach the organizational structure of the report. What is addressed in a report should serve the purpose of the report and meet the needs of the audience. These three formats are not chiseled in granite; particular sections can be substituted or combined to meet the purpose of the report.

Standard Report Format

Where the previous suggestions broke the report format up according to possible intent, a standard, acceptable format might prove to serve many report purposes.

- The Front Matter
  - ✔ Introduces the problem and its importance
  - ✔ Details limits of report
  - ✔ Summarizes point or points report will cover

- The Body
  - ✔ Details major points and support
  - ✔ Refutes possible objections

- The Conclusion
  - ✔ Draws conclusions and makes recommendations

Informational and Analytical Reports

An informational report presents data without interpretations or evaluation. The report leaves it up to the readers to examine the details and arrive at their own conclusions. There is little, if any persuasion here. Just present the evidence.

An analytical report also presents the data, but goes on to interpret that data for the audience. The writer's responsibility here is to collect the information, present it and analyze that same data for the audience. The analysis generally comes in the conclusion of the report and readers will often base decisions on the analysis.

Readability

Here we're concerned with whether or not the reader will comprehend what is being presented in the report. The reading level of the audience must be met in order to reach them effectively with the information contained in the report. Research your audience and appreciate who they are and what they require. Let the drafting process help here. Review drafts with selected members of the audience as you go through the process of putting the report together. Keep it simple, direct and to the point. How easily your message is understood is the primary stylistic factor relating to how your report will be judged.

Review

Plan your reports and conduct an objective analysis; determine what you need to accomplish. Whether it deals with cost savings, improved performance, organizational structure or analysis, part of your thrust is likely to be persuasive.

Persuade your reader to overcome objections of possible resistance. Point out the benefits and discuss the conditions that relate to the problem. Determine who will read your report.

Analyze your audience, determine who is going to read and be required to act upon the report. Discover what they already know, what they need to know and how they might feel about it.

Wrap Up

Basic report elements are detailed here. It should be understood that what really dictates the content of a report depends on the two most important factors in professional documentation. What is the primary purpose of the information you are presenting and what are the needs of the intended audience?

Try some of the following exercises and see if you can plug into your understanding of proposals and reports.

PRODUCT/SERVICE ANNOUNCEMENT

When we think about all of the products and services available today, it's a wonder most of us do eventually make a decision.

Let's go out to dinner. Where?
How big should the new T.V. be?
Happytime or Motherlove preschool?
Red car, blue car, big car, little car?
To travel agency or not?

The list could obviously go on and on, but suffice it to say that competition among products and services isn't diminishing.

For example, over the last few years the number of health clubs has grown in leaps and bounds. Many of us have even joined one of these clubs; if not, I bet most of us know someone who has. How do you choose which one is the best? Do we want to just lift weights? How about circuit training? Does it really have to have a steam room? Hey, this one has childcare available for its members. Sure, but this one is $15 cheaper a month. How do you choose? It's easy. We choose according to what appeals to us as individuals. How do these clubs know what appeals to the individual?

They don't. That's why when they're presenting their services, through ads or some other way, they concentrate on the primary features, or what makes their facility particularly unique.

A feature is generally something associated with a product or service that indicates on some level that it is unique, better if you will, than similar or like products or services. A product or service can certainly have more than one feature. A health club, for example, may concentrate on any number of features to attract the largest segment of the population.

A club wishing to appeal to the biggest potential audience may feature everything from tennis courts to treadmills. Where a club solely designed for strength training may concentrate on those features, i.e., free weights, that would appeal to that particular audience.

Basically, a feature translates as a benefit to the individual interested in the product or service.

Product/Service Report

There are a variety of ways to create enthusiasm for a product or a service. It generally requires a good dose of persuasion supported by facts, and preparation.

The persuasive element should be considered whatever our intention may be. In other words, are we trying to sell, are we seeking financial backing, or are we simply looking for permission?

- Concentrate on primary features.
- Concede to audience need.
- Be prepared; know your subject.
- Refute possible objections.
- Create desire.
- Create enthusiasm.

Depending on our intent, the design of the document could prove crucial to achieving success. Audience, like always, is an important factor to consider as well. Is it a specific audience with similar or like needs and desires, or is our audience made up of a cross section individuals? The various designs could include a report, memo, flyer, or a brochure.

The product/service document could address a variety of issues, but should consider:

* Establishing a general category
* Attracting attention
* Arousing interest
* Creating desire—best, easiest, new, improved, reliable...
* Call for action—strive for your audience to make a commitment.

Example

GREY CARE

"Grey Care is a 'home away from home' for older folks. We offer a secure, warm, friendly, social atmosphere for those over 60 to spend time at. With many planned activities and personal services, Grey Care is the place for your loved ones."

Grey Care will be a supervised day care facility that offers an alternative to a nursing home or a home health aide service for elderly people who are able to perform basic care functions but cannot be left unsupervised. We will provide a safe, secure, warm, friendly, social environment that emphasizes improving the quality of life for our elderly clients. We will accomplish this goal by providing services designed to increase physical and mental activity in a socially stimulating environment.

POTENTIAL CLIENTS

Grey Care will provide services to people over the age of 60. According to the 1990 census, there were about 78,200 people over the age of 60 living in Monroe County. The Center for Government Research projected a rise in this number to 93,000 people in 1995 before a slight decline in 2000 to about 89,000. The 1990 census also reported that, in 1990, 6370 people over the age of 65 lived in households of relatives other than their spouse. If this percentage had remained constant, this number would have risen to about 7440 people in 1995 before falling to about 7120 people in 2000. Many of these people living with relatives would be potential clients for Grey Care. Grey Care would offer them an alternative that will let families care for these loved ones and still work, volunteer, or take a break from the constant supervision they have to provide.

COST OF SERVICES

Grey Care will not only provide a much needed alternative to current elder care options, but will do so at an affordable price, much lower than nursing homes or home health aide services. The average nursing home costs about $5,000 per month and the cost for a home health aide runs about $1,200 per month. There will be additional charges for some services such as physical therapy, transportation to and from medical appointments, transportation to and from the facility, and for personal grooming services.

1990 Census of Monroe County Residents

	1990	1995*	2000*
60 to 74	50,000	49,000	42,000
75 to 84	18,200	32,000	33,000
85 and up	10,000	12,000	14,000

MARKETING STRATEGIES

Our marketing strategy is simple and cost effective. The people who most often come into contact with potential clients of Grey Care are social workers, adult protective workers, geriatric health care providers and counselors at the Monroe County Office for the Aging. We will target those people in mailings and will hold luncheon seminars to introduce Grey Care and give tours of the facilities. We will also supply these people with brochures that they can provide to clients and their families.

ACTIVITIES AND SERVICES OFFERED

- Staff licensed in Gerontology, Psychology, Sociology, Nursing, and First Aid.
- Transportation to and from facility and medical appointments.
- Secure, hospitable, supervised care.
- In-house beautician and hairdresser.
- Dining room with snacks and meals.
- Medical office with licensed personnel
- Exercise room including aerobics.
- Game room with various activities.
- A lounge to relax and/or nap in.
- Music room and dancing room.
- Field trips and outings.
- Arts and crafts room.
- Knitting room.
- Square dancing.
- Indoor bacci ball and golf.

LOCATIONS

3 Convenient Locations:
- 869 Manitou Rd., corner of Rt. 531
- 182 Hylan Dr., 2 minutes from 390
- 946 Titus Ave. in Irondequoit

Join us in a relaxed and social commune. Come every day or whenever you please.

Example

BOTTOMS UP

INTRODUCTION

We are three partners who have formed a company to bring you a new product called "Bottoms Up." This is a revolutionary simple, and effective funnel to eliminate waste from laundry detergent and fabric softener bottles.

Irene Holt holds a degree in Marketing; Cheryl Confarotta has prior small business experience and is the product designer; and Dusty Graupman holds a degree in Business Administration.

PRODUCT

Our patented product will be used by all individuals who utilize liquid laundry detergent and fabric softener; whether it be used privately or commercially. Most people prefer liquid rather than powder detergent. "Bottoms Up" was designed to eliminate waste by connecting a near empty container to another almost full container and allowing it to drip until empty. It is designed to fit 90% of the major brand containers available in the market place. This will not only help the customer's pocketbook but it will also help the environment. "Bottoms Up" is packaged in an easy to view, cost effective, clear, bubble pack with a distinct eye catching label. The label includes a UPC code, the name of the product ("Bottoms Up"), and a small diagram explaining the product use. I'm sure you will all agree this is a unique one-of-a-kind product!

FEASIBILITY STUDY

To evaluate the feasibility of our funnel, we distributed our prototype to 10 laundermats within the Rochester area. We used the *Survey Method* of collecting data by personal interviews. Out of a total of 240 interviews, 80% of the respondents liked the "Bottoms Up" product and would be willing to buy it. They found it reasonably priced, easy to use, and they recognized the benefits of the product; it would save them money and eliminate waste.

MARKETING OBJECTIVES

Our goal for our first year in production is to saturate the Rochester metropolitan area encompassing approximately 200,000 family units of house or apartment dwellers. We envision selling to 5% (10,000 units) of that market in the first year. Over the next 5 years our goal is to expand our consumer base to 1,000,000 customers throughout the United States.

DESIGN AND DEVELOPMENT OBJECTIVE

"Webster Tool and Die" has made a commitment to our company to produce each unit for $ .29. The packaging will cost $.12 for each unit. These figures are based on the production of 10,000 units (see attached sheet for cost breakdown analysis).

PROFIT PROJECTIONS

Time Frame	Number Units Sold	Distributors Profit	Company Profit
1 Year	10,000	$9,000	$5,900
5 Year	1,000,000	$990,000	$590,000

FINANCING

To obtain the capital we need to start up our business, we decided to reach into our own pockets and finance "Bottoms-Up." With the size and type of business we are launching, the capital investment needed is $5,000. We intend to reinvest our profits back into the company to establish a solid financial base for the future. Keeping our marketing objective in mind, we may need additional funds to expand our product throughout the country. At that point in time we will negotiate a loan from a bank. A successful running business with positive cash flow, a commitment to a solid financial background and the ability to collateralize a loan will stand us in good stead to secure the additional finances we need.

CONSUMER OBJECTIVES

We intend to sell "Bottoms Up" to major distributors of laundry detergent and fabric softener. Our primary focus for the first year will be to sell to Wegman's Supermarkets and Tops Supermarkets. We want our company to be perceived by the customer as a friend of the consumer and the environment. To show our commitment, 1% of the profit from our product for the first fiscal year will be donated to local recycling centers.

PRODUCT STRATEGY

With our sights set on the future, we want to expand this product line to other home and commercial containers. We intend to extend to a series of other related items such as motor oil containers, ketchup bottles, mustard bottles, salad dressing bottles, syrup bottles, etc.

PRICING STRATEGY

The recommended retail price for each 2-unit bubble pack will market for $1.99. Our wholesale price would be $.99 per unit.

DISTRIBUTION STRATEGY

As we start our company, distribution responsibility will be handled by the three owners of the company. This will enable us to keep costs down and we will be able to build a rapport with our distributors. Over the next 5 years, as we expand, we will use direct shipping from the manufacturers.

PROMOTIONAL STRATEGY

"Bottoms Up" will be strategically displayed in the laundry detergent aisle mounted at eye level on vertical mounting racks. We will perform in-store demonstrations during high volume shopping days. The product can also be introduced through the Wegman's and Tops' weekly promotional fliers. In addition, consumers will be introduced to our product as an environmental friend through their local recycling center bulletin.

CONCLUSION

We are very excited about our product, not only in a business sense but also as a money saver for our consumers and a help for a cleaner environment. We have a sound marketing plan that we are totally committed to. The bottom line for us is that we are going "Bottoms Up" all the way!

Costs For Producing and Packaging "Bottoms Up" Liquid Recovery funnel

	Qty.	1,000	2,500	5,000	10,000
Production					
Cost for 2 Cavity Mold	$1,200	1.20	0.48	0.24	0.12
Injection Costs		0.35	0.28	0.20	0.17
Packaging					
Label		0.060	0.055	0.042	0.030
Bag		0.200	0.120	0.080	0.055
Labor & Setup		0.033	0.033	0.033	0.033
Unit Price		**$1.84**	**$0.97**	**$0.60**	**$0.41**
Total (Unit Cost × Quantity)		**$1,843.30**	**$2,420.75**	**$2,976.50**	**$4,083.00**

EXERCISES

1. Write a proposal, with your teacher as audience, asking for a day off from class. Remember, you must have a good reason and clearly point out mutual benefits. (This should be a tough one.)

2. Construct a scenario where you believe some additional computer equipment is required for your place of employment. Write a proposal seeking approval to purchase this new equipment. (Some research on computers may be required here.)

3. Write a proposal requesting permission to research a discipline-related topic. You are seeking permission to research and write a report to be submitted to your teacher. He or she will be your audience.

4. Write a report detailing a seminar, presentation or reading that you attended on campus. The report should be informational and aimed at a general audience.

5. Write an analytical report on a seminar, presentation or reading you attended on campus. The audience for the report did not attend and your responsibility is to draw conclusions for them.

6. Write a report based on the proposal you submitted to your teacher requesting permission to research a discipline-related topic. Your teacher will be the audience for the report. Also consider presenting the report information to your classmates through an oral presentation.

EXERCISE

Coming up with a new, innovative product or service that will truly attract public attention is not an easy thing to do. After all, the public is not easy to please. Who would have guessed someone could get rich by marketing the "Pet Rock?" In order to interest people, whether for financial or marketing reasons, a number of issues need to be considered.

Create desire—Appeal to self-esteem, personal satisfaction, sense of responsibility.

Arouse interest—Why is your product or service better than those that already are available?

Uniqueness—What specific features make your product/service stand out.
FEATURE = BENEFIT.

Form—The physical structure of product/service-what it looks like.

Function—What product or service does.
Your group's assignment is to come up with a product or service that you will introduce through an effective marketing brochure (your design) and a verbal presentation.

Audience—Wholesalers, retailers, buyers, financial backers, eventually, the general public. Your job is to use the brochure to solicit feedback on the viability of your product/service. In other words, will there be sufficient interest to proceed.

Consider all aspects of what the brochure might include:

Marketing strategies
Cost
Competition
Uniqueness
Production
Time   *Possibilities:*
Consumer analysis   Magazine
Benefits   Health Club
Anything else   Your choice

Research Methods

RESEARCH METHODS

Understanding and appreciating the value of research is one of the most important aspects of the communication process. When you get right down to it, no one knows everything, at least no one I've met so far. So when we are faced with a communication effort we often need to discover certain information that isn't available to us. The good communicator understands that they can write about almost anything. Just because they are unfamiliar with a particular topic doesn't mean that they can't become familiar with a discipline or field of study.

IF YOU DON'T KNOW IT, FIND IT OUT

There are three primary areas in our lives where understanding research methods can be important:

Academic applications
Professional applications
Personal applications

No one will argue the importance of knowing how to do research when we're in school. Teachers, from grammar school on, are always assigning all sorts of research papers. Research is important in school; it helps us to expand our academic and disciplinary boundaries. We research information as we strive to understand, process what we discover and draw intelligent conclusions. What we discover enhances and builds upon what we learn in the classroom.

Our professional careers also offer ample opportunity to do all kinds of research. Each different career I've had besides teaching required that I do research. Whether as a counsellor, reporter or industrial professional, I had to know how to find information, discover things I didn't know. Often, in this environment, the research would run from interviewing professionals, individuals, for info that I required to better do my job, to straight library research. Remember the two primary questions we ask ourselves when faced with communication:

What do I know?
What do I need to find out?

Let's add a third question here:

Where and how to find it?

Academic and professional research ability are certainly important, but I believe that understanding and knowing how to do research is never more important than in my personal life, I realized this when one of my children became seriously ill. Anyone who has had the unfortunate experience of having a loved one ill knows about the avalanche of medical information associated with an illness.

We're constantly being presented with information that often seems like a foreign language. Certainly, doctors try their best to make themselves understood, but it's not always easy. We're required to make very difficult decisions with little or no notice. And of course, as we all know, an informed decision is the best decision.

What I did in this situation was to immediately familiarize myself with all aspects of my child's illness and the various treatments available. I wanted, needed to understand what was going on and what to expect. Too often we make decisions based on our faith in the medical professional. Well and good, but don't we want to be as sure as possible in situations such as these?

It would be naive to think that we can become as well informed as the experts, but with research, at least we might have a better chance at making a more intelligent decision. More than once through the course of my child's illness I disagreed with the professionals and rejected certain treatment. I can honestly say, with the knowledge discovered through research, combined with the love for my child, those decisions were the right ones.

When you think about it, knowing where and how to find information can be useful in all aspects of our personal lives.

- Auto Maintenance
- Home Repair
- Product Purchases
- Nutrition
- Child Development
- Travel
- Investing

The list certainly could go on, but the point is clear: the intelligent, informed decision is the best decision.

Where to Find Information

There are many different types of sources of information available to the researcher. Where to go to find what we don't know is the next step in the process here. There are three primary types of sources of information available.

Books
Periodicals
People

There are certainly other types of sources but they would fail under one of these categories.

Books are certainly a popular source of information when doing particular types of research; they sort of build the foundation for our understanding of a discipline, particularly when our background is limited. Generally speaking, most books dealing with a field of study are theoretical in nature. Like the text books we're assigned for college courses, they usually deal with theory, the foundation of a subject. We read the text books, and then go to class to build upon that foundation. Reading books helps us to formulate our basic understand of a subject.

This doesn't mean that all books are basic and theoretical. Many books dealing with a field of study can be focused and deal with specific aspects of a particular discipline. These sources would build upon the theory-based books dealing with a specific subject, like the next step in the process. The better informed we become, the better we can understand and process discipline specific data.

Once we have begun to formulate our understanding regarding a research topic, the next logical step would be to search out information in periodicals. Magazines, or periodicals are published on a regular basis. They generally deal with a specific area of interest, particularly discipline-focused periodicals. Because they are published on a regular basis, weekly, quarterly, etc., the researcher can be fairly certain that the information provided is the latest data available and is probably reliable.

Depending on our given situation, the primary source of information in the research process is probably people, recognized professionals in a field of study, discipline or area of interest. Of course we're talking about someone with professional knowledge here, not your next door neighbor who seems to have an opinion on everything.

A professional is anyone who possesses knowledge based on informed acquisition, whether through education, experience or a combination of both. These individuals have probably read, or are at least familiar with the most important theoretical-based books dealing with their discipline. In addition, they also subscribe to the most popular periodicals to keep up on the latest innovations and changes in their area of interest. In addition, they have also processed the information and come to particular conclusions, and can offer education opinions and recommendations regarding a subject of interest.

Most professionals do keep up with the latest scholarship in their disciplines; that's part of what being a professional is all about. Think about it, how long would you continue to see a doctor who didn't keep up with the latest innovations in medicine? Probably not very long. As an English teacher in a two-year college, I receive a variety of periodicals that deal strictly with that area; I want to stay informed, know what's going on in my discipline. I, like all professionals should, want to do the best job I possibly can.

STARTING RESEARCH

When faced with needing to do research, particularly when dealing with a topic we aren't terribly familiar with, where to begin is usually the first question. Some good advice might be to solicit the assistance of a librarian—they know what they're doing. Or, if they're busy, try the reference section, or *Reader's Guide to Periodical Literature.*

These areas can provide valuable background information. The reference section in particular offers general on many different areas of interest. The *Reader's Guide* provides information on articles printed in periodicals on almost any subject we could imagine. This area can help the researcher find a focus, or a specific approach to a topic when undecided.

Citing Sources

Once we've completed our research, and are beginning to construct our paper, the next step would be to incorporate the resource information into our document. Note: The most important element of anything you write is your voice, what you have to say about your topic. After all, you've done the research, processed the information and presumably have drawn some conclusions and formulated ideas regarding your topic. Your source information is usually included to lend credence and support what you have to say about your topic.

Citing sources within the text is done parenthetically ( ). This takes the place of the old footnoting, endnoting style. The new style basically eliminates the unnecessary redundancy of the old style.

Once you've quoted or paraphrased data within your text, you cite the source by indicating the author's last name followed by the page number the information came from. For example: (Brooks 76). The primary difference between a direct quote and a paraphrase is the direct quote is enclosed within quotation marks, the paraphrase isn't.

"It was the best of times, it was the worst of times..." (Dickens 13).
Times were good and bad... (Dickens 13).

If the quote or paraphrase is introduced by using the author's name, it doesn't have to appear within the parentheses.

As Dickens offered, "It was the best of times, it was the worst of times." (13).

If the data you're citing in your text does not indicate an author, you would cite an abbreviated version of the title of the article. Let's say you were quoting information from a newspaper article, "Nuclear Medicine in the Third World" (Nuclear Medicine...A2). In addition to the abbreviated version of the title, you would offer the section and page number.

The sources you cite within your paper would then be listed on your works cited page in alphabetical order.

The basic order of information included in this bibliographic style is:

BOOKS
Author (last name first)
Title
Place of Publication
Publisher
Date
Pages

ARTICLES
Author
Article Title
Periodical, Journal, Anthology Title
Date of Publication
Pages

The first line of the bibliographic entry is flush left with the margin; each following line for the same entry is indented five spaces.

Examples

Bibliography: A bibliography is an alphabetical list of sources that is placed at the end of the paper.

A BOOK WITH ONE AUTHOR

Sagan, Carl. *The Dragons of Eden.* New York: Ballantine, 1983.

A BOOK WITH TWO OR THREE AUTHORS

Caldicott, Helen, Nancy Herrington, and Nahum Stiskin. *Nuclear Madness: What You Can Do.* Toronto: Bantam, 1982.

A BOOK WITH MORE THAN THREE AUTHORS

Campbell, Ronald Fay, et al. *The Organization and Control of American Schools.* 2nd ed. Columbus, OH: Merrill, 1970.

A BOOK WITH AN EDITOR

Brandeis, Irma, ed. *Discussions of the Divine Comedy.* Boston: Heath, 1961.

ARTICLE IN WEEKLY MAGAZINE (NO AUTHOR)

"Baptism of Fire: the Guerillas Return in Force." *Time.* 12 July 1982: 45.

MONTHLY MAGAZINE

Calvert, Catherine. "The Magical Menagerie of Steiff." *Town and Country.* Dec. 1982: 204+.

   "204 +" means the article is printed on nonconsecutive pages.

DAILY NEWSPAPER (NO AUTHOR)

"Study: Disease Risk Increased by Windsurfing Polluted Waters? *Democrat and Chronicle* (Rochester, NY) 13 July 1986: 13E.

DAILY NEWSPAPER WITH AN AUTHOR

Ingrassia, Paul. "How Many Homers Will Reggie Hit in the Candy League?" *The Wall Street Journal.* 1 Feb. 1978: 1.

BIOGRAPHICAL REFERENCE

"Woolf, Virginia." *Twentieth Century Authors.* 1942.

ENCYCLOPEDIA

Sanderson, Ivan T. "Elephants." *Encyclopedia Americana.* 1984 ed.

ONE WORK FROM A COLLECTION OF WRITING ALL BY THE SAME AUTHOR

Thomas, Lewis. "The Long Habit." *The Lives of a Cell: Notes of a Biology Watcher.* New York: Viking, 1974: 47–52.

ONE AUTHOR'S WRITING IN A COLLECTION OF WRITING BY DIFFERENT AUTHORS.

Conrad, Joseph. "The Secret Sharer." *The Norton Anthology of English Literature.* Ed. M. H. Abrams, et al. 2 vols. New York: Norton, 1968. 2: 1528–61.

SHORT STORIES IN A COLLECTION OF STORIES BY THE SAME AUTHOR

Collette, Sidornie. "The Sick Child." *The Tender Shoot.* Trans. Antonia White. New York: Farrar, 1958: 338–67.

BOOK REVIEW

Culligan, Glendy. "Born Free But Not Liberated: Rev. of *The Female Eunuch,* by Germaine Greer. *Saturday Review.* 5 June 1971: 25 +.

ANNUAL REPORT

Eastman Kodak Company and Subsidiary Companies. *Annual Report, 1985.* Rochester, NY: Eastman Kodak and Subsidiary Companies, 1986.

LECTURE

Wojciechowski, Paul. "The Energy House." Instrument Society of America. Monroe Community College, Rochester, NY. 8 Feb. 1978.

INTERVIEW

Ephron, Nora. Personal interview. 6 July 1986.

PAMPHLET

Jaffe, Natalie. *Public Welfare: Facts, Myths and Prospects.* New York: Public Affairs Committee, 1977.

PAMPHLET WITHOUT PLACE OF PUBLICATION OR DATE

Clearing the Air: A Guide to Quitting Smoking. N.p: U.S. Department of Health, Education and Welfare, n.d.

    N.p. means "no place," n.p. means "no publisher"; n.d. means "no date"; n. pag. means "no page(s)."

CORPORATE AUTHOR

National Council of Teachers of Mathematics. *Insights into Modern Mathematics.* Washington: National Council of Teachers of Mathematics, 1957.

United States Office of Management and Budget. *The Budget of The United States Government Fiscal Year 1984.* Washington: GPO, 1984.

    Unless stated otherwise, most federal publications, regardless of the branch of government, are published by the Government Printing Office (GPO) in Washington, D.C.

RECORDING (SPOKEN)

Chekov, Anton. *Uncle Vanya.* Trans. Constance Garnett. Caedmon, TRS-3-3, 1964.

RECORDING (MUSIC)

Mangione, Chuck. *Main Squeeze.* A & M, SP 4612, 1976.

FILM

An Unmarried Woman. Dir. Paul Mazursky. Twentieth Century-Fox, 1978.

TELEVISION PROGRAM

"The Singer of Tales." *In Search of the Trojan War.* Writ. and narr. Michael Wood. Dir. Bill Lyons. PBS. WXXI, Rochester, NY. 2 June 1986.

AUDIOTAPE

Miller, Arthur. *Death of a Salesman.* Audiotape. Caedmon, A310, 1964.

VIDEOTAPE

"Why Write?" *The Write Course.* Videotape. Developed by the Center for Telecommunication. Dallas County Community College District, 1983. 30 min.

COMPUTER SOFTWARE

SIGI-, 1984-1985. Computer software. Princeton, N J: Educational Testing Service, 1984.

Typeset Example

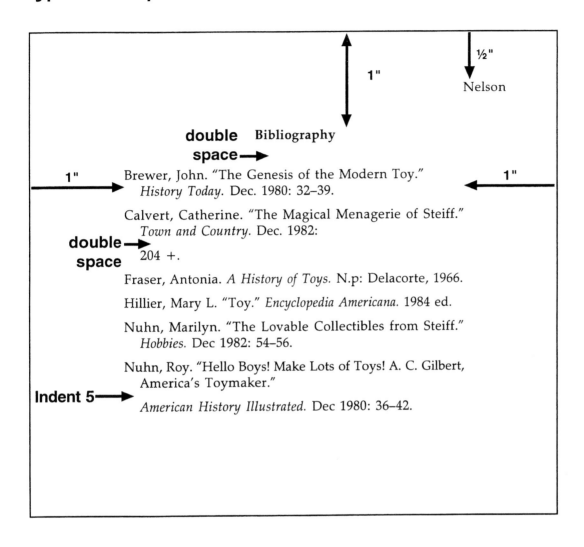

Sources Used

Brusaw, Charles T., Gerald J. Aired, and Waiter E. Oliu. *The Business Writer's Handbook.* New York: St. Martin's, 1982.

Gibaldi, Joseph, and Walter S. Achtert. *MLA Handbook for Writers of Research Papers.* 2nd, ed. New York: Modern Language Association, 1984.

Heffernan, James A.W. and John E. Lincoln. *A Guide to the New MLA Style of Documentation for Users of "Writing—A College Handbook."* New York: Norton, 1984.

Lester, James D. *Writing Research Papers: A Complete Guide.* 4th ed. Glenview, IL: Scott, Foresman, 1984.

Yaggy, Elinor. *How to Write Your Term Paper.* 5th ed. New York: Harper, 1985.

EXERCISES

Choose one of the following two parameters on which to focus your research topic.

1. Identify a significant advance or discovery in your academic discipline or a discipline that interests you outside of your educational pursuits.

    *   Investigate who made it

    *   How it was made

    *   What uses it has

    *   What benefits it offers

    *   What problems it poses

    The advance or discovery should have been made within the past 5 years.

2. Outline the dimensions of a major controversy in communications or medicine that your are, or will become aware of.

    *   What are the key issues involved

    *   What is the history of development

    *   What are the possible outcomes

    The body of your essay is your personal angle on the topic, your specific point to make about it, and your choice of methods (books, periodicals, interviews) in supporting that point. Much of the essay will come from your own ideas and observations. But the support, credibility will come from appropriate quotations, paraphrases, and summaries from outside sources.

    Find 4–6 sources that have some bearing on your topic. Give credit to your sources with parenthetical citations and a bibliography using the MLA format that will be provided to you.

    Length: 5–7 typed pages, plus bibliography page.

    Verbal: in addition to your typed research paper, you will deliver a 8–10 minute oral presentation on your findings to me and the class.

Additional Considerations

FACE TO FACE COMMUNICATION

One of the most difficult tasks in industry is effectively communicating verbally with one or more individuals. Most people can understand and relate to the fear associated with getting up in front of a group and delivering an oral presentation. But speaking with one individual or a small group can often be more difficult.

Most of us probably spend a good portion of our work day talking with colleagues or people outside of our company in an effort to solicit information. We need to speak with others for many different reasons:

- Work related information (we need it to do our jobs).

- Receiving assignments (whether we like it or not, someone tells us what to do).

- Vendors, or professionals outside of the company (you need it by when?).

- Customers (face it, most jobs today are service oriented) want fries with that?

- And many others who may cross our path daily.

It certainly won't do anyone any good if we don't get what we professionally require from others. Ensuring that we are successful in our efforts might not be as difficult as we might imagine. As stated earlier, the Human Factor is something to keep in mind.

People Have Good Days, Bad Days; Likes and Dislikes

But it's also important to appreciate what motivates people to communicate willing and positively; for that matter, what just basically motives people. There are certainly many different ways to motivate individuals.

We've all been motivated to do our homework when we were in school. We did our homework because we didn't want to get a poor grade; we wanted to pass. The higher the grade, the better we felt

For those of us who played organized sports growing up, we were motivated to play our best in order to win. Winning is good; it makes us and others proud.

We've all been motivated to please our parents, most of the time anyway. Praise from a parent is very important to self esteem.

Most people are quite motivated to do a good job at work. Everyone wants to receive raises, get promotions, be recognized by our colleagues for performance. It's human nature.

Unfortunately, particularly in our society, recognition often comes as criticism for not doing what's expected of us. This results in negative motivation.

Sure, we may behave in school because we don't want to get yelled at, not because we've been convinced or many times even informed of proper behavior.

Consider this: A four year-old has been playing quietly in the family room for a period of time. He's not making a mess, puts toys away when finished, is even being creative in his playing. But no one says anything to him. No one praises him for behaving in what can be considered a preferable manner. He's not learning that's he's acting appropriately. Suddenly he accidently spills his glass of Ovaltine.

He's immediately recognized and often chastised for not being more careful. He may even get into trouble for his mistake. What does he learn from this? Unfortunately he learns that he will be noticed and addressed when he does something that he perceives as wrong. He will be encouraged to act based on a negative response.

This attitude often carries over to school as well as to the work place.

Perform as Expected to Stay Out of Trouble

I had a boss in the private sector once who would basically manage by using intimidation—negative motivational management. This individual would keep her employees on their toes by basically making them afraid.

Sure most of the workers made an effort to do a good job, but not out of pride for their work or loyalty to the company; they performed effectively so they wouldn't get into trouble. I vividly recall her yelling at people on many occasions. This would accomplish two of her goals.

1. Put the employee on notice.

2. Put everyone within earshot on notice.

Do what I want you to do and the way I want it done or else. Sure, it might have been effective to a degree, but it was effective for the wrong reasons. Often in these situations, workers would make the minimal effort just to avoid hassle. This is obviously a negative way to motivate people. So what's the solution to this problem?

Positive Motivation

Sure, not a profound revelation, but facts are facts. Praise a kid for doing well in school and they'll probably strive to continue to do well. It's about figuring out what motivates people; what people want.

There are basically two things people want in regards to motivation. The first is reward. Most people are willing to do almost anything, within reason of course, if the reward is big enough.

Consider this: Many things in life are figuratively considered painful. It often depends on the situation and the individual.

School

Work

Standing in line

Relationships at times

Driving

Housework

As an educator, I don't necessarily like to admit it, but some students don't like being in school. It's a pain for them to get up in the morning, drive to school, go to class, prepared or not, and sit there for 50 minutes or so. So why do they do it? They do it because there is a reward to be had for their efforts. A grade and eventually credit for the course. And the size of the reward, the grade, is associated directly with their efforts. The more pain they put up with, studying, homework, the larger the reward will probably be.

Of course students recognize the reward of knowledge, but sometimes, at least when we're younger, that isn't quite enough. I once asked a 15 week, three credit class if they would still come all the time if the course only offered one credit? The majority of them said that they wouldn't, probably wouldn't have even signed up for the course. There wouldn't have been enough of a reward for 15 weeks of effort, or pain.

Often, the amount of pain is directly associated with the size of the reward. Consider the professions. To become a doctor, an individual must go to school for a long time—eight years of college, internship and so on. So, with that degree of pain, the reward has to be worth it. That's one reason doctors make the money they do.

Education, pain, provides choices directly associated with the amount. Think about it. How many choices does a person have with only a high school diploma? Their pain was limited, therefore their professional choices are equally limited. It's all about reward.

The amount of money one makes certainly isn't the only type of professional reward. Many people get satisfaction in the job itself. Why do people who collect your garbage make more money than nurses?

Collecting garbage doesn't have a lot of job satisfaction associated with it. Unless you find some good stuff on the curb. So the reward at the end of the effort has to be large enough to compensate for the pain. Nurses make less because part of the reward is in the effort itself. Again, most people will deal with almost anything as long as the reward is larger than the pain.

REWARD IN THE WORKPLACE

Reward can also be considered when trying to understand what encourages people to be cooperative in the professional environment. Obviously, the money we make for the job we do is probably one of the primary rewards we receive. But it isn't necessarily the only reward available. Often, job satisfaction is in itself an important reward. Other work-related rewards could include:

- Praise, recognition
- Promotion
- Coveted assignments
- A corner office with a window

- Successful efforts
- Prime parking spot
- People knowing who you are
- Respect

The point here is, knowing that reward motivates people to cooperate can assist the professional in doing his job more effectively. There are many ways this theory can be applied; just being aware of it is the first step.

Feeling Important

Feeling important is the second thing that motivates most people to be cooperative and serve particular purposes. Remember the kid who spilled his milk and got yelled at? Well had he been praised for playing so quietly instead of getting in trouble he would have been made to feel important and understand we're recognized as important for cooperating. It all ties in: pain and reward, and feeling important.

As children, we all dream of being famous. Little boys often hope to be a great sports star, or an astronaut. Little girls dream of fame on the stage, or being an astronaut. Why? These people are loved by millions; regarded as very important. It makes us feel good to be recognized and respected; we seek it out.

Why else would seemingly ordinary people want to go on all of these talk shows currently being offered and discuss the personal aspects of their lives. Well maybe they're not quite that ordinary. Some of the topics border on the ridiculous. Why do they do it? They do it because it is probably the only opportunity they've had to become important, even if only for a moment. Think about it. They get flown first class to a major city; get put up in a nice hotel; get driven around in limo's and are basically treated as though they are important. Why? The producers want to guarantee that they will appear and will discuss what they promised to discuss no matter what anyone may think. Some people are just desperate to feel important.

There are certainly positive ways we can help others to feel important.

This helps to establish a rapport for better and more positive communication. You assist people in feeling important and you motivate them to be cooperative.

- ✔ Use a person's name when you speak to them.
- ✔ Smile, make eye contact.
- ✔ Praise them for prior efforts.
- ✔ Be positive. Give the you approach.
- ✔ Give credit.
- ✔ Seek their advice.

Remember, the key here is that we all want to feel important in all aspects of our lives. It is particularly so in our professional lives. Understand and appreciate that the people you work with, communicate with, want to feel important just as much as you. With that in mind and practiced, motivation and positive communication can be the only result.

ORAL PRESENTATIONS

You've been talking most of your life; by now you should be an expert at it. So why are you so reluctant to get in front of a group of people and give a presentation?

It's been reported that Americans fear speaking in public more than they fear heights, bugs, or death. Sure, most of us can appreciate why people would like to avoid speaking in public—it creates a lot of stress; don't forget the fear. Logically, what's the worst thing that could happen? No, forgetting your material or having the audience laugh at you aren't the worst things that could happen. The worst thing that could happen is that you'd wet your pants and have a heart attack. I've never heard of anyone having the worst thing happen to them when speaking in public.

Lots of people speak in public; many are even quite good at it. They weren't born with the ability; they learned it through experience and practice. The more you do something, the better you get at it.

I remember the first time I had to speak before a group. I was in college and had to give an oral presentation in front of my art history class. I was a nervous wreck for two weeks leading up to presentation day. I came up with dozens of excuses why I shouldn't, or didn't have to do it. Of course, none of them were legitimate. If someone would have offered me a valium on the day of the presentation, I probably would have taken it. Thank goodness no one did because I did fine, I think.

I don't remember much of that presentation other than I did get through it and the audience did applaud at the end. Once I got to the podium and began speaking it went relatively well, because I knew my material. My nervousness didn't get in the way of presenting the information. Thankfully, I did enough preparation to know my topic and present the data to the audience.

Speaking on the Job

The more responsible your position, the more you'll be called upon to express your ideas orally, and the more important it will be for you to present information effectively. It's all about communicating, and talking is communicating.

It's a Performance

- Stage Fright—It can be natural and beneficial. Accept the tension as a normal reaction, like any normal anxiety prior to the testing of our abilities.
- Plan—It's essential to create a positive attitude about your presentation—planning helps you to understand the importance of your information.
- Rehearse—Practice your presentation in front of friends and family, before a mirror, or with a tape recorder. Get comfortable with it.
- Appearance—What you wear and how you look creates a favorable impression upon the audience.
- Begin and End Strong—Your introduction should be as audience grabbing as you can make it. Your conclusion should be forceful and memorable. Remember, it's often how you finish that counts the most.

Planning the Presentation

- Establish your statement of purpose for the presentation.
- Outline the material for the presentation.
- Prepare the introduction, body and conclusion with the audience in mind.

By developing a statement of purpose you narrow your topic to meet the needs of your audience. Establish your intent also by determining whether you want to amuse, persuade or inform. By doing a preliminary outline, you give yourself the opportunity to make changes throughout the process. You can determine the organization of your presentation and the information you want to include.

Organization

Your oral presentation organization can often follow the outline of a written report. There are basically three things you want the introduction to accomplish in your oral presentation.

- Attract the attention of your audience, get them interested and involved.
- Establish your image and style to make sure your audience is comfortable.
- Clearly indicate the focus of the presentation and the related points to be covered.

The body of the presentation can pretty much follow the organization of a written report, but you need to hold the interest of your audience.

Hold Their Attention

Once you get your audience all fired up with the introduction to your presentation, it's important to hold their attention throughout. Once you've got them, don't lose them.

- Look at your audience—let them know you know they are there. There's no presentation as boring as the one given by an individual who just reads from notes. Let the audience know that you are interested enough in the topic to have some of it committed to memory.
- Make eye contact—make contact with selected members of the audience. Eye contact keeps the presentation lively. Choose audience members who have friendly faces or are smiling. Don't look at the ever present sourpuss who shows up at every presentation. Looking at them will just throw you off your pace.
- Hand gestures—use them sparingly and only to emphasize a point. Animated hand gestures may take the audience's attention off what you're saying and focus on your hands.

The conclusion to your presentation should basically pull all of the elements together, reiterate briefly what you've told them and summarize. Again, end strong and the presentation will be remembered.

Types of Oral Presentations

- Informative—probably the most common type of presentation. You are, in essence, educating here.
- Persuasive—you're trying to sell something here, get your audience to agree with you.

- Special Occasions—here you could be dealing with everything from retirement dinners to corporate get-togethers.
- Impromptu—here you don't have a lot of time to prepare. You're called upon to give a speech, generally, because of your knowledge and presence.

The best way to deliver an effective presentation is to know the topic you will speak on and to prepare. Use whatever nervousness may exist to your advantage to create the energy required to give an oral presentation. If you would have asked me twenty some years ago when I was anticipating my first oral presentation if I thought I could do it for a living someday, I would have said, heck no. Well here I am doing it every day in the classroom with little difficulty. Does the anxiety ever go away? I don't think it does for most people. When I'm about to give a presentation to members of industry or other specialized groups, I still get nervous. But I know the key is preparation—know your subject and how you'll present it.

SURVIVING and SUCCEEDING in INDUSTRY

Remember the Human Factor? Being aware of this as you embark upon your career path will lead you to success. Understanding people and their needs is directly related to success.

One of the primary things most people want out of life is to feel important. Let others know that you regard them as important for who they are and for their efforts, and they will more than appreciate it. That's the primary way to influence people. Be sincere and honest, and it will pay off. Most people recognize insincere praise as shallow. Be honest, and let others know what you appreciate.

- Don't criticize, condemn or complain.
- Give honest, sincere appreciation.
- Arouse in others an eager desire to succeed.
- Encourage others, don't fault them.
- Call attention to mistakes indirectly, begin with your own.
- Talk in terms of other's interests—make them feel important.
- Don't give orders or make demands, ask questions.
- Praise and encourage, don't argue.
- Look at people when you talk with them—be a good listener.
- Smile.

Everyone has his or her own needs they want met. The closer you can come to helping people meet their needs, the more professionally you'll be regarded with respect and credibility. Be known for your cooperativeness, not for your difficulty to get along with. Respect others and they will respect you. Remember, we're all in this together, so why not make it work for everyone, not just the few.

CONTINUED STUDY

With the constantly increasing need for effective communicators in industry comes the need for communicators whose skills transcend those acquired in a single course. Although what's contained in here is a very good start when it comes to how to apply theory in the workplace, it certainly can't cover everything. Explore beyond the boundaries of what's required. Take advantage of any and all opportunities to increase your skills as a communicator. You don't have to aspire to professional writing; it's okay if you do, there are lots of opportunities out there for professional writers. Just aspire to be the best you can be in whatever you choose to do. And part of what will lead to your success is the ability to communicate. Remember, THE ABILITY TO COMMUNICATE DOUBLES YOUR VALUE TO YOUR EMPLOYER.

Take advantage of this beginning and explore the other areas of interest relating to writing for industry. Take an in-depth look at what else may prove valuable to your success as a communicator. There are a wide variety of sources available to study for increased understanding. Although we have touched upon many of the important elements of effective professional communication in industry, we certainly couldn't give every area the in-depth treatment a second or third course could. What else is available, what other areas you can discover is limited only by your commitment.

- Instruction Design Principles
- Document Design
- Designing Manuals
- Scientific Reports and Journal Articles
- News Releases and Brochures
- Audiovisual Presentations

These are some of the advanced communication skills required by industry today. And the list for the serious communicator can go on.

- Promotional Writing
- Project Management

Basic courses in professional writing just don't have the time to go into the depth required to address some of the advanced aspects of communicating in industry. If the interest is there, we can take it upon ourselves to explore the more advanced areas. Most introductory courses in professional writing can prepare us to communicate in industry. It is where the need for advanced communication courses can be anticipated for the engineer or professional writer that additional courses can build upon the basic concepts to better prepare for success.

Additional Examples of Professional Documentation

MATERIAL STANDARD

Standards are generally the authoritative source of information for promoting uniformity and economy in industrial design and manufacture. They are used when selecting material for a new design, product, or alteration. They include preferred materials judged most suitable for a particular industry's manufacturing. The following example deals with sheet metal

Sheet-250	Sheet	55527
Aluminum Alloy, 5756, Sheet: Annealed (Special Tolerance)		

USAGE

Sheet-250 is a bright, corrosion-resistant aluminum alloy material that is suitable for making nameplates.

This material has special thickness tolerances that are compatible with the Coin-Paint-Mill (CPM) process used to make nameplates.

HOW TO SPECIFY

Specify thickness, thickness tolerance, specification number and material.

EXAMPLE

.016 + .000, Sheet-250, Aluminum Sheet
     – .001

TYPICAL PROPERTIES

Modules of Elasticity	10,000 ksi
Hardness	28HB
Basic Chemistry	0.60% to 1.00% Mg, 0.08% Si max, 0.10% Fe max, 0.10% Cu max, 0.03% Mn max, 0.03% Zn max, Balance Al
Tensile Strength	16 ksi
Yield Point	6 ksi
Yield Strength (0.2% offset)	-
Elongation (2 in)	2.0%
Specific Gravity	2.70
Density lbs per in^3	-
Electrical Conductivity	45.0% IACS
Electrical Resistivity	-
Magnetism	No response
Thermal Conductivity: Btu. ft/hr. ft^2. °F	97.0
Thermal Expansion: in/in/ °F (320 to 2120F)	13.2 x 10 -6

PROCESSING DATA

Corrosion Resistance	Good
Machining	Poor
Blanking	Fair
Forming	180, flat
Drawing	Deep
Welding	Good
Silver Brazing	No
Soft Soldering	No
Copper Brazing	No
Hardening	Not pardonable
Finishing (Coatings)	Anodize, anodize and dye, organic finished, plate (most metals)

STANDARD THICKNESS (INCH)

.016+ .000/– .001

.020+ .000/– .001

STANDARD SHEET SIZE (INCH)

Coiled sheet widths used are 3 ½ inches, 4 ½ inches, and 6 inches

GOVERNMENT SPECIFICATIONS

Information is not available

And that is an example of the information contained in a material standard. It obviously doesn't offer a lot of room for creativity, but then again its intent is to inform, not entertain. The material standard is one of the basic writing tasks a professional writer is expected to be able to perform. The primary challenge here is correct research and organization. The information has to be exact. There is no room for error.

DATA SHEETS

Product and manufacturing data sheets are also fast becoming one of industry's most viable ways to communicate. They offer information and data aimed, generally, at the experienced manufacturer searching for better or alternative services and processes. They too require care, thought, research and interviewing. Data are, basically, items of information presented for analysis, or required for making a decision. The following is an example of a data sheet.

SURFACE MOUNT TECHNOLOGY
BY ELECTRICAL ASSEMBLY

Surface mount technology is up and running at Buildrite. Our knowledge and expertise are supported by over five years of concentrated experience. Our organization is firmly established and eager to serve your surface mount assembly needs. Electronic Assembly's 5600-foot production facility is equipped with the automation and flexibility required to deliver your job professionally and at a competitive cost.

Buildrite Electronic Assembly is a consolidation of experienced personnel committed to the application of surface mount technology. As an organization, our goals include maintaining the highest quality service available. As these efforts are directed toward a positive conclusion, the entire process is monitored by a host computer system. Our organization is devoted to close customer service, and that service is supported by the considerable resources of Buildrite Company.

Services Offered Include:
* Computer-aided design layout
* Worldwide component sourcing
* Low, medium and high volume production
* Automated testing

Some of Our SMT Production equipment:
* 1505—Printer
* DYNAPERT MPS500—Placement
* SANYO TCM40—Placement
* VITRONICS SMD718—IR Oven
* CORPANE VP18—In-Line Vaport Phase system
* DETREX—Solvent Cleaner
* HOLLIS GBS 11—Dual Wave Solder
* HEWLETT PACKARD—Host Computer

For More Information Call or Write:
Ted Wally–Buildrite Company
555-1111

CORPORATE ANNOUNCEMENT

A corporate announcement takes as much care and thought as a procedure or material standard. There are few professional writing tasks that don't involve some kind of research, and this example is no exception. The information has to be totally accurate and reliable.

The following is an example of a corporate announcement.

TO: Customers of Product Development and Manufacturing
FROM: Lawrence Mondello, Superintendent, Product Development and
           Manufacturing
SUBJECT: New Department Numbers

Our new departments are now in place and functioning smoothly. Our recent reorganization has made us better able to serve your entire product development needs. This letter with the attachment is meant to make you aware of our new department numbers and provide some phone numbers. We also want to give you a closer look at the range of services we can provide.

We welcome your continued support.

DEPARTMENT	DEPARTMENT NUMBER	DEPARTMENT	PHONE
Business Operations & Engineering	270	James Monroe	22725
Mechanization & Custom Products	199	Fletcher Smith	29947
Special Machining	302	Ward Haskell	11239
Electronics Development & Manufacturing	978	Ed Cleaver	87456

A seemingly simple document, maybe, but one the practicing technical writer is quite familiar with.

BROCHURE

The brochure is fast becoming one of the most important communication outlets for industry today. Its function is, basically, to provide information and entice prospective customers into utilizing services. Again, the information has to be accurate and reliable. There is often extensive research involved as well as interviewing.

The following is an example of a page that might be found in an industrial brochure.

The Engineering Service Department provides important services to the Custom Products Manufacturing Model Shop. In that effort, it links each of our areas, forming a cohesive whole to better serve our customers. The support here is concrete and goal-oriented.

- We provide open lines of communication between the engineer and shop.
- We serve the customer and the job with the preparation of paper, stock, and hardware.
- Our preliminary evaluations provide for more accurate estimating
- We have the flexibility to purchase special items and material.

- Our experience in organization allows for the stocking of all finished parts and subsequent release for assembly.
- Our tool crib helps maintain the sustained operation of the shop.
- Our floor control procedures were one of the first to be computerized.
- We maintain strict control on all jobs subcontracted to vendors, and monitor their progress and performance.

This particular page from a brochure would have to support and complement the entire publication. Besides the research and interviewing involved here, a professional writer would also coordinate organization, brochure design, illustrations and photographs, typesetting, and publication.

MEMORANDUM

TO: Dr. Douglas Brooks, Vice President, Curriculum & Program Development
FROM: Cheryl Confarotta, Cooperative & Experiential Learning Office
SUBJECT: Proposal For Membership in the National Society for Experiential Education
DATE: April 1,

Introduction

At your request, I have done some exploration and research into publications that will assist us here in the Cooperative & Experiential Learning Office to better serve our students, to stay abreast of the changing environment in the experiential education field, and to advance experiential learning on campus here at MCC.

Proposal

After considerable research, I would recommend the *NSEE Quarterly* to be the publication of choice. *NSEE Quarterly* is published by the National Society for Experiential Education located in Raleigh, North Carolina. It is published four times yearly—winter, spring, summer, and fall. The *NSEE Quarterly* is available only to members of the National Society for Experiential Education; a subscription to this publication cannot be purchased separately. An individual membership is $75 yearly. The circulation is to over 2,000 members of this professional organization.

Support/Background

After careful review of several issues of this periodical, I found each issue to contain three recurring sections which I feel could be a timely source for future development of our department.

- *BOOK REVIEW SECTION*
  The purpose of this section is to review published books that relate to experiential learning.
  In the Spring,   issue, the book *Sit Down. Be Quiet. Pay Attention.* by Robert L. Sigmon was reviewed. This book relates the phrase sit down, be quiet, pay attention to service-learning and community service as well as all other aspects of experiential education programming.

- *PROFESSIONAL DEVELOPMENT CALENDAR*
  This area announces conferences and/or workshops throughout the country related to experiential education.

- *PUBLICATIONS AND RESOURCES*

This section lists by topic publications and resources pertinent to all areas of experiential learning. Also, there is a synopsis of each item listed, where it can be purchased, and the cost of the publication.

I feel that the *NSEE Quarterly* will prove to be a useful tool for our department for other reasons as well. All the articles are well-written, very informative, and can provide us with valuable experiential learning information. This publication contains a wide variety of articles encompassing all areas of experiential learning. One type of article I saw in several issues was a report on other experiential learning programs currently in place in different cities and/or colleges throughout the country. The Winter, 1995 issue reports on the establishment and results of the Fall, 1992 experiment in higher education undertaken at the University of Richmond with the establishment of the Jepson School of Leadership Studies. The statement "Experiential education is an essential element in the innovation and improvement that the Jepson School pursues" summarizes the concept behind the program.

Conclusion

In conclusion, I recommend that we become members of the National Society for Experiential Education in order for us to receive the *NSEE Quarterly*. In addition to regularly receiving this publication, membership will entitle us to receive other important and useful benefits for our office. Included among these other benefits are the following:

- a *Membership Directory* to assist you in maintaining contact with colleagues around the country.
- discounts on NSEE publications and NSEE resource materials.
- reduced registration fees at the NSEE National Conference.
- participation in NSEE Special Interest Groups and Committees.
- opportunities for participation in special projects.
- discounts on NSEE's consulting services.
- full voting privileges as well as eligibility for election or appointment to the NSEE Board of Directors.

In comparison shopping of other professional organizations involved in this area of education that would provide a publication of the NSEE type, I found the $75 membership fee to be quite reasonable. Most other professional organizations' membership fees averaged $100–$120 a year. I feel the benefits our department will acquire from this investment will far outweigh the cost.

If you have any questions or would care to discuss this proposal, please give me a call and we can set a time to meet that is convenient for you.

BROOKS AND ASSOCIATES, CPA'S
Interoffice Memo

To: Douglas Brooks
From: Patrick Michael
Subject: Proposal to subscribe to the *Journal of Accountancy*
Date: March 25,

Statement of Problem

In order to provide our clients with the finest professional service our employees must stay informed of the latest changes in accounting. This is most important in the ever changing area of tax accounting which comprises a majority of our practice.

Proposed Solution

Subscriptions to the *Journal of Accountancy* would be a useful component of a continuing education program for our employees.

Supporting Data

The *Journal of Accountancy* (JOA) is a monthly publication of the American Institute of Certified Public Accountants, Inc. (AICPA). I researched several publications that cater to accounting professionals and found JOA was best suited to meeting our needs.

Every month the JOA has articles and recurring columns on a wide range of subjects with an emphasis on tax accounting. Each issue has four recurring columns that deal with tax issues:

- Tax Matters—contains updates and news releases from the IRS. The updates and news items would be very helpful in keeping our employees abreast of recent IRS technical advice memoranda, announcements and proposed changes to the tax law.

- Tax Briefs—details IRS rulings and court decisions that affect corporate, small business and individual taxes. At the conclusion of each piece the author offers his or her observations and analysis of the ruling clearing up some of the gray areas created by the decisions/rulings.

- Small Business Tax Solutions—answers questions involving tax procedures for small businesses. This column would be of particular interest as our number of small business clients keeps growing.

- From The Tax Advisor—reprint of recent articles published in The Tax Advisor on a wide range of tax topics.

In addition to these recurring columns the JOA generally has at least one full length article that deals with tax matters. Recent issues included articles on tax reform, how organizational form affects tax liability and tax consequences of family loans. The JOA's full-length articles have two unique features I found to be very useful.

The first feature is the "Executive Summary." This summary highlights the major points in the article and lists the credentials of the author, most of whom have post graduate degrees in accounting and/or law. This feature is printed in a shaded box making it easy to find. This feature is a great time saver as it allows the reader to skip articles that have no interest to them and by being aware of the article's main points the reader can read the article quicker without sacrificing comprehension.

The second useful feature is a case study of the material presented in the article. Most full-length articles, and all articles involving tax matters, have the case study. Practicing CPAs give their opinions and shows how the material discussed in the articles relates to the real world.

The JOA also focuses on other areas of the accounting profession that are changing, such as:

* The use of computers and technology in accounting. The JOA has a continuing series of articles called "CPA 2000" that reports on areas such as accounting software, computer systems and communication technology. Staying on top of the technological advances can help the firm be more productive.

* A review of recent court decisions that affect the liabilities and responsibilities imposed by case law. This column can help minimize the possibility of malpractice suits being filed against the firm.

* Discussions of current events and how they could effect the financial world and the accounting profession.

Recommendation

I recommend the firm purchase five subscriptions to the *Journal of Accountancy* and make the copies available to all the employees. Five subscriptions will ensure our employees will have access to this information in a timely manner. The JOA has much to offer and at a cost of $56.00 a year per subscription the benefits far outweigh the cost.

PATRICK W. MICHAEL

266 Blackwell Lane
Henrietta, NY 14467
(716) 334-8758

February 20,

Elizabeth H. Riley, Director
Monroe County Department of Human Resources
39 West Main Street-Room 210
Rochester, New York 14614

Dear Elizabeth Riley:

On February 18,   First Assistant District Attorney Richard Keenan informed me of the job announcement for the position of Confidential Homicide Coordinator with the Monroe County District Attorney's Office. This sounds like an exciting, challenging position and I would like to be considered. I believe you will find my combination of experience and education make me well suited for this position.

During my twelve years with the Monroe County Sheriff's Department I have learned first hand how important it is to properly handle physical evidence. How evidence is handled and documented can mean the difference between winning and losing cases. Through my combination of hands-on experience and education I have learned how to correctly collect, preserve and present evidence to ensure it passes the scrutiny of the court.

My experience with the Sheriff's Department includes:

- Investigating thousands of crimes.
- Locating, collecting, documenting and securing hundreds of pieces of physical evidence.
- Testifying at hundreds of trials, hearings and other judicial proceedings.

In addition to my experience I have earned an A.A.S. degree in Criminal Justice-Police Science from Monroe Community College. I have also completed numerous courses at the Regional Criminal Justice Training Center. These courses include:

- Crime Scene Photography
- Crime Scene Management
- Evidence Collection Procedures
- Criminal Investigation Procedures
- Interview and Interrogation
- Basic Fingerprint

I feel this combination of experience and education would ensure my success in this position. I have enclosed my resume for your review. I will call you on February 28,   at 11:00 AM to determine your interest and, if appropriate, arrange for an interview. I thank you for your time and consideration. If you have any questions please call me at (716) 334-8758.

Sincerely,

Patrick Michael

pwm
Enclosure

PATRICK W. MICHAEL SR.

266 Blackwell Lane
Henrietta, NY 14467

October 15,

Dr. Seymour Schwartz, DDS
1000 Dewey Avenue
Rochester, NY 14612

Dear Dr. Schwartz:

Recently my long-time dentist, Dr. Yankem, retired and referred me to your office. On October 12, 1995 I had a 1:00 P.M. appointment with you for an exam. The appointment was to last one hour, however I did not leave your office until after 3:00 P.M. This delay caused me problems at work and additional expense.

I am the Store Manager at PayLess Shoes in Northgate Plaza and had made arrangements for Al Bundy, the Assistant Manager, to cover for me while I was at your office. I arrived at 12:50 P.M., 10 minutes early, but was not taken back to the examination room until 1:20 P.M. During the exam you found a cavity and offered to fill it at that time. I explained to you that I had to be back to the store by 2:00 P.M. as Mr. Bundy had to leave at that time. You assured me you would be done with time to spare. Due to an allergy to Novocain I was rendered unconscious with nitrous oxide. While you were filling the one cavity you found eight more cavities and decided to fill them at that time. I did not leave your office until after 3:00 P.M. and did not get back to the store until almost 4:00 P.M.

To make matters even worse, when I returned to my car I found I had received a parking ticket for overtime parking. I had parked in a metered spot and had deposited a sufficient amount of money into the meter for one and half hours, more than enough time for my appointment.

Things continued to go downhill when I returned to work. I was greeted by a very upset District Manager (Joyce VanStringy) who was making a surprise visit to the store. I was reprimanded for not returning to the store at 2:00 P.M., thereby leaving a clerk in charge of the store. A letter was placed in my personnel file and she also docked me for the two hours I was late returning to the store.

I understand the added difficulty and risk involved when using nitrous oxide and can appreciate your decision to fill the other cavities at that time. However, I did make you aware of my need to return to my store by 2:00 P.M. Your unilateral decision to fill the other cavities has caused me much stress and added expense.

I would like to be reimbursed for the $20.00 parking ticket I received and for the two hours of pay I was docked ($18.00 per hour), for a total of $56.00. I would also like you to send a letter to my District Manager, Joyce VanStringy, explaining that my late return to the store was due to circumstances beyond my control. The letter can be sent to Ms. VanStringy at PayLess Shoes District Office, 1123 Filmore Avenue, Buffalo NY 14321. Thank you for your attention to this matter and I look forward to your speedy response.

Sincerely,

Patrick Michael

LAURIE A. ALIANELL

73 Wyndham Road
Rochester, NY 14612
716/722-4537 (w)
716/581-0843 (h)

WORK HISTORY:

3/93 – Present **Eastman Kodak Company**
Rochester, NY
Title: Secretary to the Director of Finance
Responsibilities: Provide secretarial support for the Director of Finance, 4 Supervisors, and 15 Financial Analysts. Schedule meetings and travel, maintain calendars and attendance records. Submit, track, and maintain the department budget. Distribution of all financial reports (electronic and hard copy). Maintain Research Accounting Manual, backup for PROJCARD, Corporate Close, Opening/Closing of EWOs, and closing TMS Level 2 & 3.
Special Skills: Government Rates Administrator, RDIMS Administrator, Division Records Management Coordinator, Division Chairman United Way Campaign, Core Team member of KNECT (Kodak-News-Education-Communications-Team). Computer Skills: Macintosh (Excel, Microsoft Word, MacDraw, MacPaint), McCormick & Dodge and General Ledger financial system, Lotus 1-2-3, MS DOS, "Documents" (EKPROFS) and OARS.
Courses: Introduction to SAS, 10X, 6 Sigma, and Leadership in a Diverse Workforce.
Awards: Special Recognition (KNECT) — Team Achievement Awards

8/90 – 3/93 **Eastman Kodak Company**
Rochester, New York
Title: Laboratory Secretary (Labs 756, 795, 797)
Responsibilities: Provided secretarial support for 2 Laboratory Heads and 175 Technicians in the MCED laboratories. Scheduled meetings and travel, maintained calendars and attendance records. Tracked capital assets, suggestions, and film distribution and allotment. Processed employee transfers and office moves.
Special Skills: PNSpread and PROJCARD
Courses: QLP, Excel, Hard Disk Management, Lotus 1-2-3, MS DOS, MacDraw, Microsoft Word, "Documents" (EKPROFS)

9/89 – 8/90 **St. Mary's Hospital**
Rochester, New York
Title: Administrative Secretary — Director of Emergency
Responsibilities: Provided secretarial support to the Director of the Emergency Department. Scheduled meetings and maintain calendar. Created and updated spreadsheet tracking patients admitted to emergency on monthly basis. Process time cards for the Emergency Department nurses. Scheduled training classes for BLS, CPR, and BTLS.

8/82 – 9/89 **United Way of Greater Rochester**
Rochester, New York
Title: Secretary — Communications Department
Responsibilities: Provided secretarial support to the Director of Communications and 5 Writers. Scheduled meetings and maintain calendars. Tracked the departmental budget. Set up for all campaign meetings. Inventory and ordering of office supplies, awards/special recognition, and campaign materials.

EDUCATION:

1/96 – **Present** A.A.S., Computer Information Systems, Monroe Community College, Rochester, NY, expected graduation 1999
8/80 – 5/82 A.A.S., Secretarial Science, SUNY Canton ATC, Canton, NY 1982

PROFESSIONAL PORTFOLIO & REFERENCES AVAILABLE UPON REQUEST

Additional Examples of Professional Documentation   **229**

AROUND THE WORLD TRAVEL
Interoffice Memo

TO: Douglas Brooks
            President
FROM: Laurie Alianell
            Sales Manager
SUBJECT: Proposal For Magazine Subscription
DATE: March 25,

Purpose

The purpose of this memo is to recommend that Around The World Travel subscribe to *Travel Holiday* magazine.

Background

For the past three years, year-end sales and earnings for Around The World Travel have remained constant. There has been no decrease nor increase in sales and earnings over this period of time.

Proposal

I would like to implement the policy of Around The World Travel subscribing to *Travel Holiday*. To do this effectively, we should order a total of 12 subscriptions. One for each department. After researching available travel magazines at the library, I have selected *Travel Holiday* as the magazine that will best serve our needs at Around the World Travel. *Travel Holiday* offers a wide variety of travel news and tips in every issue. Listed below are a few examples of what you will find in each issue of *Travel Holiday*.

- Five feature stories on travel to a specific city, state or country. We can use this information to build a library on travel to specific areas. This will give us additional information to provide to customers traveling to these locations.

- "What's On Your Mind?" — Poses questions to readers on a specific topic. The best 15 answers are published in the magazine. (I.e., What's the biggest rip-off of travel? Where in the world is your favorite island getaway?) Since the traveler is our customer, this will benefit our agency because we will be receiving direct input from our customers on what their likes and dislikes are.

- "Travel Adviser" — Recommends vacations for those seeking a peaceful vacations, off-season travel, early spring getaways, fall foliage "Autumn's Best Package," and other topics of this nature. This can be used in the same aspect as the feature stories are used to be included in the library.

- Health Tips — Gives a listing of phone numbers to call regarding questions on health. (I.e., traveling with oxygen, English speaking doctors overseas, traveling with a disability, etc.) This will allow us to better serve our customers with disabilities, overseas travelers, etc.

- "Globetrotter's Indispensable Index" — A listing of approximately 25 destinations and gives information on the following for each destination:

  Best way in (bus, train, etc.)/hotel $/dinner $/water yes or no/local beer $/Big Mac/ postcard home, gas (gallon) $/per diem/weather now/before you go (books to read, movies to watch)/favorite food/spot light/book store/don't miss/best buy.

  As with the "Travel Adviser" and the feature stores, this is just another piece of information we can supply to our customer. The more information we are able to give them on their location of travel, the more satisfied they will be. The more satisfied the customer is, the longer they will continue to be a customer and recommend our agency to others. The outcome will be increased productivity.

These are just to name a few of the interesting articles you'll find in *Travel Holiday*. 95% of the magazine contains information on travel. There are very few advertisements.

Some of the other magazines I considered but rejected were *Cruise Trade, Travel Weekly* and *National Geographic Traveler*. I found *Cruise Trade* to be too limited. As the title reads, it only discussed travel by cruises and contained many advertisements. *Travel Weekly* had no articles on travel itself. It's main focus was on corporate issues around travel. It was more of a travel industry magazine. *National Geographic Traveler* is only issued bi-monthly and is more expensive.

Budget

Travel Holiday is a monthly publication costing $2.50 per issue. The total cost for 12, one year, subscriptions would be $360.00 less a 10% group discount of $36.00. Resulting in a total cost of $324.00.

Conclusion

Not only is *Travel Holiday* available in magazine form, but also on the Internet. *Travel Holiday* resides on the Internet as *Cyber Travel*. Since our travel agency already subscribes to the Internet, this magazine could now be accessed by each employee via this route. It is my recommendation that Around The World Travel subscribe to *Travel Holiday* for a one year trial period. It's my belief that subscribing to this magazine will increase productivity, which will, in turn, increase sales and earnings. If you would like to discuss this further, please feel free to contact me.

Example

73 Wyndham Road
Rochester, NY 14612
March 4,

Wegman's Corporation
Mr. Daniel Wegman
1500 Brooks Avenue
Rochester, NY 14624

Dear Mr. Wegman:

On Sunday, March 3, 1996, I was doing my weekly shopping at your Driving Park Wegman's and the following situation occurred. Two of the items I purchased were chicken salad, from your deli, and a brick of cheddar cheese. When I returned home, I discovered that the cheese I'd purchased had a "remove from shelf" date of three months ago. In addition to this, my chicken salad was spoiled.

Immediately I packed up the cheese and salad and returned to the store. However, I could not locate my sales receipt at this time. With the excellent reputation Wegman's has, I felt that this would not be a problem. Also, the chicken salad that I purchased was clearly stamped with the price as well as today's date so I was sure this would be sufficient.

Upon my return, I proceeded to the Customer Service counter and spoke with the Assistant Manager, Brian Rogers. I told Brian what had happened and he asked for my receipt. I explained that I couldn't find it and showed him the label on the chicken salad with today's date. He informed me that without a receipt, I could not receive a refund. I'd have to exchange the salad and cheese for other items in the store of equal or greater value. I informed him that I had completed my shopping and did not need any more groceries at this time. I did not wish to purchase any more salad as it was spoiled. I also informed him that there were 13 more bricks of cheese in the cheese section which should have been removed from the shelf three months ago. He still insisted, that without a receipt, I could not receive a refund. At that time, I asked to see the Store Manager and was told he was not there. The only option I was left with was to exchange the spoiled items for more groceries.

I realize that your stores must have policies such as receipts required for returns to run a successful business. However, I believe that the policies should keep in mind the welfare of the customer. You might want to review your store policies to prevent this situation from happening to another customer in the future. I've always done my shopping in your stores and have never been dissatisfied until now.

Sincerely,

Laurie Alianell

THE INTERNET

As technology progresses, so does the information highway. The internet has become one of the most important and consulted sources of information. It is now one of the fastest ways to find out what we all need to find out; to discover. The ease of using the internet can't be disputed; its reliability can.

The internet can be a good source to begin research. But it shouldn't be the only source. With the professional need to discover reliable information so important to our jobs and lives in general, we need to treat most sources as non-conclusive. Check and double check. As the internet stands today, we all know, almost without exception, anyone can post information. There aren't the checks and balances that exist in publishing, and the professional's approach to research. Certainly use the internet in research efforts, but not as the beginning and the end to your search for reliable information.

THE COMPUTER TODAY

Way back in the day when computers first began to find their way into the work-place, the capabilities were limited. The MAC was one of the first to be introduced and used in many companies and organizations. It was often used to manipulate text and for its simple graphic designs. In addition, many companies also began to incorporate publishing systems into their documentation efforts, such as the ATEX system. Comparatively, these PC's and systems were quite limited considering what's available today. Today's computers and systems provide workers with so many possibilities, constant training is often required to keep abreast of changes and the latest innovations.

We no longer rely on our computers just to produce text and simple graphics. We now count on the computer for everything from power point presentations to keeping in touch with fellow workers, friends and family through the use of a wide variety of e-mailing systems, and instant messaging. We not only have these capabilities in the work place, many of us have personal computers at home with the same potential for doing all of the things we use the computer for in the work-place. Just one more thing to make our lives, personally and professionally, easier and more challenging at the same time.

③ p.40

E-MAIL ADDRESS

Two or threes years ago, I probably would have been reluctant to suggest that job seekers add their e-mail addresses to their resume. The point was, why give potential employers too many choices as to how the get a hold of you to offer an interview. I figured, keep it simple. With the advent of all the potential ways people have of communicating today, it could often prove frustrating. I mean, there are faxes, beepers, cell phones, answering machines, e-mail here and there not to mention good old fashioned snail mail. I still believe

234

it's important to keep it simple; not give the reader too many options as to how the reach you. And today, e-mail should be one of those ways along with a reliable phone number.

Currently, the advantage of including your e-mail address on your resume gives the reader the opportunity to contact you ensuring you will sooner, or later, hopefully sooner receive and respond to their inquiry. Many organizations today are requesting potential employees respond with their resumes submitted on-line for consideration. Providing your e-mail address satisfies, and responds directly to this mode of operation. Also, with the advent of computer knowledge required with almost all professional positions today, including your e-mail address on your resume indicates computer use and knowledge--so important to the professional environment. Including your e-mail address indicates to the reader that you are familiar with computers and support their importance in communication.

④ p.107   7. Try This One...Your Great Aunt, Fay Day, was coming to your house to celebrate your birthday. The morning of, it snowed over 36 inches covering the streets. Your Aunt was bound and determined to still celebrate with you. She even baked you a chocolate cake. Her son, Ray, who works in the local shoe lace factory, was to drive her over about 4 p.m. in his 1974 Buick Electra. Upon arrival he discovered he couldn't pull into your driveway because a plow truck was parked in front. The B & O Construction company truck's driver, Willard Durtz said the gears were locked and he couldn't move. So Ray parked up the street and proceeded to assist his mother through the snow covered sidewalk. At one point Aunt Fay slipped and fell in the snow on top of the cake. The chocolate was smeared all over her $259 cashmere coat, a present from her late husband, Jay. In addition, Aunt

Fay twisted her ankle and had to be taken to emergency. The emergency bill was $150.

Write a letter to the appropriate party requesting what you believe to be fair

compensation.

5. p-198 By combining periodicals, books, people with the internet, the research professional

should be able to explore and discover the information necessary for them to do their job

and communicate effectively and accurately with the audience. Remember, the internet is a

good place to begin research, but should not be the only source we rely on in our efforts

to find accurate information. It is important to know how to use the internet, but it is

equally important that we also know how to explore print material, and use a library and

all of its resources. In my experience, most people today are quite comfortable exploring

the Net, but many are either missing, or totally without library skills. The professional

should be adept at using all research sources in order to secure the best information.

Suggested Readings

All good writing, whether prose or poetry, whether for a business letter or the sports page or a presidential speech or a novel, has some things in common, and all bad writing has other things in common. In this book, the focus has been on professional and business writing, but any writer would be making a mistake if he or she believed that writing a business speech or an article about a business or a business memo allowed him or her to ignore the practices of good writers. That's why it's useful for any writer to become familiar with the principles of good writing. This book has attempted to both use and teach those principles. But it will be helpful to anyone who values a well-crafted piece of writing to be reminded that those principles appear in all good writing and are absent in most bad writing. That's why it would be useful to read about writing outside the confines of a book about business and professional writing. Therefore, I suggest you read each of the following works. Each is, in its own way, a classic about writing.

***The Elements of Style* by William Strunk, Jr., and E.B. White.** This book was first published in 1957 and has been in print ever since. It is the best selling book about writing ever published in the United States, and with good reason. It contains sound, easy-to-follow advice. The first half of this thin book was written in the early 20th Century by Strunk for the students he taught at Cornell University. The second half was written by White, who was a student of Strunk and who went on to become a famous writer. Strunk's part is dictatorial; that is, he says, here's a rule, follow it. White's part is discursive; that is, he discusses those rules. The first half if a handy reference book; the second half encourages careful thinking about the act of writing. This book can be found in almost any library and any bookstore.

On Writing Well **by William Zinsser.** First published in 1976, this book is the second best selling book about writing ever published in the United States. It is an outgrowth of a writing course Zinsser taught at Yale University. In tone, it is friendly and easy to read. It's chapters of "Clutter," in which he helps you identify and avoid words that add no information to your writing, and "Business Writing," in which he scorns the idea that writing for business purposes in some allows the writer to have different standards than other writers, will be particularly helpful to the business writer. This book, also, is available in most bookstores and libraries.

"Politics and the English Language" by George Orwell. This British author is best known for the novels *Animal Farm* and *1984*, both of which are about totalitarian societies. "Politics and the English Language" is one of the best known essays about how the language can be used to subvert logic, to manipulate people, to tell lies while being technically accurate. It's a warning about bad writing, about the damage it does to democracy. You'll find this on-line or in a library in a collection of essays by Orwell.

"The Literary Offenses of Fenimore Cooper" by Mark Twain. The author of *Huckleberry Finn* and *Tom Sawyer* thought the novels of James Fenimore Cooper weren't very good, and in this humorous essay he explains why. You do not need to have read Cooper's novels in order to appreciate Twain's sarcasm. The essay is about fiction, but its principles are easily applied to non-fiction, including business writing. This also is easy to find on-line or in the library; it's reprinted in many anthologies of Twain's works.

"How to Tell a True War Story" by Tim O'Brien. This work—part essay, part short-story—is part of O'Brien's book *The Things They Carried*. It's about war, but its principle argument, that you should always try to tell the truth, is applicable to any writing. It's also a reminder that sometimes telling the truth is a very difficult thing to do. *The Things They Carried* is easy to find in most bookstores and libraries.

That's it. There are lots of other good books and essays to read that will help make you a more careful, more thoughtful writer, but I want to keep this list short to encourage you to actually use it.

PROFESSIONAL COMMUNICATION
ENGLISH :
FINAL LIBRARY RESEARCH PROJECT (FLRP)

It's very important to understand how to use all resources a library has to offer.(The stupid internet isn't reliable) Once you have completed this project, you should have little difficulty locating information in the future. If you already know how to find stuff in the library, this should be a walk in the park.

Locate and, where indicated, briefly summarize the items listed below. Following each summary, you will parenthetically cite the source and provide the complete source listing on the bibliography page (Brooks 93).

1.) Headline from the New York Times on the date of your birth. (summarize)
2.) Major news story from a periodical on or about ten years after your birth. (summarize)
3.) Any periodical article on aids. (summarize)
4.) Article on a medical advancement appearing in a periodical other than aids. (summarize)
5.) Article on a popular entertainment figure appearing in a periodical the year you were born. (summarize)
6.) Novel by an American Nobel prize winning author.
7.) Review of the same novel from # 6 appearing in a periodical. (summarize)
8.) Bibliographic or critical study(book) of author from #6.
9.) Poem from any book or periodical. (Briefly explicate)
10.) A published book dealing with your discipline/career plans.
11.) Story on a historical or political figure appearing in a periodical year you were born. (summarize)
12.) Any article dealing with a sports figure appearing in a periodical the year you were born. (summarize)

What you will be turning in includes the summaries as indicated as well as a bibliography page citing the complete source for all twelve items.

How to list your sources on a bibliography page as well as all research issues are presented quite well in your book. Also, you may rely on the teacher for assistance. You may also rely on each other for help...just turn in your own work.

(5)

"Flowing From Forests to Faucets"
By Jane Braxton Little

The scene has shifted somewhat from forest conservation, inventory and management for the assured production of forest products. While this is the concern of 1952, ecological events have turned the argument towards assuring the water supply for the greatly expanded urban centers of this century.

With ever-greater demands, government officials are peering closely at forest management techniques that provide a sustainable resource of potable water. Many municipalities have some control of their watersheds and are trying to balance their water needs with forestry jobs. This article suggests that some logging actually improves the filtering action of the new forests that spring up from the harvesting of the older ones.(Little, 40-43)

(6)

"Life So Far: A Memoir"
By Betty Friedan

Renowned feminist, Betty Friedan, introduces her book as a reaction to the works of modern biographers who would write her unauthorized history. She felt the need to get her own perspective accurately and personally represented.

Friedan, a co-founder of the National Organization of Women, traces her life from her earliest recollections at age three, to the present. It is a life of early frustration, with the first chapter focused on her "perfect" mother, and her unworthy offspring. Born in

Peoria, Illinois to a relatively wealthy Jewish home, Friedan recounts her frustration with being discriminated against on two counts: that of being a woman and a Jew.

She writes frankly of her failed marriage and attendant physical abuse by her husband, Carl, who she has since reconciled with. Her 1963 book, *The Feminist Mystique*, originally garnered Friedan's fame. Being self-employed empowered her to publicly represent the widespread anguish of professional women in government and industry in their struggle to implement Title VII of the 1964 Civil Rights Act, which bans sex discrimination.(Friedan)

(7)

"Rendezvous With Destiny: A History of Modern American Reform"
By Eric Goldman

This a book written by an avowed liberal, and published in an historical era quite inhospitable to its tenants. Goldman has written a history of progressive movements in the United States from the post Civil War period to his present with particular emphasis on Franklin Roosevelt's Administration. The title is taken from a speech Roosevelt gave in 1936, suggesting not only the pressing events leading to World War II, but the culmination of efforts to effect social and economic justice. Goldman's work is fast paced for a scholarly history punctuated by numerous footnotes and forty pages of biographical notes.(Goldman)

(8)

An Interview With Lori Wallach
By Moisés Naím

Lori Wallach was a leader of the anti-WTO (World Trade Organization) protests in Seattle last November. A graduate of Harvard Law School, and Director of (Ralph Nader's) Public Citizen's, Global Trade Watch, Wallach describes herself as a progressive. Interestingly, she notes that the difference between progressives and liberals is that the latter think that big government is the answer to our problems, while the former "puts a higher value on process issues that have to do with power and equality and accountability, and is more suspicious about big anything (Naím, 31)." Wallach sees global trade as inevitable and desirable, but that the crucial issue is who decides the rules and how are they accountable. With these concerns being decided by unelected officials with a eye towards profit, how can there be any meaningful responsibility and sanction for deeds gone wrong?

Wallach correctly points out the serious WTO disagreements over crucial issues such as sweat shops, child and prisoner labor, and environmental obligations, the last being a shining failure of the North American Free Trade Association (NAFTA).(Naím, 29-55)

(9)

American Socialism- A long Time Creeping

By Irving Brant

Brant is a serious conservative who begins his article by denouncing the "Ohio Socialist", long time regular Republican and Eisenhower supporter, Robert A. Taft. He expresses further doubt about Eisenhower as well, who has "rendered himself suspect by declaring in favor of Federal pump priming in periods of depression" (Brant, 13).

Brant claims Benjamin Franklin to be America's first Socialist Bureaucrat in his capacity of first Postmaster General and paints George Washington as similarly tainted by his acceptance of a fifteen thousand acre parcel of land in exchange for his participation in the French and Indian War. Brant begins a foaming litany of socialist "monstrosities" found throughout American History. He cites government expenditures in Education, Transportation, Banking, Agriculture and Social security as travesties and bemoans "the saddest story of all- the origin of Socialized Medicine" (Brant, 14).

A Madison scholar, Brant takes his most vicious swipe at Alexander Hamilton, noting him to be one of the most nefarious of Socialists. He suggests that a proper

243

remediation of Socialist Doctrine should include the removal of Hamilton's works from high schools throughout the land. "If anybody objects, it can be pointed out that he was born outside the United States and that his parents were not married (14)." (Brant, 13-14)

(10)

"The Old man and the Sea"

By Ernest Hemingway

Mixed reviews for the old expatriate. Edward Weeks of the *Atlantic* magazine (Weeks, 72)) calls it top shelf stuff with a philosophy true to the sea. Seymour Krim of *Commonweal* believes that "we have gotten all we can get from him now" (Krim, 584). Krim believes that we've seen his best work and *Old Man* only repeats it. Having read much better works by this author, I am in Krim's corner. This was, to me, a book that not only suggested the sea, but the emphatic sense of despair when lost upon it forever- the sensation I experienced toughing through this book.(Hemingway)

(11)

"Governor Asserts Victory 'In Air'"

By W. H. Lawrence

Two days before the Presidential Election, news headlines are split between the political prize and the ""Red Menace" in Indochina, Korea and West Germany. I chose the article, dedicated to the Democratic Presidential Candidate, Ohio Governor Adlai E. Stevenson. Stevenson predicts his own victory and excoriates his opponent, former General Dwight D. Eisenhower, for having played "irresponsible, dangerous, sorry and cheap politics" (Lawrence, 1) in the Republican Party quest.

The atmosphere is charged with the inflammatory rhetoric characterized by McCarthyism and excerpts from one of Stevenson's recent speeches underscore the tone. Stevenson sees "an America where no man fears to think as he pleases and say what he thinks." (Lawrence, 1) The crux of the political battle was the situation in Korea, which Eisenhower vowed to resolve by going there personally, if elected. Stevenson presents this as a strategic weakness that will be exploited by the Communists manipulators of Soviet Russia, "which has the iron crust but the hollow center of all tyrannies." (Lawrence, 87)

(12)

Adventures of Humphrey Bogart

By Cameron Shipp

Humphrey De Forest Bogart is a "whiskey-drinking actor who has been hooting at Hollywood and making fun at its pretensions for twenty-two years" (Shipp, 32). According to Cameron Shipp, Bogart is devoted to the creation of image contrary to the popular American belief in the mystique of entertainers; that they are pretty good people who wash dishes just like the rest of us.

Not since the "martini –loading" W. C. Fields, has Hollywood had a celebrity so devoted to slamming down bourbon as his public persona. Shipp quotes an acquaintance of Bogart, writer-producer Nunally Johnson, on the notion of celebrity drinkers. These folks are "outfitted with an alcoholic thermostat in their foreheads...[to keep them]...fueled up to the correct temperature (Shipp, 33)." Shipp goes on to relate the drinking session between Bogart, director John Houston, and Katherine Hepburn that resulted in the creation of *African Queen*, the film which had just landed Bogart an Oscar, and turbocharged his career.

The entire history of Bogart seems anchored in his "tough guy" image with some interesting anecdotal evidence, such as when a former French Resistance fighter ate his champagne glass challenged Bogart to do the same. Initially balking, Bogie bites down a manly morsel and lacerates his mouth. Both with bleeding mouths, Bogie and the patriot sally forth together, confident that they had the right camaraderie and image to "insult women"(Shipp, 33).

245

Works Cited

Brant, Irving. "American Socialism-A Long Time Creeping." New Republic.
7 July, 1952: 13, 14.

Friedan, Betty. *Life So Far: A Memoir*. New York: Simon and Schuster, 2000.

Goldman, Eric.*Rendezvous With Destiny: A History of Modern American Reform*.
New York: Alfred A. Knoph Inc., 1952.

Hemingway, Ernest. *The Old Man and the Sea*. New York: Charles Scribner's Sons,
1952.

Kazin, Alfred, ed. *F. Scott Fitzgerald: The Man and His Work*. New York: Collier
Books, 1952.

Krim, Seymour. "A Review of *The Old Man and the Sea*." *Commonweal*. September
19, 1952: 584.

Lawrence, W. H. "Governor Asserts Victory 'In Air'." *New York Times*. 2 Nov.1952: 1+.

Little, Jane Braxton. "Flowing From Forests to Faucets." *American Forests*. Spring 2000:
40-43.

Long,E.B. *Personal Memoirs of Ulysses S. Grant*. New York: Da Capo Press, 1952.

"Medicine." *Time Magazine*. January 21, 1952: 68.

Naím, Moisés. "An Interview With Lori Wallach." *Foreign Policy*. Spring, 2000: 28+.

Ryan, David P. M.D., et al. "Medical Progress: Carcinoma of the Anal Canal." *New
England Journal of Medicine*. March 16, 2000: 792-797.

Shipp, Cameron. "Adventures of Humphrey Bogart." *Saturday Evening Post*. 2 August,
1952: 32+.

Wilson, Tyler, ed. *Nobel Prize Winners: An A.H. Wilson Biographical Dictionary*.
New York: H.W. Wilson, 1987.

Weeks, Edward. "A Review of The Old Man and the Sea." *Atlantic*. September, 1952.

Weldon, Martin. "The Other Side of Babe Ruth" *Coronet*. June,1952.

Zipser, Alfred R. "Reactions Mixed to Timber Study." *New York Times*. 2 November
1952: Section 3: 1+.